A Place for Wayfaring
The Poetry and Prose of Gary Snyder

A Place for Wayfaring
The Poetry and Prose of Gary Snyder

Patrick D. Murphy

Oregon State University Press
Corvallis

The paper in this book meets the guidelines for permanence and durability of the Committee on Production Guidelines for Book Longevity of the Council on Library Resources and the minimum requirements of the American National Standard for Permanence of Paper for Printed Library Materials Z39.48-1984.

Library of Congress Cataloging-in-Publication Data
Murphy, Patrick D., 1951-
   A place for wayfaring : the poetry and prose of Gary Snyder / Patrick D. Murphy.
      p.   cm.
   Includes bibliographical references (p.) and index.
   ISBN 0-87071-479-1 (alk. paper)
   1. Snyder, Gary, 1930- —Criticism and interpretation. I. Title.

PS3569.N88 Z788 2000
811'.54—dc21

99-088384

Oregon State University Press
101 Waldo Hall
Corvallis OR 97331-6407
541-737-3166 • fax 541-737-3170

http://osu.orst.edu/dept/press

For Mary

Whose courage, strength, patience, and good cheer
are truly an inspiration

Contents

Preface vii

Acknowledgments viii

1 "Membership in a Real World"
   An Introduction to the Writer and His Work 1

2 From Myth Criticism to Mythopoesis
   Myths & Texts 20

3 Working Rhythms
   Riprap and Cold Mountain Poems 43

4 Passing and Returning
   Passage Through India and *The Back Country* 63

5 The Waves of Household and Marriage
   Earth House Hold and *Regarding Wave* 89

6 Reinhabiting the Land: *Turtle Island* 104

7 Handing Down the Practice
   Axe Handles and *Left Out in the Rain* 123

8 Of Wildness and Wilderness in Plain Language
   The Practice of the Wild 143

9 Sifting and Selecting
   No Nature and *A Place in Space* 155

10 The Calligraphy of Water on Rock
    Mountains and Rivers Without End 178

   Conclusion: As Mountains and Waters Remain,
   The Poet Continues Walking 209

Notes 216

Bibliography 235

Index 243

Preface

A much shorter version of this book was originally published as *Understanding Gary Snyder*. It was written for the Understanding Contemporary American Literature Series and as a result had to conform to series constrictions. With the publication of *Mountains and Rivers Without End* in 1996, I knew I had to update my overview of Snyder's work. My original publisher was not interested in publishing a revised edition; but fortunately for me, Warren Slesinger enthusiastically endorsed the idea of my writing a new book on Snyder's poetry and prose for Oregon State University Press, and so here it is.

Not only have I added detailed treatments of all of Snyder's book publications since 1992 and consideration of previously uncollected materials in the new *Reader*, but I have also expanded my earlier analyses of the volumes published before that year. In some cases, I have changed my interpretations of particular poems; in other cases I have altered my emphases, being, for example, more attentive to issues of gender in his writing and Buddhist allusions, symbols, and concepts. In all cases, I have expanded the number of poems and the amount of prose from any given volume that I analyze and have made a special effort to comment on the poems and essays reprinted in *The Gary Snyder Reader*.

Dialogue with several Snyder critics has benefitted this study. In particular, I would like to thank Timothy Gray, Anthony Hunt, Eric Todd Smith, and Katsunori Yamazato. Preston Houser of Kyoto aided me by sending some Snyder publications from the *Kyoto Journal*, a beautiful and extremely valuable journal. Michael J. Hoffman and Peggy Bogeman welcomed me into their home in Davis, California. David Robertson spared me time out of his busy schedule and John Skarstad in the Special Collections Department at the University of California, Davis, not only aided me with his expertise on the archival material, but also his insightful remarks on several Snyder-related subjects helped me focus my research and sharpen my analysis. Jeff Bartone, my graduate assistant at Indiana University of Pennsylvania, read the manuscript with an astutely critical eye, and made numerous helpful comments—any errors that remain persist through no fault of his but are exclusively my responsibility. Knowing my writing schedule, the graduate students at IUP were quite graceful and considerate about allowing me the time to concentrate on this project despite their anxieties about exams and dissertations. I owe Gary Snyder an unrepayable debt of gratitude for providing me with the literature that is the source for this study, for graciously responding to a variety of questions with clarity and patience, and for granting me permission to quote from archival material. Finally, I owe thanks to all those people who bought and commented on *Understanding Gary Snyder*, since their interest has enabled me to continue to pursue mine in print.

Acknowledgments

Quotations from published and unpublished materials in the Gary Snyder Archives are used by permission of the Department of Special Collections, University of California, Davis, California.

Quotations by Gary Snyder, from *Myths & Texts*, copyright © 1978, by Gary Snyder; quotations from Gary Snyder, from *The Back Country*, copyright © 1968, by Gary Snyder; and quotations by Gary Snyder, from *Turtle Island*, copyright © 1974, by Gary Snyder, all are reprinted by permission of New Directions Publishing Corporation.

Quotations from *Riprap and Cold Mountain Poems*, copyright © 1958, 1959, 1965, by Gary Snyder; *Axe Handles*, copyright © 1983, by Gary Snyder; and *Left Out in the Rain: New Poems 1947-1985*, copyright © 1986, by Gary Snyder, are reprinted by permission of North Point Press, a division of Farrar, Straus & Giroux.

Quotations from *Mountains and Rivers Without*, copyright © 1996, by Gary Snyder, are reprinted by permission of Counterpoint.

1

"Membership in a Real World"
An Introduction to the Writer and His Work

Gary Snyder was born on the 8th day of May, 1930, in the early months of what would become a decade-long period of dire hardship for millions of Americans known today as the Great Depression. During Lois Wilkie Snyder's pregnancy, her husband Harold was on the road looking for work, and Lois stayed with relatives in San Francisco, California, where Gary was born. Eighteen months later, the family moved to Lake City, north of Seattle, Washington, an area that "essentially was the aftermath of a giant clearcut."[1] The significance of this land having been clear-cut for Snyder's psychological and environmental-ethical development should not be underestimated. In *The Practice of the Wild*, he remarks that "I know now that the area had been home to some of the largest and finest trees the world has ever seen. . . . And I suspect that I was to some extent instructed by the ghosts of those ancient trees as they hovered near their stumps."[2] Harold Snyder may have chosen this area because he had grown up in "Kitsap County and Seattle," and Harold's father had "homesteaded some land directly after it had been logged" in Kitsap. There the Snyders eked out a subsistence living through farming, cutting stumps to make shingles, and bartering. Into these conditions Snyder's sister Anthea was born. The Snyder family was generally poorer than their neighbors and "lived in a house that was covered with tar paper," rather than siding.[3] Carol Baker has remarked that Snyder "suffered from rickets as a child due to his poor diet."[4]

Gary Snyder learned to work early in life as did many of the children of his generation. By his own account he did not feel deprived by the lack of money and material goods. His mother, who aspired throughout her life to be a writer, introduced Gary to books at the public library.[5] Snyder had the good fortune, then, to become at an early age attached to both literature and the physical world around him. "I developed," he has said, "a certain amount of self-discipline and an enjoyment in doing a certain amount of work, and then a great attachment to nature."[6] As he explained his early years to Nicholas O'Connell in 1986, "I grew up in terms of planetary normal, which is to say growing up in close contact with the fabric of nature, rather than removed from it. . . . Growing up in that fabric gave me a powerful moral perspective of respect and regard for all sentient beings and gave me a powerful sense of membership in a real world."[7]

Snyder's family moved to Portland in 1942 as jobs became more plentiful due to the growth of war-related industries. By the time Gary started high school, his parents had separated. Although Lois Snyder and the two children were living in a working-class housing development, Gary's mother arranged for him to attend Lincoln High School in downtown Portland because it had the best academic reputation in the city. There, according to Jerry Crandall, who also attended Lincoln, Snyder participated in the journalism club and the drama group.[8]

Despite moving to the city, Snyder remained a child of the mountains and forests and became involved in studying Native American ways of life. He spent some high school summers at a YMCA camp on Spirit Lake at the foot of Mount St. Helens and became committed to camping, backpacking, and mountain climbing; and Crandall claims that Snyder was already a defender of wildlife in his early teens.[9] While attending high school, Snyder joined the Mazamas, an adult mountaineering club, and the Wilderness Society. He also worked part-time as a copyboy with the *Oregonian* newspaper where his mother worked. In these teenage years he began to write poetry because, as he recalls, "I couldn't find any other way to express what I was feeling about mountaineering on the great snowpeaks of the Northwest. . . . That was a powerful teaching for me. It was an initiation by all of the great gods of the land here. And so I began to write poems."[10] Snyder's juvenile writing, then, was primarily oriented toward his experiences in the wild, an orientation that has remained the staple of his poetry. That direct experience was reinforced by his avid reading in the Mazama clubhouse library. Not only did mountaineering initiate Snyder into poetry writing it also led to his first prose publication, an article in the December 1946 issue of *Mazama* magazine.[11] Mountain climbing and mountain hiking also became a lifelong practice for Snyder. Not only did he climb and hike while in Japan in the 1950s and 1960s, but also went on climbs during his visits to the U.S. He continues climbing in the U.S. and other parts of the world to this day.

Snyder received a scholarship in 1947 to attend Reed College in Portland and selected a double major in anthropology and literature. In the summer after his first year, with the help of a friend of his father, Snyder set sail from New York City on an oceangoing ship, working in the steward's department. This experience turned out to be the start of an engagement with seamanship that continued into the 1960s. It also became a source of trouble with the government during the anti-communist McCarthy days of the Cold War, because of the political connections between the Communist Party and the union Snyder joined in order to have his job.

Midway through his undergraduate years Snyder learned a lasting lesson about mountains and wilderness that came not from physical immersion in the land but from a poetic perspective on a very different land of mountains and rivers, forests and plains. In 1949, he discovered Chinese poetry in English translation, which was being popularized by poets and veterans interested in Asia and Buddhism. These poems left a deep impression on Snyder because, as he has remarked, they "freed me from excessive attachment to wild mountains, with their almost subliminal way of presenting even the wildest hills as a place where people, also, live."[12] As the language of Snyder's remark suggests, he not only gained a new aesthetic perspective but also an introduction to an applied Eastern metaphysics that would soon lead him to serious Buddhist practice.

The following year, 1950, Snyder worked for the Park Service, helping to excavate the archaeological site of Old Fort Vancouver. And in the summer of 1951 he was employed at a logging camp on the Warm Springs Indian Reservation in Oregon, where he worked as a timber scaler, but also "came to know Indians there, and he collected oral literature," according to David H. French.[13] The anthropological/ archaeological impulse has remained strong for Snyder. While he has not continued to excavate sites in the way that he worked in the summer of 1950, he has continued to excavate the heritage of what he has called "The Great Subculture" of mystics and visionaries. Recovering the past, imaginatively reconstructing gaps that remain, and envisioning the future have always been intertwined activities in Snyder's research and writing.[14] At the same time, such intellectual archaeology and imaginative mythmaking have remained grounded in physical labor as my pairing of his 1950 archaeology and his 1951 logging activities is intended to suggest.[15]

Reed College was a tremendously stimulating experience for Snyder and crucial in shaping the intellectual and creative directions of his life. He was, first, deeply influenced by some of the teachers that he had, such as the co-advisors for his thesis, David French, who introduced him to anthropology, and Lloyd Reynolds, who introduced him to calligraphy. Second, he was also influenced by a community of students who came to Reed from across the United States, especially the creative writers. In addition, Snyder experienced his first heartbreak with Robin Collins and was also briefly married to another Reed classmate, Allison Gass.[16] Both of these women are the subject of various poems.

Snyder wrote an extremely sophisticated undergraduate thesis that was eventually published unrevised in 1979 as *He Who Hunted Birds in His Father's Village*. By the time he graduated from college in 1951, Snyder had developed into a truly working class intellectual, "deeply imbued," as he claims, "with a lot of western American political and literary lore," such as "labor history, strikes, IWW, early socialism, people like Charles Erskine Scott Wood and Joe Hill."[17] He has said of Reed that

> I had some marvelous teachers, I learned how to use a library, I was in an atmosphere that challenged me and pushed me to the utmost, which was just what I needed. They wouldn't tolerate bullshit, made me clean up my prose style, exposed me to all varieties of intellectual positions and gave me a territory in which I could speak out my radical politics and get arguments and augmentations on it.[18]

French, in fact, argues that Snyder has intertwined anthropology and poetry ever since: "It is as if he has been a teacher of anthropology to audiences who did not always know that it was anthropology they were learning. Often, he told them it was."[19]

For most of the first twenty-one years of his life, then, Snyder shuttled among the rural and the urban, the lowlands and the highlands, of the Pacific Northwest; he had also begun oceanic forays with his first seafaring work. He learned a series of jobs and gained experiences in wilderness, particularly the mountains, that would provide ample material for poems and essays integrating the routines of physical work with the life of the mind. In a sense, Snyder's experience could be depicted as a combination of discipline and innovation, which in turn could be viewed metaphorically as being "on the path" in the first instance and "off the trail" in the second instance—concepts that he would elaborate nearly forty years after graduating from Reed in "On the Path, Off the Trail" in *The Practice of the Wild*.

At Reed he participated in a group affiliated with the student arts magazine, *Janus*. Many of the members of this group became lifelong friends, such as Philip Whalen and Lew Welch. And while Welch became heavily influenced by William Carlos Williams and Gertrude Stein,[20] Snyder looked more to Ezra Pound for technical guidance and to D. H. Lawrence and Robinson Jeffers for thematic guidance.[21] He was also influenced by Robert Graves's recently published *The White Goddess* with its emphasis on the relationship of poetry and myth; Timothy Gray, however, argues that the artist Morris Graves was a far more important influence. Morris Graves "was steeped in Japanese aesthetic practices" and "believed that the landscape of the Pacific Northwest had much in common with the landscape of Asia."[22]

But Snyder's decision to become a poet was not made simply or immediately. Initially, he, along with Dell Hymes—another Reed graduate in anthropology and literature—enrolled in graduate school at Indiana University, anticipating earning a Ph.D. in linguistics.[23] But the academic life for Snyder quickly palled, and after a semester he decided to set himself "loose in the world to sink or swim as a poet."[24] But even though he had made this commitment, it would be a few more years before he clarified his own poetic voice. And that clarity would come from immersion once again in wilderness, specifically the Yosemite California high country in 1955.[25]

In the summer of 1952, back on the West Coast, Snyder went to work in northern Washington state as a lookout on Crater Mountain for the U.S. Forest Service, and the following summer he returned as a lookout on Sourdough Mountain. In the winter months, he lived in San Francisco and enrolled in graduate school in Oriental languages, studying Chinese and Japanese, at the University of California at Berkeley. Snyder did not attend Berkeley in order to earn a degree, but rather to prepare himself to go to Japan to study Buddhism. While at Reed, he had already begun practicing sitting meditation, *zazen*, and in Berkeley "became acquainted with the warm, relaxed, familial, and devotional Buddhism of traditional Asia in the atmosphere of the Berkeley Buddhist Church."[26] He also felt a strong affinity for China, in part as a result of an experience he had as a child, which he has retold in several different interviews. He recounts going into the Seattle Art Museum and seeing a room full of Chinese landscape paintings. At that moment he felt a deep shock of recognition because they looked to him exactly like the Cascades, with which he was already familiar. He felt that "the Chinese had an eye for the world that I saw as real."[27] Visting China in the early 1950s, however, was not an option.

As a youth, he had gravitated toward Native American cultures in his search for an alternative to Judeo-Christian Western capitalist culture because it seemed the cause of so much suffering in the world. And although he had read widely as a youth,[28] worked on a reservation, done archaeological and anthropological work on Native cultures, and become friends with individuals from various tribes, he realized that the kind of spiritual study he wished to undertake of Native American culture was not accessible to a white person. Mahayana Buddhism, in contrast, is by its own doctrine open to anyone who seeks to learn its ways and follow its path. So Snyder worked on his Japanese and Chinese and dreamed of Japan for three years before actually being able to get there.

In 1954, life became complicated. He was blacklisted from the Forest Service while on his way to a summer job. Unable to work as a lookout, he returned to the Warm Springs Indian Reservation and worked for the Warm Springs Lumber Company as a choker setter, engaging in selective cutting of ponderosa pine: "The logging was under contract with the tribal council. The proceeds were to benefit the people as a whole."[29] The following summer he was able to work on a trail crew in the high country of Yosemite National Park. Eventually, Snyder learned that he had been branded a subversive by two different governmental agencies. One was the U.S. Coast Guard, which did so because he had gotten his seamen's card back in 1948 through the assistance of a communist-affiliated maritime union. The other was the F.B.I., which considered some of Snyder's teachers and friends at Reed College to be either members or supporters of the Communist Party. Through a series of letters, queries, and negotiations, including the writing of a loyalty statement of sorts, Snyder eventually cleared his record, which enabled him to obtain a passport.

His letter to the State Department is an interesting document.[30] While Snyder disavows any affiliation with communism, he does admit to having considered himself "an intellectual Marxist" at nineteen—a self-definition he soon dropped in favor of "anarcho-pacifist." He also stands by the statement attributed to him that he "would rather go to a concentration camp than be drafted" into the Korean War. He states unequivocally in his letter that his is a legitimate opinion to hold and one that he continues to support. And, while pledging not to speak out against the U.S. government while abroad, he also distances himself from any political loyalties. In opposition to large, centralized modern nation states, Snyder supports decentralized land-based social organizations. These would be communities based on more ancient models of traditional societies, with territories defined by the lines of the natural boundaries and regions of a particular place. Snyder's foreshadowing of a basically bioregionalist definition of political organization in his 1955 letter to the State Department is truly impressive.

The year 1955 proved to be a pivotal one for Snyder during his early adult years. He worked out his problems with the government, found himself writing a new kind of poetry, and participated in the famous October 13th Six Gallery reading in San Francisco. At that reading Allen Ginsberg first performed *Howl* and Snyder read "A Berry Feast." Snyder had not only found his own voice and cleared the way to pursue his journey to the Far East, but he also established himself as one of the rising young stars of the San Francisco Renaissance.

I refer here to Snyder as part of the San Francisco Renaissance rather than as one of the Beats for several reasons. One, Snyder views himself as part of that renaissance but strongly dissents from identification with the Beat Movement. Edward Halsey Foster in *Understanding the Beats* argues quite convincingly that there were "four major beat writers: William S. Burroughs, Gregory Corso, Allen Ginsberg, and Jack Kerouac." The confusion arises, he believes, "from the fact that various beat writers were living in the Bay Area during the San Francisco Renaissance."[31] Foster, however, like Michael Davidson, author of *The San Francisco Renaissance*, argues that the distinction between the Beats and the San Francisco Renaissance poets goes beyond individual affiliations to matters of poetics and sensibilities.[32]

The confusion, however, is quite understandable since the media lumped them together and treated both groups in a sensational fashion. Also, the innovative poets of both coasts tended to be published alongside each other in the same literary magazines and frequently commented on each other's work. The perception of Snyder as a Beat also resulted from Kerouac's idealization of him as Japhy Ryder in *The Dharma Bums* (1958). Even though Snyder has repeatedly stressed that Kerouac's novel is a work of fiction, many still equate Ryder with Snyder, perhaps in part because a good portion of the novel does accurately record real events and conversations.

Nevertheless, in the midst of this literary ferment, Snyder left San Francisco for Japan, and studied and worked there at a Buddhist temple in conjunction with the activities of the First Zen Institute of America's Kyoto facility, which was directed by Ruth Fuller Sasaki.[33] He had left behind with Robert Creeley the manuscript of *Myths & Texts*, but it would pass through many hands and be rejected by several editors before its publication in 1960. Although it was published a year after *Riprap* (1959), it was completed and organized as a book by 1956, before many of the *Riprap* poems were even written. So, not only did Snyder continue to publish individual poems in literary magazines while in Japan, but he was also circulating one book manuscript and working on another.

Despite the seriousness with which he was approaching Buddhist study, Snyder wrote to a close friend, Will Petersen, in September,

1956, shortly after arriving in Kyoto: "have come to realize that I am first most a poet. . . . So I don't think I'll ever commit myself to the role of Zen Monk, as free as that role seems to be, because it calls for too much sense of serious responsible behavior, & no faith in letting poems & such flow out free to everybody."[34] Even after making this statement, however, Snyder did have his head shaved, took the Bodhissatva precepts, and studied in and out of monasteries with Buddhist teachers for over ten years in Japan.

Snyder's immersion in Buddhism also involved extensive linguistic, cultural, and historical study as well as religious training. He commented on this training in an article written in 1969 for *Wind Bell*, the magazine of the Zen Center of San Francisco:

> I was studying Japanese and Chinese at Berkeley before I ever went over there and I had a kind of feeling for sinology and for that kind of scholarship so I enjoyed doing it, but at the same time it always seemed a little bit paradoxical because one of the things that first attracted to me to Zen in Suzuki's books was getting away from scholarship and learning and not relying on books, words and doctrines. . . .
>
> . . . . you have to become as Oriental as possible, because a lot of what goes down in traditional Zen training involves certain references which connect with the whole cultural background of China and Japan, even down to modes of expression. Someone who is going to do long term Rinzai study would do well to thoroughly acquaint himself with the great Chinese T'ang and Sung Dynasty poets. . . . Chinese proverbs are often made into koans or used as part of koans with just a slight twist. So much of the culture becomes involved in ways that we don't realize.[35]

A year later, wanting some time to reflect on Zen and Japan and taking the opportunity to earn some money, Snyder took a job as a wiper in the engine room of an oil tanker, *Sappa Creek*.[36] For eight months the ship wound its way back and forth to the Persian Gulf, stopping in Italy, Turkey, Okinawa, Ceylon, and various Pacific Islands before reaching the United States.

Snyder landed in California in April, 1958, and spent nine months in the Bay Area, heavily involved in the poetry scene. The next year *Riprap* was published as his first book by Cid Corman in Japan and distributed through City Lights Books in the United States. During this period he met Joanne Kyger, a fellow poet. A year later, Kyger agreed to travel to Kyoto to live with and marry Snyder. It was her first marriage and Snyder's second, and it lasted a stormy, intense four years.[37] The year they were married also witnessed the publication of *Myths & Texts*. And for Snyder, back in Japan, there came a moment of spiritual enlightenment, duly acknowledged by his Zen master.[38]

The entire time he and Kyger were together, with the exception of their six-month sojourn to India in late 1961 and early 1962 (which Snyder treats in *Passage through India* [1983]), Snyder studied Buddhism with Oda Sesso Roshi, Rinzai Zen master and Head Abbot of Daitoku-ji Temple in Kyoto. In February, 1964, Kyger returned alone to San Francisco. By the time Snyder arrived that fall, the possibility of reconciliation seemed distant and the two resolved to divorce. Snyder briefly taught creative writing at Berkeley and participated in Buddhist "protest meditation" demonstrations against the Vietnam War; he then returned to Japan in October, 1965.[39] That year *Riprap* was republished with the addition of the Han-shan translations that he had first published in *Evergreen Review* in 1958. Also that year, the first six sections of *Mountains and Rivers Without End*, a long poetic sequence that Snyder had begun shortly after completing *Myths & Texts* and which he would not complete until 1996, was published.

The following year Oda Sesso Roshi died and Snyder returned briefly to the United States in time to help preside, with Ginsberg, over the Great Human Be-In at Golden Gate Park in early 1967. When he returned shortly after that to Japan, he turned more outward from the Buddhist community and its many expatriates to the Japanese equivalent of the hippy community, making connections with Nanao Sakaki, a military veteran and wandering poet who was organizing communes in various parts of Japan. He and Snyder have remained close friends ever since. Snyder was also introduced to an Okinawan graduate student in English literature, Masa Uehara, and they married in 1967 on the lip of an active volcano on Suwanose Island south of Kyushu. The two of them were living there with Sakaki and a dozen or so others in a subsistence communal experiment. The poems of the first three sections of *Regarding Wave* (1969, limited edition) come from this period of 1967 and 1968, when Gary and Masa were first married and she gave birth to their first son, Kai, in Japan.

Shortly after Kai's birth, the Snyders returned to the United States. It was the end of Snyder's long sojourn in Japan. Now he was looking forward to establishing a homestead and participating in the rising ecology movement in the U.S., even as he renewed his involvement in the anti-war movement and with Native American struggles. In 1969, Gary and Masa's second son, Gen, was born. During this period Snyder was busy publishing books with New Directions—*The Back Country* (1968), *Earth House Hold* (1969), and the expanded edition of

Regarding Wave (1970), as well as publishing differently organized collections in England. During these years he received various awards and increasing recognition in the United States for his poetry.

What accounted for such attention? Dan McLeod argues that it was far more than Snyder's poetry: "the example of Snyder's life and values offered a constructive, albeit underground, alternative to mainstream American culture." He goes on to claim that "Snyder's main impact on the Beat Generation, and on American literature since, has been as a spokesperson for the natural world and the values associated with primitive cultures. But his poetic use of Asian sources has also been influential."[40] Also, Snyder's poetry offered people in the 1960s a counter-modernist poetics, which took many of the features of modernist poetry and turned them on their heads in the rhythms of a very different lifestyle and sensibility and in the service of a very different vision of the world. The prose of *Earth House Hold* and the poems of *Regarding Wave*, in particular, were filled with possibility, optimism, and ecstasy arising from lived experience filled with alternative pathways. This kind of spirit can be seen in a reply Snyder wrote to a query sent him by a poetry collective in 1970:

> I should say struggle has always been a joy to me and much identity—as a man as well as a poet—is to be found in struggle itself. Struggle for what? In my case, struggle to maintain a line of study, a style of living, a certain forward momentum, that would not give up, betray, some powerful visions I had as a very young man—a child even—visions of man and nature. The key vision had to do with wilderness and its great teaching and healing powers; and that intelligence is to be found in all being—even stone. I became a poet that I might give voice to the songs I heard in nature and my inner ear, and that also, by the power of song, I might contribute to the downfall of the technological-industrial world, its total destruction, in favor of a world based on closer knowledge of nature in man himself.[41]

After his return to California, Snyder's influence spread farther afield to environmental and American Buddhist circles. His 1970 Earth Day speech at Colorado State College and the following year's talk at the Center for the Study of Democratic Institutions in Santa Barbara, California, formed part of a growing practice of lecturing on environmental and international issues, as well as giving poetry readings across the nation. During this time, with the help of others, he built his home outside of Nevada City, California, on the edge of the Tahoe National Forest in the midst of land heavily damaged by hydraulic mining. He named it Kitkitdizze, "the Indian word for a local plant called Mountain Misery."[42] In 1972, he participated in the United Nations Conference on Human Environment in Stockholm, Sweden. Such lecturing and conference participation led to his writing an increasing amount of prose, as evidenced by *Earth House Hold*, *The Old Ways* (1977), a variety of uncollected pieces, then in 1990 *The Practice of the Wild*, and in 1995 *A Place in Space*, which incorporates *The Old Ways* with selected essays written between 1960 and 1995.

Poetry, of course, has never been left behind. In 1973, he published *The Fudo Trilogy*, a limited edition chapbook. The next year *Turtle Island*, his most overtly political volume, was published and won the Pulitzer Prize for poetry in 1975. Snyder defines this volume as "the first literary surfacing of the bioregional concept."[43] He was heavily involved during these years in the California Arts Council and ecological work, both locally and internationally. And from such involvement came *Axe Handles* (1983), a collection with a very different tone from that of *Turtle Island*. *Axe Handles* is less apocalyptic, less confrontational, and more focused on the building of family and community. Just as the shift from *The Back Country* to *Regarding Wave* displays a transformation from doubt, struggle, and difficulty to rapture, attainment, and immersion, so too is there displayed a transformation between the later two volumes. Snyder may be said, with the differences between *Turtle Island* and *Axe Handles*, to move from an immediacy and confrontational approach to political struggle to a long-range, evolutionary attitude toward the processes of cultural change.

In addition to the social changes within the United States itself, Snyder's own aging may have been a factor in his change of emphasis; also, the growth of his children and promise of another generation to carry on the lessons already learned may have enabled him to feel less anxious about the future. Snyder commented on this change during an interview in 1983: "If *Turtle Island* was a statement about what life in North American could be . . . *Axe Handles* is a much more low-key presentation of what the moves are when you really make a place your home."[44] That same year *Passage Through India*, an edited version of the journals of his trip in the early 1960s, was published. And in 1986 *Left Out in the Rain: New Poems 1947-1985* appeared, pulling together some 150 previously uncollected poems beginning with ones from his high school years.

The year 1985 also witnessed Snyder accepting an appointment at the University of California at Davis. Soon thereafter he was named a member of the American Academy and Institute of Arts and Letters.

In 1987, his family life underwent a change as well. He and Masa Uehara divorced after twenty years of marriage. Snyder then began a relationship with Carole Koda, a third-generation Japanese American with two daughters, and they were married in April of 1991. As Snyder turned toward the 1990s and the entering of his seventh decade of life, he characterized his artistic practice from a particularly long-term perspective: "I see my role as trying to present some alternative, and to tell people what the normal world was or could be like if we took on the job of reknitting our connections with each other and with the natural world. The fact is that the modern human condition in the last 60 or 70 years has gone against the norm of the last 40,000 years, and we don't know yet what it means."[45]

With the publication in 1990 of *The Practice of the Wild* and then *A Place in Space* in 1995, it seems that Snyder may increasingly rely on essay writing to continue such "telling." In his interview with John P. O'Grady, Snyder expresses pleasure in *Practice* being adopted as a text in college classes around the country.[46] But that's not to say that his prose has taken an *academic* turn, but rather that it reaches across audiences and generations, just as Snyder's activism and writing reach from the research university in Davis to the Yuba Watershed Institute in rural northern California.[47]

In 1992, in between the publication of his prose volumes, Snyder released *No Nature: New and Selected Poems*, which includes approximately 150 of his previously published poems and fifteen new poems. This volume, like *The Practice of the Wild*, has the potential to become a textbook and will likely be the most widely taught of Snyder's poetry volumes. The major publishing event of the 1990s for Snyder, however, was the completion of his poetic sequence *Mountains and Rivers Without End*, which was forty years in the making. At the end of this sequence, Snyder has appended a prose piece, "The Making of *Mountains and Rivers Without End*," that succinctly identifies major developments in his thinking about it over the years as well as key aesthetic and philosophical influences. In connection with its publication, Snyder has been awarded a Bollingen Prize, the Orion Society's John Hay Award for Nature Writing, and an award for the promotion of Buddhism by the Bukkyo Dendo Kyokai of Japan. As the 1990s draw to a close and Snyder faces toward the "fiftieth millennium,"[48] he continues teaching at the University of California at Davis, remains vigorously active, continues to lecture and travel, and has various writing projects underway, but he also stays closer to home. His wife Carole has a serious illness (one of the new poems in *The Gary Snyder Reader* obliquely addresses her health).

For Snyder, perhaps more so than for any other twentieth-century American poet, his life and his art are fully intertwined. Charles Egan concludes his 1995 interview with Snyder with these words:

> Snyder hopes that the broader range of his work—not just any one poem, or even his writing, but everything including his environmental work and his teaching—will have a deeper, more long-lasting effect on humanity. For him the power of his life and work are in the mosaic it creates. "And that is where I am an artist. I haven't just been writing poems. I have been creating a much larger picture in my work. I look at it as one large project in which all of these things are part of the picture."[49]

Such a unity seems particularly appropriate for a writer who remarked a decade earlier in a different interview that "what's really interesting to my mind is the 'political' work of poetry on the fundamental myth-archetypes, transforming the very way we see the world."[50]

The preceding pages set out the highlights of Snyder's career by means of a chronology of events in his life. In this section, the focus will shift to the major features of Snyder's spiritual, intellectual, and artistic development. Snyder frequently resorts to the Buddhist imagery of Indra's jeweled net to depict the interconnectedness of all existence. In such terms, then, it can be said that while the individual trajectory of a single physical life may be laid out linearly, the life of the mind does not conform to such a structure. A more appropriate image for intellectual growth is that of the net, which has threads that radiate out from one another, forming eventually a circle, a curved universe. New experiences, new ideas, new aesthetic influences are connected to each other and to what is already known by a variety of threads linking nodes that initially might seem to be discrete and disparate. For instance, Snyder reads a book about the migratory patterns of birds while waiting to travel to Japan and draws connections between the birds and himself. But perhaps also he draws connections about cultural differences between societies that rely on linear paradigms of development and knowledge and societies that rely on recursive, net-like paradigms of change and wisdom. And those connections will produce the poem "Migration of Birds" in *Riprap*. Later, however, Snyder will experience birds flying in and out of a shed where he is working, and the linearity/circularity issue will again arise, but this time in connection with the seasonal cycles of work for all sentient creatures, producing "Six-Month Song in the Foothills" in *The Back Country*.

Like a curved universe, Snyder's concerns loop back and circle out from identification with the "ghosts of trees," whom he feels were teaching him in his youth, to learning to write "about a pine tree as a pine tree would want to be written about, from inside," to becoming a biosphere spokesperson: "part of my life project has been proposing the possibility of speaking from the nonhuman to the human, because the human does not hear enough from the nonhuman."[51] Such a role can be seen in Snyder's participation in the Buddhist Peace Fellowship founded in 1977. Speaking about its purpose before a benefit poetry reading in 1985, Snyder stated that "it's part of our mission—as we've defined it—as Buddhists to extend the concern for peace outside the human realm to the nonhuman realm."[52]

A quick reading of Snyder's *Left Out in the Rain* and *No Nature* reveals a poet who practices an amazingly diverse array of poetic styles. Although he primarily practices the kind of free verse developed in Anglo-American modernism in the first half of the twentieth century, he has learned and utilizes elements of poetic forms from both European and Asian traditions. As of 1996, each end of his book publishing career is marked by a major book-length poetic sequence, with *Myths & Texts* at one end and *Mountains and Rivers Without End* at the other. Of these two, the former is more modernist, more derived from the poetics of Ezra Pound, than is the latter, which has a greater range of styles within it. Part of what makes these works difficult, especially for the novice poetry reader, is that Snyder uses such a vast range of allusions. He refers to Japanese folklore, Native American myths and songs, Hindu mythology, Buddhist philosophy and religious practice, international historical figures, artists, and places. He also employs structures that affect meaning, such as that of the Japanese Nō drama in *Mountains and Rivers Without End*.

These devices make it difficult to capture the full range of meaning playing through a poem. Often, the densely allusive poems are more readily understandable through reading them within the context of the volume in which they appear, rather than trying to understand a poem with no context to aid interpretation. As part of a carefully arranged collection, the allusive poems often resonate with each other and frequently one poem, perhaps a more direct and simpler one, helps to explain another, more abstract and complex one. Sometimes Snyder produces poems of such direct observation or re-enactment that readers become suspicious of their simplicity. Some of the brief poems, however, can be quite difficult because Snyder has so integrated diverse cultural materials into his own life that the context in which the poem is written and the context most suitable for its reading are often not evident. In a collection like *Turtle Island* this problem may not be as great as in one like *The Back Country*, because the poems in the former book were mostly written relatively close together. The poems in the latter book, however, were written across a span of nearly fifteen years.

Part of the difficulties I have raised here arise from the intellectual tradition in which he has developed. Early influences, such as Ezra Pound, William Carlos Williams, and Robinson Jeffers, were poets who wrote large-scale mythic poems, and in the case of Pound attempted to incorporate Asian poetic aesthetics and structures into his writing. Such poetic ambitions were reinforced by the San Francisco Renaissance years with senior figures such as Kenneth Rexroth, who was steeped in Asian aesthetics. Snyder's own reading, writing, and speaking knowledge of Chinese and Japanese, particularly the use of ideograms in both languages, affect his poetic style. Another contributing factor to the matter of difficulty also arises from the Pound tradition and that is the sense that the poet is an educator and a visionary, who must lead readers to new understanding, new knowledge, and images of the future. As a result, Snyder frequently points to, names, and suggests new areas of study for the reader. He also put materials together in unfamiliar ways. Two small but representative examples of such practice appear in *Earth House Hold*, when he writes: "(In San Francisco: I live on the Montgomery Street drainage—at the top of a long scree slope just below a cliff)" and "the desk is under the pencil."[53] In the first instance, Snyder describes an urban location in geological terms; in the second, he reverses the usual sense of foreground/background relationship.

There are four areas that comprise the heart of Snyder's resources for his poetry. The first consists of the cultures of inhabitory or indigenous peoples, particularly the Native American tribes of the Pacific West. Other peoples who have influenced him are the Ainu of Japan, the Hawai'ians, the Alaskan Eskimos, and the Australian aborigines. The specific and practical relationships of these peoples' cultures to the land are crucial for Snyder. His concern is not with genetic heritage, but with cultural heritage—the skills, wisdom, and behaviors learned through inhabitation in a particular place over many generations and maintained and modified by each succeeding generation. Before Snyder knew anything about Buddhism, he was learning about Native Americans, and he renewed that study and contact when he returned to the United States.[54]

The second area consists of the Asian cultures of China, Japan, and, to a lesser extent, India and Tibet, particularly in terms of their Buddhist practices and life-styles, and Buddhism's religious precursors. Snyder identifies himself as a Zen Buddhist, but even within Zen he showed an eclectic and interdisciplinary tendency through his contact not just with the Rinzai sect of his own temple but also with the Soto, Yamabushi, Jodo, and Kegon sects of Buddhism. His explanation of the Zen practice at the Ring of Bone Zendo near his home, which he helped build in 1982, gives some sense of this syncretic spirit: "It was not so much Zen as it was Chan. By that I mean not so narrowly monastic and Japanese, but more 'Chinese'— earlier, less codified, more ecumenical, ecological, and playful."[55]

The third area consists of ecology, a concern of Snyder's throughout his life. Clearly, when he was very young he intuited a harmonious relationship with nature and sensed that American culture was violating that harmony. As the years went by, his sense of ecological criteria for evaluating philosophies, beliefs, and practices deepened. His permanent return to the United States largely coincided with the recognition of ecology not simply as a legitimate science but as a long-term movement for major, evolutionary and revolutionary cultural change. In the Earth Day speech he gave at Colorado State College, Greeley, on April 22, 1970, he stated unequivocally that "the moment I stepped foot on this soil after having been away that long [almost fifteen years], I immediately got into the ecological battle—the only battle that counts now, the only thing that matters to me anymore."[56] And twenty years later, in another Earth Day speech, he looked back at that moment: "It marked the gradual closing of the Viet-Nam War and anti-war activism, and the turning of that energy toward another war, the war against earth."[57]

Snyder's remark that ecology was the only thing that mattered has never meant the exclusion of his concerns for other issues, such as the rights of indigenous peoples or the cultural significance of Buddhist practice, but rather that these issues are all interrelated and understood through the lens of ecology. For Snyder, to be a Buddhist and not an ecologist would be a travesty because the practice of Buddhism requires compassion for all beings; and to be an ecologist means that a person, consciously or not, is living a life that shares practices found in Buddhism and inhabitory cultures. He also remarked in his 1970 Earth Day speech that "the people who are beginning to understand how these networks and relationships function are the ones who can also comprehend that ancient, primitive, archaic religious world view which is the true ethic, the biological ethic, morality that includes all beings."

The whole spinning universe, humans included, is interconnected, interdependent, and interanimating for Snyder, and he would have his readers see that too. It is not surprising that Snyder was attracted at one time to the Gaia hypothesis, which posits that the biosphere is one living organism in which humans participate.[58] Through a variety of mechanisms and mythic names, including Gaia, as in "Little Songs for Gaia" in *Axe Handles*,[59] Snyder has imaged the earth as a living entity, most often in gendered terms as a goddess and as a mother.[60]

The fourth area of resources is distinct from the first three in that it is formal, a matter of poetics rather than thematics. Three major sources for Snyder's poetics need to be recognized. One is the free verse tradition of Anglo-American modernism. In particular, Snyder's form involves in many, although not all, poems a specific development in free verse known as field composition. In field composition, the entire page provides a canvas for laying out the lines of a poem. Such field composition can involve cascading lines, hyphenated words broken across stanzas, varied margins, font changes, and the insertion of symbols and designs.

For Snyder, free verse and field composition open up the poetic form to the utmost flexibility and variation possible on the printed page. They in turn enable the presentation of differing perceptions of relationships between words, between language and thought, and between words and things than is possible in more traditional fixed forms. For example, in the mid-1970s Snyder claimed that "each poem grows from an energy-mind-field dance, and has its own inner grain."[61] Snyder sees written poetry as arising from and continuing to be based on oral performance. Field composition, then, is a way of *scoring* the poem, as in musical composition, for the way in which it ought to be performed when read or sung aloud.

And this matter of scoring raises another important source for Snyder's poetics: orality. When Snyder uses the word *song* in a poem title he is using it literally rather than figuratively in most cases.[62] There are several different cultural traditions that converge here. One is Native American song. Another is the memorization and recitation tradition of Buddhism. A third is the cross-cultural shamanistic concept of healing songs, which are not descriptions or representations of experience but are actions. Woody Rehanek discusses this idea of healing songs in his study of *Axe Handles*, while Timothy Gray discusses the idea of "Song as Reorientation" in relation to the second section of *Regarding Wave*.[63]

Another source of significant formal influence on Snyder has been classical Chinese and Japanese poetics. Some of Snyder's first translation work at Berkeley involved translating the Chinese poems of Han-shan into English. These exercises became the "Cold Mountain Poems." The specific characteristics of the Chinese and Japanese languages contribute to the differences between these poetics and that of the Anglo-American tradition. Spoken Chinese is a relatively monosyllabic, word-order language, using tones phonemically (the same sound with a different tone means an entirely different word in Chinese). Written Chinese intensifies that language's differences from English, because it relies on characters rather than on an alphabet building individual words. Chinese, then, expresses poetic images in blocks and concise phrases, often without verbs and with no equivalents of English-language prepositions and articles. And classical Chinese, the language of much of the Asian poetry Snyder initially studied, does not employ any tenses.[64]

Likewise, the Japanese language has a very different syntax and grammar than English, more similar to Latin or German than any of the Romance languages. Like Chinese it is uninflected so that neither Chinese nor Japanese poetry can be written in the metrical structures that dominated English-language poetry from the time of Chaucer through the nineteenth century. Also in Japanese, sentences can be constructed with no explicit subject and the first person pronoun is rarely used in conversation. Snyder eschews metrics, and in his poems the frequent absence of articles, *a* and *the*, stands out along with the frequent absence or lengthy delay of the appearance of any pronouns. By often using infinitives and participles, *to go* and *going*, rather than subject + verb constructions, he can depict actions as occurring with no "I" claiming control. Also, he can place emphasis on the action or event rather than on the person causing or witnessing such an event. The poems of *Riprap* are replete with such Asian poetic influences.

Another evidence of Asian influence in Snyder's work is that thematic or emotive points are often made by means of the juxtaposition of two images rather than through metaphor or simile. As Laszlo Géfin notes, "in its unadorned, unpretentious simplicity and quick juxtapositions of natural data, the Snyder poem comes closest perhaps to the Fenollosian definition of the Chinese ideogram: 'a vivid shorthand picture of the operations of nature.' "[65] Finally, from the Japanese haiku form—extremely compressed seventeen-syllable poems, with many formal rules—as well as the classical Chinese poems he studied, Snyder learned to write poems that have no explicitly stated moral or authorial observation but do have very direct depiction of the things and events perceived. While Snyder's poems are populated with human beings, they are frequently not the center of attention, nor are they the reason for the existence or behavior of other beings.

Many of Snyder's poems require of the reader no special preparation to be enjoyed and appreciated, whether or not all of the nuances are noticed, allusions registered, and styles recognized. Much of the learning that the more complex poems demand is provided at least in outline in Snyder's many essays and interviews. And the continually increasing amount of Snyder criticism is making much of the exotic and arcane more accessible. A sense of Snyder's poetics is also helpful for reading his prose, since some of his essays are surprisingly direct, literal, and thematically explicit, while others are more circuitous and indirect, poetically rather than rhetorically structured whereby a recursive linkage of images accumulates a meaning that is nowhere stated outright. "The Porous World" in *A Place in Space* is an example of the former, while "The Woman Who Married a Bear" is an example of the latter.

Snyder's writing poses questions and offers solutions about the most critical questions facing American culture today and the global relationship between humanity and the rest of the planet. He offers possibilities and defines potentials for humanity's development of a balanced relationship with the rest of nature, as well as criticizing and analyzing the errors of present and past ways, not only of Western societies but also of Eastern societies as well. Snyder, alongside other contemporary writers, such as Susan Griffin, John Haines, Joy Harjo, Linda Hogan, Ursula K. Le Guin, Barry Lopez, David Mas Masumoto, Leslie Marmon Silko, and Alice Walker, is working to help shape a new cultural paradigm, one that he hopes will support the building of a new culture based on healing rather than ravaging the world.

2
From Myth Criticism to Mythopoesis
Myths & Texts

In the first half of the 1950s Snyder produced two full-length works, one critical and one poetic. *He Who Hunted Birds in His Father's Village* (not published until 1979) and *Myths & Texts* (1960).[1] The former is his undergraduate thesis written in 1951. While it is of interest in its own right as an anthropological study of a particular Native American myth, it is more important as a document informing the directions and concerns of Snyder's poetry. As he says in the foreword to the published edition, "I went on to other modes of study and writing, but never forgot what I learned from this work."[2] And Nathaniel Tarn, in the preface, claims that "the basic themes of Snyder's work, many of which appear in filigree in the thesis, are all set out in *Myths & Texts*" (p. xvi). This connection is not surprising given that Snyder started writing the poems for this sequence within a year of graduation.

Myths & Texts shows Snyder practicing mythopoesis, handling existing myths and synthesizing a new one. It also shows Snyder working toward his own voice as a poet. This development can be discerned through a comparison of *Myths & Texts* with *Riprap*. The latter collection is the one that most critics start with when analyzing Snyder's career. But starting with *Riprap* because it was published first creates confusion, as when Tim Dean attempts to compare it with the first edition of Walt Whitman's *Leaves of Grass*.[3] Some critics see Snyder's style floundering, turning back toward modernism, rather than forward to something more innovative, because they fail to realize that *Myths & Texts* was nearly finished before *Riprap* poems was started.[4]

As various critics have noted, *Myths & Texts* is far more indebted stylistically to Ezra Pound and T. S. Eliot than to direct Asian influences. As a result, the references to Hinduism and Buddhism are based primarily on reading rather than experience, and Japanese allusions are rare.[5] Certainly Snyder's own study of Chinese and Japanese were quickly taking him beyond Pound, but these are revealed more in *Riprap* than *Myths & Texts*. The ideas, however, are definitely Snyder's and those ideas are informed by a wealth of Native

American myths and practices, as well as "animal patterns he saw transforming the west coast landscape he loved."[6]

This anthropologically based Native American influence also may account for part of the difficulty of Snyder's coming into a poetics for his own voice. As Timothy Gray cogently argues,

> Snyder was never so bold as to claim sole authorship of *Myths & Texts*. The volume does not portray an individual's monomythic quest romance . . . but is instead indebted to the various agents whose movements through the centuries have traced the geographic boundaries of a Pacific Rim culture region, and indebted as well to the oral literatures that have kept their stories alive. . . . a myth is oftentimes a joint authorship, dynamically conceived and geographically routed.[7]

Gray has hit on a key explanation for the problem of voice at this stage in Snyder's poetic development. In setting out to write a poetic sequence not only did he undertake a highly ambitious project but also he chose the difficult strategy of making it polyphonic, so that multiple voices can be heard with the author's voice just one component of the book's *hero*. By hero I do not mean a single character but rather the collective life force or agent of the book. This agent could be understood in one sense as matter seeking consciousness; in another sense it could be understood as the path by which entities of the world can come to live in the balance of mutual interdependence; in a third sense it could be understood as Western humanity finding the trail to a new culture.

These notions of *path* and *trail*, along with the title of the sequence itself, suggest that Snyder's undergraduate thesis might provide some clues for understanding *Myths & Texts*. In *He Who Hunted Birds*, Snyder states: "Original Mind speaks through little myths and tales that tell us how to *be* in some specific ecosystem of the far-flung world" (p. x). Snyder surmises: "Myth is a 'reality lived' because for every individual it contains, at the moment of telling, the projected content of both his unarticulated and conscious values simultaneously ordering, organizing, and making comprehensible the world within which the values exist. One might even reformulate the statement to say 'Reality is a myth lived' " (109-10). Myth, then, places people in a cultural and physical matrix, providing them with a coherent sense of presence in place and time. Snyder also defines the role of the poet: "The poet would not only be creating private mythologies for his readers, but moving toward the formation of a new social mythology" (112). The poet acts as a vehicle for a social mythology that seeks to reintegrate individual, society, and ecosystem.

Myths & Texts produces an interplay between the kinds of information linked in the title, "the two sources of human knowledge" (vii), until at the end of the sequence they become complementary descriptions of one experience/one world. The "texts" consist of sensory experiences undergone by speakers in the poem as well as the previous experiences of historical figures who are either the speakers or the subjects of little stories. Similarly, one finds two kinds of "myths" in the poem: allusions to and brief stories about indigenous and ancient myths of previous cultures; and little stories and mythopoeic elements—figures, events, locales—that contribute to "the formation of a new social mythology," a task of the sequence explicitly stated in "Hunting 1." For Snyder, as William J. Jungels notes, "it is probably generally true that myths serve as much to sustain and encourage a culture in its practices and values as to simply reflect them."[8] In this context, then, what may have been or may be at the moment a "text," an external sensory experience, may become through the work of mythopoesis part of a little "myth" that will "tell us how to *be* in some specific ecosystem."

"Logging"

The first passage of *Myths & Texts*, "Logging 1," opens with "The morning star is not a star." This line functions as a text making a factual statement about the planet Venus, while suggesting that the mind can misinterpret sense impressions. Paraphrasing Thoreau's remark in *Walden* that "the sun is but a morning star," it also functions as a myth element. It alludes to *Walden* not simply as a literary work but as an American myth, because that book has become an element of the romantic image of American individualism and self-reliance. The negation itself, implying a false vision, begins the section on an ominous note, one prefigured by the epigraph from Acts 19:27, which refers to Christian attacks on the worship of the goddess Diana. The second and third lines, "Two seedling fir, one died / Io, Io," present another text and then a refrain alluding to one of the manifestations of the Great Mother and a myth with a wandering hero.[9] This refrain also responds to the epigraph by referring to another form of goddess worship. The next two lines describe the initial garbing for a mythic celebration. The quotation "The May Queen / Is the survival of / A pre-human / Rutting season" then produces a textual gloss of the myth. In these few lines "myth" as the religious story about a universal cultural experience and "text" as the record of specific, actual experiences are woven together.

The second stanza of "Logging 1" reads:

> The year spins
> Pleiades sing to their rest
> > at San Francisco
> > dream
> > dream
> Green comes out of the ground
> Birds squabble
> Young girls run mad with the pine bough,
>
> > > > > > Io (3)

The first line presents a text connecting human conception of time with earth's physical cycles. The next line mixes myth and text: a setting constellation is described by means of an accompanying myth. The reader is given a physical location, but the relationship of this location to what precedes it and what follows it remains ambiguous due to the lack of punctuation. If it refers in both directions simultaneously, then the myth pertaining to the setting of the Pleiades has to do with beliefs of Native peoples who lived in what is now the San Francisco area, while the invocation to "dream / dream" places the dreamer in that city as well. The invocation suggests the sensory realm of the collective unconscious, the locus for mythic vision.

Springtime is then indicated in the following lines through descriptions of animal and plant life. This text is linked to another myth of that season, in addition to the one about the Pleiades, by the last two lines, which describe "the thyrsus, carried by maenads worshiping Dionysus."[10] In some myths, Io is the mother of Dionysus, who was forced to wander for years before regaining human form. Dionysus was also a wanderer, but more importantly he is associated with rituals of the changing seasons. Snyder may be making connections not only between Spring and fertility but also between wandering and homecoming. Already influenced by Buddhism, Snyder would understand *wandering* as a potentially positive spiritual practice, one possibly far more fruitful and important than *questing*.

Jungels argues that the physical location of the Pleiades actually indicates the season as Autumn and thus: "With the goddesses retired and the earth devastated it is only in dream that spring and Io . . . can be conjured" (17), which would suggest that the Earth-worshiping values have become completely submerged. Tom Lynch, however, believes Jungels's remark about the location of the Pleiades is erroneous and that Snyder is referring to Coastal California myths in which the disappearance of the Pleiades is marked as one of the signs of Spring, and hence the use of the word "sing."[11] In this interpretation, then, "Logging 1" displays a marshaling of pagan/native myths honoring Spring and fertility in opposition to the death and destruction figured in the epigraph from Acts and the quotation from Exodus that opens "Logging 2."

In this regard, Timothy Gray's remark about the entire "Logging" section becomes relevant: "Much of the material in 'Logging' . . . derives from the summers of 1951 and 1954 when Snyder worked as a timber scaler and log setter. . . . Snyder came to see the havoc that greedy lumber companies, and Western civilization in general, had inflicted on his beloved west coast wilderness areas."[12] At the same time, it is important to remember that Snyder worked these summers on the Warm Springs Reservation involved in selective cutting rather than clear-cutting. As Snyder states in *The Practice of the Wild*, "I had no great problem with that job" because "I don't doubt that the many seed-trees and smaller trees left standing have flourished, and that the forest came back in good shape."[13] Thus one can argue that, while Snyder is aware of destructive logging and will condemn it in this section of *Myths & Texts*, he also has experienced a native-influenced alternative way of working that makes the power of Spring/fertility myths not merely psychic supports in dream time but also cultural supports for economic decisions in real time.

Snyder opens "Logging 2" with a quotation from Exodus 34:13 that prefigures the poem's epigraph, Acts 19:27. Both, however, depict attacks on matrifocal, nature-worship religions. The next line describes ancient China's denuding of its forests and subsequent ground erosion. This juxtaposition links the destructive character of widely divergent urban civilizations, indicating that Snyder recognizes that the anti-ecological drive of much human economics is not limited to the so-called West. In the following lines, the use of "killed" in relation to the forests asserts the living quality of trees and "in their own praise" places the entire description within a religious, mythic framework.

The narrator comments in stanza 4: "I wake from bitter dreams," a contrast with the invocation of "dream / dream." The bitterness, readers may presume, results from the reality of destruction that invades the dream time. The line may also reflect a desire to imagine the present-day anti-ecological activities of American culture as something unreal, a period of time that will be remembered in the future by humanity as only a brief bitter dream.

Snyder follows this bitter stanza with one that again interweaves myth and text:

> "Pines grasp the clouds with iron claws
> like dragons rising from sleep"
> 250,000 board-feet a day
> If both Cats keep working
> & nobody gets hurt (4)

Although the pines and Cats form part of an experiential text, they also can serve as symbols for the creation of a logging myth. An essential difference exists, though, between the pines-as-dragons myth, with its Chinese fertility symbolism (Jungels, 26), and any modern logging myth. The "iron claws" grasp but do not devour the clouds, while the Cats devour the pines as dead "board-feet." Gray points out the irony of this passage, in that if a forest can be "killed" then it makes no sense to claim that "nobody gets hurt," unless the concept of life is limited only to human beings.[14] The term "board-feet" contributes to such exclusion because, as with much other consumer/production terminology, it disguises the living origin of the product and defines its existence only in terms of its use/exchange value, rather than its intrinsic value.

"Logging 3" opens with a quotation describing the lodgepole pine. In juxtaposition to the preceding quotation, this one is a textbook definition that produces a phoenix-like archetypal symbol: a tree whose new life arises from seedcones gestating in the ashes of the tree-consuming fire. This symbol counters the destructive burning of "Logging 2." The second stanza describes the process of hooking felled trees. Snyder follows this vignette with a tale of the ancient Chinese figure Hsü Fang, who lived a life diametrically opposed to the destructive one that demands the rape of forests.[15] A story of modern life follows and concludes with a regenerative remark: "The kids grow up and go to college / They don't come back. / The little fir-trees do" (5).

"Logging 3" ends:

> Rocks the same blue as sky
> Only icefields a mile up,
>   are the mountain
> Hovering over ten thousand acres
> Of young fir. (5)

This text of sensory experience contains essential elements of Snyder's mythopoesis. The mountain plays a crucial role in "Burning" as its height provides the physical opportunity for a different perception of the world, paralleling the opportunity for a changed psychological perception that dreaming can provide. The stanza concludes by reiterating the image of natural regeneration that began it. Gray aptly notes:

> The "Logging 3" through "Logging 11" sections show the variety of creatures who populate the forest wasteland. Some are clearly in danger of getting hurt, while others have proved their ability to endure. Consider, for instance, the resilient species of trees and insects, which have adapted themselves to the present environment and accompany anyone who moves in this domain.[16]

The rest of "Logging" continues these patterns of interweaving. Passages "4" and "5" produce an intermixing of myth and text similar to the first three. Passages "6" and "7" produce stories from the recent past that are already beginning to take on aspects of "little myths," with "6" being a story by Snyder's father, which McCord reveals Snyder tape-recorded without his father's knowledge. This passage tells of the natural plenitude of second-growth regeneration through the rapid spread of new kinds of trees and bushes on logged-off land. "Logging 7" tells of the Wobbly (Industrial Workers of the World—IWW) days in Washington state, part of the Snyder family's political heritage in a period of explicit and violent class conflict. Those events have led to slogans that have developed their own symbolic, and potentially, mythic characteristics. Also, here, Snyder introduces Ed McCullough, one of the human "creatures" of the forest, who has also been rendered *obsolete*, like the other animals and the forest itself, by modern industrial development.[17]

Passages "8" and "9" focus almost exclusively on individual physical experiences, with a theme of the development that has disenfranchised McCullough causing an increasing homelessness for all the animals of the forest, from insect to human. Passage "8" ends with an attempt to come to terms with the destruction depicted, by recognizing that this land has been subjected to a late lava flow and so animal and plant species have been displaced before. From "Logging 10" until the end, the mythic elements increase in length in relation to the text elements, with the exception of a lull in "13." And through these passages the notion of homelessness, or displacement, takes on increasing importance. In "11," for instance, Snyder contrasts the type of work that Ray Wells must do as a chokersetter with what Ray relates of his father-in-law's life working with ponies. And in "12" Snyder presents the bleak prophecy of Drinkswater, recorded in *Black Elk Speaks*:

> "You shall live in square
>> gray houses in a barren land
>> and besides those square gray
>> houses you shall starve." (13)

One can read this prophecy as both a vision about the plight of Native Americans on reservations, but also as a curse on the Americans who displace the native peoples in order to live in boxes made of killed trees. Gray sees "Logging 12" as "a pivotal section, not merely for 'Logging,' not even for *Myths & Texts* in general, but for Snyder's larger body of work" because it sets up the irreconcilable contradiction between indigenous and exotic cultures in relation to the environments of their habitats. Gray states that "Snyder implies that the civilization's 'fortune,' by which I mean both its wealth and its fate, is a squared-off version of the Indian's circular harmony, or a capitalist version of a holistic relationship whose loss Drinkswater sadly prophesies and Snyder belatedly laments."[18] Ray Well's circular tipi in "Logging 11," then, is not only a text element but also a myth element in that it symbolizes the native circle of life in opposition to the industrial square of destruction.

Also, in "Logging 12" Snyder pens the lines "Where Crazy Horse / went to watch the Morning Star" (13), linking native vision with the narrator's observation at the opening of the sequence and, as readers will eventually discover, with the sequence's conclusion as well. As the tone of "Logging" suddenly lifts midway through "12," it becomes clear that the mythic vision of native and ancient peoples is not merely of historical interest or a dream time psychic salve, but an opening into an alternative culture by which humans, in league with "the four-legged people, the creeping people, / The standing people and the flying people" (13), could live in this world at this time. The very last parts of "12," however, suggest that Snyder realizes that the development of this alternative culture requires more than the study of Native American myths. Thus, he invokes Han-shan, the Chinese mountain hermit poet he was translating at Berkeley in 1955, and writes of "Looking off toward China and Japan" (14). Gray trenchantly notes that "by combining the cosmic unitary vision of the

Oglala Sioux with the shamanistic voice of Haida spokesmen, the Ch'an poetry of Han-shan, and the pragmatic advice of the logger [the last three lines of "12"], 'Logging 12' suggests the diverse cultural riches upon which Snyder's poetry would continue to draw."[19]

In "Logging 13," the narrator describes a natural forest fire and observes it as a lookout rather than as a logger, reflecting Snyder's own lookout experiences in the summers in between his logging work. He concludes this short section of "Logging": "The crews have departed, / And I am not concerned" (14). This passage, like the last stanza of "Logging 3," uses description of natural processes to develop reader awareness of a state of mind. The narrator's lack of concern suggests a changing perception of ecological activity. From this psychological vantage point, "Logging 14" looks back through history at all the destruction wrought by various societies and brings the survey up to the present. It also specifically condemns the destruction of Native American societies. This passage closes with an experience rendered as myth, contrasting regenerative fires identified elsewhere with this destructive one:

> Sawmill temples of Jehovah.
> Squat black burners 100 feet high
> Sending the smoke of our burnt
> Live sap and leaf
> To his eager nose. (15)

This stanza serves first as a mythic representation of a text experience; second, as an experiential evaluation of the results of a still-functioning religious myth: Christianity, which continues to guide much of American society.

The "Logging" section of *Myths & Texts* concludes with a passage entirely composed of myth fragments. "Logging 15" proposes a source for society's guiding myths other than the Judeo-Christian tradition. It draws on Hinduism and Buddhism for its perception of the interpenetrating movement of natural life and human social life and culminates by seeking solace in the Hindu teleology of the kalpa cycle.[20] This seeking produces a multiplicity of tonalities, from anger to sorrow and confidence to pessimism, which suggests the conclusion's tentative character. The way of modern life so far portrayed proves insufficient to cope with the relationship of society and nature. In like manner, the culmination of insights proves insufficient to resolve the contradictions of that relationship.

The first of half of "15" reads:

Lodgepole
    cone/seed waits for fire
And then thin forest of sliver-gray.
    in the void
    a pine cone falls
Pursued by squirrels
What mad pursuit! What struggle to escape!

Her body a seedpod
Open to the wind
"A seed pod void of seed
We had no meeting together"
    so you and I must wait
Until the next blaze
Of the world, the universe,
Millions of worlds, burning
    —oh let it lie. (16)

Here the lodgepole pine stands as a symbol of earth's regenerative cycles, including fiery destruction. The pursuit of the squirrels followed by the line from British Romantic poet Keats's "Ode on a Grecian Urn" produces both a lighthearted tone and an emphasis on fertility. The second stanza, though, abruptly reverses the tone, embedding a text of unfulfilled pairing between myth fragments of sterility and cleansing. Snyder intensifies the reversal through the diametrically opposed uses of "void." In the first stanza its use combines the positive Buddhist sense of it as emptiness with the description of an area where the forest has been cleansed of underbrush and dead wood to enable new growth. In the second stanza it is used with the American sense of sterility. Snyder suggests that hope lies in the mythic cycle of rebirth, rather than in the physical regeneration of the society depicted in "Logging."

The third stanza picks up the apocalyptic image of the kalpa cycle's end initiated in the previous stanza. The first two lines—"Shiva at the end of the kalpa: / Rock-fat, hill-flesh, gone in a whiff"—state the mythic apocalypse of the world's body, but with a significant element of hope in that "Shiva, known in the Hindu pantheon as the phallic 'Lord of Destruction,' is succeeded by the beneficent and non-grasping Ganesh, known as the 'Remover of Obstacles.' "[21] The next four lines denounce modern society and its Judeo-Christian antecedents, including its refusal to attend to the teachings of Buddha. But the narrator pulls himself up short with "Let them lie." He has condemned but not as yet offered an alternative. Further, his own seeking of solace in the cycles beyond humanity's meddling encourages passivity because he does not commit himself to changing the present human condition. The resignation of the second stanza is reiterated at the end of the third by the variation on the refrain from "oh let it lie" to "Let them lie," thereby undercutting the stanza's tone of anger.

The naming of Gautama in this stanza may be aimed more at reproaching the speaker than reproaching society. The bodhisattva vow, which will be introduced in the "Burning" section, would call on the speaker to renounce his own achievement of nirvana in the service of bringing all sentient beings into Buddhahood, an act of compassion that he does not seem ready to undertake at this point in the sequence.

The opening lines of stanza 4 present a text of natural activity, but one of mythic proportions. In opposition to the cutting down of groves, "flowers crack the pavement." The images here return to the upbeat mood of the opening stanza. The Chinese aphorism that closes the passage—"The brush / May paint the mountains and streams" / Though the territory is lost" (16)—however, questions nature's ability to succeed in its regeneration, providing no reassurance that the "territory" will not "be lost." The question stands at the end of "Logging": can the damage of modern society be undone, or will humanity so damage the biosphere that it must collapse before regenerating? And its corollary, addressed to both poet and reader: can anything be done or must people merely wait, watch, and record the death, while preserving the valuable myths and texts of past experience that may be of use when the entire cycle of life starts back up again? The use of the word "may" in this aphorism leaves an opening for the value of art, whether painting or poetry, in salvaging the wisdom of the past for the practice of the future in relation to humanity's interaction with the rest of nature.

"Hunting"

The "Hunting" section of *Myths & Texts* opens with the "first shaman song," which provides the beginning of a response to "Logging." If "Logging" exemplifies by reference to a Judeo-Christian based capitalist society that "Myth is a 'reality lived,' " then "Hunting," by means of Snyder's uses of indigenous beliefs and shamanistic practices, exemplifies that "Reality is a myth lived." Or, as Jungels puts it, "Snyder sees hunting, meditation, and shamanism as all part of the same complex of human perception" (61). Gray places a related but slightly different emphasis on the transition from "Logging" to "Hunting": "*Myths & Texts'* second phase, 'Hunting," solidifies the poet's compact between humankind and wildlife. At this juncture, Snyder assumes the aboriginal role of shaman in order to better understand the wisdom of animal behavior."[22] The experiences of animals, mythically rendered, are part of the process of learning "how to *be* in some specific ecosystem." Here the emphasis remains on the Pacific Northwest. "Hunting 1" ends with the speaker sitting "without thoughts" at the edge of a logging road "Hatching a new myth" (19). Snyder uses the participle "hatching" with precision. Throughout "Hunting" humanity's life will be intimately tied to the life cycles of animals and the myths surrounding them. The background Native American hunting and food-gathering myths, with their attendant shamanistic beliefs, that run throughout this section of the sequence bolster the narrator in his own hunting and gathering of the mythic materials that the next culture will need. At the same time, Snyder has not ceased to be "looking off toward China and Japan," and so "Hunting 2" links Northwestern hunting practices with animal images on ancient Chinese pottery.

"Hunting 3" and "Hunting 4" focus on birds. In "3" Snyder defines the text of living birds, then describes their role in divination and links that religious role with writing: "Form: dots in air changing from line to line" (20). The last line of the stanza, "the future defined," suggests that not only do myths define the future through ritual but also that the birds, as a synecdoche for all of nature, determine humanity's future. The second stanza begins with a description of Native American ritual and then moves to physical description of California coastal hills in a rainstorm. The last two lines, "Mussels clamp to sea-boulders / Sucking the Spring tides" (21), contrast with "Hunting 1," in which "Soft oysters rot now, between tides" (19). The following two-line stanza of "3" identifies by name another bird species, ducks, in addition to the ones already named in the first two stanzas, and further develops the rainstorm description. The long concluding stanza first adds to that text description and then symbolically develops the color imagery as the sky darkens in the storm. The "Black Swifts" assume a mythic divinatory role in the closing two lines: "—the swifts cry / As they shoot by, See or go blind!" (21). An ambiguous imperative, it warns that humanity must change its perception in order to "See." With the ironic use of the word "shoot," Snyder turns the birds into the hunters and the observing human the hunted.

"Hunting 4" opens with an animal-medicine myth and animal-song myths. It then moves more deeply into bird myths, with the second stanza concluding "Brushed by the hawk's wing / of vision" (22). The narrator has apparently gone on "blind," but the birds help him to gain vision. The next stanza links the migration of the Flathead tribe with a bird myth. As Jungles argues, this story about disputes over how the Golden-eye Duck makes a whistling sound may serve to emphasize the importance of accurate naming both in terms of "a fidelity to the text of objects" and "a correspondence to the inner world of myth" (80); i.e., accuracy in both dimensions of human knowledge.

"Hunting 4" closes by following the Golden-eye Duck story with a description: "Raven / on a roost of furs / No bird in a bird-book, / black as the sun" (22). The narrator of "Hunting," through his increasing perception of birds as mythic creatures, gains an understanding of the limitations of book knowledge and, by extension, of "texts" in general. Snyder ties this perception to a recognition of the most notorious symbolic bird in American literature, the raven, a Northwest trickster figure. Viewing Snyder's physical and mythic portrayals of "Raven" in terms of Native American lore, Jungels states that "the result of these associations, both visual and mythic, is to merge Raven and sun as reciprocal aspects of a single reality embodying both the object and source of vision" (80). The reality of physical appearance remains a useful source of information, but one that is limited to historical and individual sensory experience. For such experience to be understood and properly acted upon, it must be placed in context by the mythic consciousness of spiritual knowledge, which in archetypal terms resides in the collective psyche of the community rather than being created in an individual mind.

At the same time that Snyder has carried the poem into a storm's darkness, the blindness of humanity, and the sinister blackness of mythic birds, he has also prepared the reader emotionally for a strong response to the regenerative ritual of "Hunting 5." "The making of the horn spoon" presented here is drawn from Kwakiutl ritual (Jungels 82). The ritual shows respect for dead animals by its example of using all of their parts; its sacred character is reinforced by the passage closing with an untranslated chant.

"Hunting 6" and "Hunting 7" are bear and rabbit poems respectively, while the dedication for "Hunting 8" reads *this poem is for deer* (26). "Hunting 6" provides both textual information about bears in North America, and introduces the mythic story of "The Woman Who Married a Bear." "Hunting 8" opens with a myth-song sung by "deer," a sacred animal, as is the bear and the rabbit for various tribes. The second stanza describes a hunting experience without any redeeming ritual. As a result, the narrator and his cohorts are pursued by the sacred deer, "howling like a wise man," because the deer recognizes the hunter's sacrilege. The second part of "8" describes someone driving home drunk, shooting a buck caught in his headlights, ironically echoing the swifts' warning earlier in the sequence. The description ends with "the limp tongue," signaling the loss of the deer's singing voice. This loss represents one danger of "the future defined," in that current American cultural behavior may produce the permanent loss of this voice as well as that of other animals, both in its physical and mythic manifestations.

In reading this passage one needs to distinguish the individuals who narrate it. Just as with other passages in various sections, the speaker is not always the same person as the narrator. Nothing here indicates that the narrative "I" of "Hunting" as a whole is necessarily the same person as the one who kills the buck. Elsewhere in "Hunting" there occur similar narrative shifts suggesting that the narrator of the entire *Myths & Texts* is not limited to representing the voice of only a single ego in his sense of identity. As Tim Dean argues, "the characteristically Snyderian voice is one in which many voices can be heard."[23]

The description of wanton murder of the buck is followed by a brief epilogue:

> Deer don't want to die for me.
>   I'll drink sea-water
> Sleep on beach pebbles in the rain
> Until the deer come down to die
>   in pity for my pain. (28).

This promise of penance describes a type of shamanistic journey into the wilderness to seek vision, based on coastal Salish practices. The vision achieved during this penitential journey is described in "Hunting 9" and "Hunting 10," while "Hunting 11" compares it with the myth of Prajapati, "Lord of Creatures, Brahma as Creator," again linking Native American and Hindu beliefs. Only through delving deeply into animal consciousness and sensuality and then assuming a shamanistic-tickster role at passage's end can the speaker begin to renew his necessary relationship with nature. Such a relationship is absolutely essential for any kind of hunting magic to bring a hunter game. All three of these sections are predominantly myth elements, with the first two being derived from Native American myths while in "11" the first half of the passage is Hindu-based and the second half is Haida-based.[24]

While "Hunting 11" is almost entirely myth, "12" is entirely text, ostensibly describing the "I" who opens "Hunting" coming out of the mountains after being purified through his wandering. Through the course of "Hunting" this "I" changes from the one who sits by the logging road into a variety of historical and mythical figures who represent different aspects of the narrator's changing perception of humanity's relationship with nature, a key element of his developing consciousness. Here, the text is undergirded by the myth of the Garden of Eden and the fruit of the "Tree of Knowledge." But in this instance the speaker is protected from being stung by hornets because he has been purified through a mountain-hiking fast with "the smell of the mountains still on me" (31). The fruit he picks consists of apples "gone wild" (30); in other words the wilderness has recovered the tree and its fruit from civilization's domestication, just as the speaker has recovered his animal sensibility, as Gray would have it, through his shamanistic journey.[25]

Although most of "Hunting" focuses on Native American and shamanistic myths and rituals, "Hunting 11" introduces Prajapati and "14," "15," and "16" expand the integration of Hindu-Buddhist myth elements, linking the two belief systems. This linkage prepares the reader for the predominantly Hindu-Buddhist references in "Burning." "Hunting 16" closes this second section of the tripartite *Myths & Texts* with an explicit statement:

> Meaning: compassion
> Agents: man and beasts, beasts
> Got the buddha-nature
> All but
> Coyote. (34)

Here uncompassionate Coyote is a trickster, derived from Native American mythology, who can serve as an alternative to Christ. In particular, as "16" suggests, salvation has to include all sentient beings, not just humans and, hence, the appropriateness of an animal-savior figure. Closing "Hunting" with Coyote serves to carry over the mythic Native American beliefs into the next section, with Snyder's little story of animals bringing Gautama tribute serving as a bridge between these worlds.

"Burning"

"Burning 1," "*second shaman song*," explicitly continues the references to shamanistic experience. The first stanza ends: "Seawater fills each eye" (37), reiterating the theme of vision. The second stanza produces an image of an infant in the birth canal, while the third stanza introduces the Buddhist concept of *karma*—cause and effect or affinity, even across reincarnation. That it is a "congestion of karma" suggests that the individual in past lives has built up, like the sedimentation implied by the "streaked rock" that precedes it, layers of responsibilities and harmful actions that require him to continue to be reborn into this world. The fourth stanza, however, ends "River recedes. No matter," while the final stanza concludes the poem in celebration: "The sun dries me as I dance" (37). The willingness to be reborn carries over the concept of compassion from the end of "Hunting" to "Burning" through the nonchalant phrase "No matter" and the dancing celebration of rebirth.

The distinction between myth and text, ritual and real experience, is undercut by a series of evolutionary and empathetic images in "Burning 1," signaling a beginning of the movement toward synthesis that will culminate the sequence. The "congestion of karma" will be unclogged through acts of compassion across the human/nonhuman divide. Sherman Paul claims that "self-transformation is the work proposed by 'Burning,' " but this remark overvalues individual achievement by not attending to the point that it is a "shaman song."[26] The shaman and the poet are *public* figures, whose transformations serve the community, as emphasized later in "Burning 10."

"Burning 2" provides a philosophical gloss of "Burning 1" in its opening stanza. The last line, "Attentive to the real-world flesh and stone" (38), suggests a development of the concept of "consciousness" named in the opening line. Being attentive to the external world is a necessary part of human consciousness, but someone who sees *only* that world may remain unaware of the "other" within oneself. In the second line of this stanza, Snyder defines that "other" as "totally alien, non-human," which is to say wild nature or unacculturated life. Only if people can learn to be attentive to the "real-world" as both flesh and stone, and by extension both "non-human" and human, can they begin to enter into an expanded consciousness beyond the anthropocentric one of ego-consciousness.

And yet, from a Buddhist perspective the "real-world" is illusory in terms of any notion of fixity or stability. Thus the second stanza of "Burning 2" raises a second philosophical position. In response to ego-consciousness that posits the dichotomy of self and other, this stanza posits that the two concepts and the perception of them as a dichotomy are "forms" lacking permanence. The error that produces the dichotomy is that of "clinging" to appearances. The final stanza of "Burning 2" reinforces this recognition of impermanence through the example of the avocado shedding its leaves in the spring when the cherry tree is just coming into bloom. Then Snyder intrudes a reference to books, which pivots the stanza away from the cyclical, nonconscious actions of trees and birds to the conscious actions of people. The passage ends, "& not a word about the void / To which one hand diddling / Cling" (38). As Gray suggests, there may be an implication here that animals do not suffer from the illusion of form and that human beings must adopt such an animal-consciousness in contrast to ego-consciousness in order to gain the Buddhist release from "clinging" to illusions.[27] This argument sounds persuasive to me as I also hear an echo of D. H. Lawrence's poem "Wild Thing," in which he claims that no wild animal ever felt sorry for itself.[28] In brief, the shaman is responsible for developing or reinforcing a collective awareness not of the "real-world" but of the balanced relationships among entities in flux, a permeable rather than fixed consciousness.

As Sherman Paul notes, there are clear echoes of T. S. Eliot's "The Love Song of J. Alfred Prufrock" and *The Waste Land* in this stanza and the final one, both of which deal with male projections about women, sterility, and lost love, while the latter also treats myths of rape[29]; Eliot will be alluded to again later in the section as well. But Paul emphasizes Snyder as an individual, the author in the poem, rather than the relationship of these allusions to the overall theme of *Myths & Texts*. In regard to love and sexual relationships, readers will note that the topic arises only once in the first two sections of *Myths & Text*: in a text version in "Logging 9," which emphasizes the woman's loneliness and the way that work separates the man from the woman; and in a myth version in "Hunting 6," in which Snyder tells the Native American myth of the woman who married a bear, which emphasizes love across species lines. But in "Burning," love and sexual relationships, particularly erotic imagery, appear with some frequency. Love as a relationship is distinguished from the perception of sex and the lover as an object, since the former requires a surrender of control and a mutual interaction, while the latter involves an assertion of control through domination. Also in "Burning" Snyder uses the female lover as a symbol of the Void and the Earth, with all of the attendant problems of objectification that one might suspect. As Gray suggests, the sexism within this "sex-typing" of the Earth undercuts Snyder's project and, unknowingly, reinforces his more sensitive commentary on the failure of love as a relationship in distinction from sex/lover as object.

Thus, "love" is mentioned again in "Burning 3," subtitled *"Maudgalyâyana saw hell,"* which consists of two stanzas. The first relates the myth of Buddha's descent to the underworld. Reinvoking sight imagery, line three states: "The mind grabs and the shut eye sees" (39). Snyder uses "mind," which is more encompassing than the "consciousness" of "Burning 2," while the "shut eye" refers to the mystical "third eye." The mind moves beyond and below consciousness to gain spiritual vision through alternative forms of understanding. Love is now defined as part of "nature rising fragile"; and the "real-world flesh and stone" of "Burning 2" has now become "sentient stone and flesh," perhaps through the transformation suggested near the end of "2": in the line "Bones & flesh knit in the rock" (38). Thus not only is there a movement from consciousness to mind, but also sentience and love move from being perceived as part of a separate-from-nature human realm to part of nature's relational processes. In the second stanza, the narrator states that "We learn to love" and then "Burning 3" ends with "Dropping it all, and opening the eyes" (39). This opening does not block out what the "shut eye sees" but unites the two visions. This unity enables the narrator to recognize both the "forms" of the physical world and the "intricate layers of emptiness" of the spiritual world described in "Burning 2" (38).

"Burning 4" looks to the future as a mythic piece on *"Maitreya the future Buddha."* Although brief, this celebratory passage directly replies to the pessimistic aspect of "Logging 15." "Burning 4" focuses on a spiritual rebirth embodied in the promise of a future Buddha. Passages "5" and "6" provide a collage of myths, reintroducing Native American beliefs, the Beat interest in drugs, sexuality, and various moments of enlightenment. "Burning 7" focuses on Prajna, the mother of all bodhisattvas, "The Mother whose body is the Universe" (43). The quotation that closes this passage claims that one must worship Prajna to gain immortality; it can also be read in the context of "Burning" to imply that human beings must extend their love and nurturer/nurtured relationships beyond the realm of the human to the rest of nature.

"Burning 8" quotes an experience of enlightenment John Muir had when he ceased trying to solve a mountain climbing crisis through conscious analysis: "I seemed suddenly to become possessed / Of a new sense" (44). He experienced *kensho*, in Zen terminology a brief moment of enlightenment, or seeing into "essential nature," enabling him to unite with the rock rather than fight it.[30] The excerpt concludes: "My limbs moved with a positiveness and precision / With which I seemed to have / Nothing at all to do" (44). The last line suggests both *wuwei*, the action of non-action, and the letting go of consciousness, that release of the self from the limitation of rationality and will, which enables Muir to breach the self/other dichotomy. This text embodies the unity of inner and outer vision mythically propounded in "Burning 3" and demonstrates the interpenetration of physical and spiritual realities. Gray fruitfully suggests that this episode represents a response to the problem of "clinging" raised earlier in "Burning." Further, he argues that Muir's *kensho* can be compared with the narrator's conversion to Prajna worship in "Burning 7" and thus: "As Muir comes to rely upon his instincts, he is transformed by Snyder into Buddhist sage and a creaturely mover who urges us to seek uncanny release in the landscape of our dreams."[31]

"Burning 9," like "5" and "6," produces a collage of political and philosophical images from the Wobblies in the Northwest to Native American leaders, Lenin, and Chinese figures, including Confucius. Amidst these images is placed the paradoxical statement, "Surrender into freedom, revolt into slavery" (45), which returns readers to the issue of clinging-versus-letting-go and Buddhist belief, which paves the way for "Burning 10," "*Amitabha's vow*." This passage presents a humorous sequence of updated bodhisattva vows, in which the traditional Buddhist vows to forego nirvana in order to bring all sentient creatures to enlightenment are presented in Beat language. The last lines of "10" echo "Hunting 12," which describes the narrator coming out of the mountains after fasting. Here the "we" decide not to "come down" but to continue ascending. "Burning 10" marks a transition in the poem, a commitment to a way of perception made here that will culminate in the epiphany of "Burning 17" in which the illusory dichotomy of myth and text dissolves.

"Burning 11" and "Burning 12" treat the difficulties of embarking on this path. "Burning 11" imitates koan study in which the student tries to answer the question "What is the way of non-activity?" (46). The answer begins with a description of the meditation posture, then blossoms into myth elements, initially beautiful but increasingly presented in terms of pain and fire. It closes with a Coyote-as-savior legend in which he and Earthmaker contemplate rebuilding the world. This section thus links the fire imagery of the end of "Logging" with the Coyote figure introduced at the end of "Hunting," indicating the increasing momentum toward synthesis as the sequence draws to a close.

Such looping backs continue in "Burning 12," which begins with the narrator describing a nightmarish meditation reiterating the impermanence of the body addressed in "Burning 2." The second stanza tells of "The city of the Gandharvas," a beautiful fairy-tale place, but, as Snyder notes, "an Indian trope for a 'mirage.' "[32] The passage closes with a reference to another bird, the nighthawk, "Circling & swooping in the still, bright dawn" (47). These lines underscore the difficulty of experiencing enlightenment along the path of meditation, reiterate the hope that nature will assist in the experiencing of vision, and foreshadow the tranquil state of knowledge presented in "Burning 17."

"Burning 13" returns to the more unsure tone opening "Burning 12." The first stanza presents the difficulties of gaining release from the distraction of the senses. The second contrasts the experience of writing poetry with the text of life in which that writing took place. The third briefly intermingles text and myth fragments, while the fourth begins with a myth of Emperor Wu putting an end to war. This story is brutally contradicted by the lines that follow it: "Smell of crushed spruce and burned snag-wood. / remains of men, / Bone-chopped foul remains, thick stew / Food for crows—"(48). The first line alludes to the world of "Logging," while the pun on "foul" and the reference to "crows" call into question the vision gained from birds in "Hunting."

The rest of the passage confronts this deepening doubt by acceding that conditions are bad, then responding "As long as you hesitate, no place to go" (49)—a gloss on the John Muir vignette of "Burning 8." After casting doubt on meditation, poetry, and politics, the narrator then defies the darkness: " 'Leap through an Eagle's snapping beak' / Actaeon saw Dhyana in the Spring" (49). The narrator calls on readers to leap beyond the living of reality to the living of myth, turning the latter into the former to gain a glimpse of the world beyond appearance. The use of "Dhyana" instead of Diana emphasizes in this pun not only the danger of such a leap—after all Actaeon is destroyed as a result of his vision—but also the power of myth to concentrate the essence of experience if one opens oneself to such perception. Snyder punningly alludes to meditation as a powerful goddess with "Dhyana," which is a transliteration of Sanskrit meaning "absorption; the form of meditation."[33] The passage ends with a haiku-like description of a moment of enlightenment, written in the understated language typical of Zen humility.

Looping back occurs once again in "Burning 14," which returns to "Burning 10," providing a text for the narrator's marrying. After "a marriage has been" (50), the couple hikes Mt. Tamalpais in Marin County near San Francisco. "Burning 15" then returns this now-married narrator to civilization. Paul accurately emphasizes that this unity with the "other" is predicated upon an adoption of matrifocal values.[34] The return occurs through a series of locations expanding outward from a farm in the Pacific Northwest to the universe, symbolized by its mythic center "Mt. Sumeru L.O." (51; L.O. is the abbreviation for Lookout). Text and myth alternate until the closing two lines where they come together as a description of the physical reality of the lodgepole pine of "Logging 15"; the "hot seeds" are not only the source of future trees but also a new mythic vision; they "steam underground" beneath the destructive civilization of "Logging" waiting for the right conditions to burst forth.

After this foreshadowing of "Burning 17," the next passage, "16," briefly relates a set of songs of different cultures, then reiterates the invocation of "Logging 1," "Dream, Dream, / Earth!" (52). This passage speaks of a human transformation from living a superficial physical reality to living a deep spiritual reality, and closes with the signature of Coyote.[35] In line with the *Amitabha's Vow* of "10," this transformation does not only refer to human beings but to all "those beings living" on the planet.

"Burning 17," the final section of "Burning" and of *Myths & Texts*, brings the alternation of myth and text fragments together. It consists not of two stanzas, but of three. The first is labeled "the text," the second "the myth," while the third has only three lines: "The sun is but a morning star / Crater Mt. L.O. 1952-Marin-an 1956 / end of myths & texts" (54). The first stanza presents a text of fighting a forest fire. The second retells the text as myth: "Fire up Thunder Creek and the mountain— / troy's burning!" and then "The cloud mutters / The mountains are your mind" (53). The link is made between physical experience and psychological experience, between myth and reality, demonstrating the unity of Snyder's remark that "Myth is a 'reality lived,' . . . Reality is a myth lived."

The myth stanza does not replicate the text stanza. To do so the line, "The sun is but a morning star" (53), would need to end the stanza to maintain a parallel with "The last glimmer of the morning star" (54). But Snyder sets the line apart so that it returns readers to the start of this experience of changed perception, the opening line of "Logging 1." In terms of emotional power, the setting off of this line, taken directly from *Walden*, reverses the ominous tone of the opening and posits unlimited possibility before the sequence's readers.

The myth presents an awareness that readers can gain by recognizing that "the mountains are your mind." This identity is reinforced by the location line, "Crater Mt. L.O. 1952-Marin-an 1956" (54). The sequence has been written as a wandering journey in which there is no end or goal, but only the experiencing of the journey itself, which directly contradicts the argument that some critics make that *Myths & Texts* replicates the separation-journey-return motif of the monomyth.[36] The first location, while a physical place, alludes to the Mt. Sumeru of "Burning 15," a mythical, mystical vantage point. "Marin-an 1956" presents the text equivalent, the physical place of Marin County, California; the use of "an," however, allies the location with Japan, and by inference to Buddhism, because this suffix in Japanese would refer to a hermitage and also a Zen temple annex.[37]

The argument for including the location line as part of the sequence is based on considering the poem's final line to be "end of myths & texts." The closing of the sequence represents the end of myths and texts because readers can no longer view them as separate categories of experience or perception. Snyder's "little myth" of *Myths & Texts* can help readers to learn to recognize the two "sources of human knowledge" as one *myths'n'texts*. The completion of the poem opens up another arm of the spinning galaxy of experience, which would involve the entire mind, not just consciousness. Through *Myths & Texts* Snyder works out the public responsibilities of the poet, as well as the contributions of mythopoesis, to the cultural transformation that he believes the United States must undergo.

Readers coming to *Myths & Texts* today might very well view it initially as a very postmodern poem, given its structure, indeterminacy, and extensive playfulness. Formally, however, it is written very much in emulation of Pound's modernist techniques practiced in the *Cantos*. Like that work, and unlike postmodernist sequences, *Myths & Texts* very much reflects the ambition to produce a poem that will provide a visionary and ethical guide for the transformation of culture, a master narrative. Yet, at the same time, it exceeds the modernist project of Pound and his peers in that it encompasses the world beyond human culture as a key element in such cultural transformation; and in so doing it denies popular premises in postmodernist literature, which are that language signifies concepts but does not refer to the material world and that surface phenomena are the only reality without any ontological depth or teleological meaning.[38] At the time of writing *Myths & Texts*, Snyder very much believed in the possibilities for language to refer people to the phenomenal world and to the larger-than-phenomenal world, and he believed in the possibility of human agency to effect positive social change; he continues to believe in these possibilities to this day.

3
Working Rhythms
Riprap and Cold Mountain Poems

Throughout the 1950s Gary Snyder was publishing poems in various small magazines. After he left for Japan, the submission of his poems, as well as the efforts to get *Myths & Texts* and a collection of short poems published, was largely handled by his friends. Much letter writing and many conversations about various book and journal projects took place with the editors publishing the Beats and San Francisco writers. Out of such discussion came the publication of Snyder's translation of Han-shan in 1958 in *Evergreen Review* and the collection titled *Riprap* in 1959. These two projects were combined in 1965 under the title *Riprap & Cold Mountain Poems*. A new edition with an afterword by Snyder was published in 1990 and in the title the ampersand was changed to an "and."[1]

Riprap became Snyder's first published book of poems only by circumstance. He was more concerned in the latter half of the 1950s with getting *Myths & Texts* published. It is clear from the correspondence available that Snyder did not initially write the poems in *Riprap* to be unified in any particular way. At the same time, the poems as arranged do represent a sequence, although one much looser in structure and content than *Myths & Texts*. James Wright, therefore, errs when he remarks that "*Riprap* was a simple collection of occasional poems."[2] In contrast, Sherman Paul claims that "as always, composition is by book, which is more than the sum of its parts and a greater achievement than any poem."[1] As his small press publications and the table of contents of *Left Out in the Rain* indicate, Snyder had written dozens of other poems between 1952 and 1958 that could have gone into *Riprap*. Instead, he chose only twenty-one, which cover some of his experiences from 1953 through 1958.

These twenty-one poems record a rite of passage, which took him from the western mountains of the United States to Japan and back again. The arrangement of these poems both reflects and prefigures the actual journey of Snyder's life from the early 1950s to 1968. The Han-shan translations, or Cold Mountain Poems, actually fall into the middle of the first leg of Snyder's journey. They were begun in the San Francisco Bay Area while Snyder studied Asian languages at

Berkeley and attended the Berkeley Buddhist Church. And as his knowledge of Buddhism and Asian cultures deepened, he reworked the translations. With the help of a Japanese specialist in Chinese poetry in Kyoto, he refined them prior to their publication in *Evergreen Review*. One could argue that the translations ought to be read between the last of the poems set in the United States and the first of the poems set in Japan in the *Riprap* cycle rather than at the end of the volume, since they represent a process of personal development experienced by the translator. They help clarify some of Snyder's own poetics and show a sense of identification between Snyder and Han-shan. One should not, however, draw biographical conclusions about Snyder by analyzing his depictions of Han-shan.[3]

In 1959, Snyder wrote a statement on the poetics to be found in *Riprap* for Donald Allen's anthology *The New American Poetry*. There he actually made two quite distinct statements. First, he claims that "the rhythms of my poems follow the rhythm of the physical work I'm doing and life I'm leading at any given time." Therefore, " 'Riprap' is really a class of poems I wrote under the influence of the geology of the Sierra Nevada and the daily trail-crew work." Second, he claims that "I tried writing poems of tough, simple, short words, with the complexity far beneath the surface texture. In part the line was influenced by the five- and seven-character line Chinese poems I'd been reading, which work like sharp blows on the mind."[4]

In *Riprap and Cold Mountain Poems*, the poems of Han-shan are examples of just that type of poetry described in this second claim, and one can see in this volume the affinities between the translations and some of the English-language poems. But four of the other poems in the volume come from Snyder's first year in Japan and five others from the experience of working on the tanker *Sappa Creek*. The style, then, of the poems ought to shift if Snyder's claim that they are based on specific places and types of work holds true. And indeed, to some extent, the poems written in Japan and aboard ship do differ from the others. This accounts for Snyder's own view of the volume as a loose collection, as well as for the complaints of some critics about the uneven quality of the poems. In correspondence with Timothy Gray, Snyder wrote that "*Riprap* is entirely North American, with just a trace of Chinese flavor, and is actually NOT a play of Chinese poetics, which is formal, rhymed, strict, parallelistic and elegant."[5] In my view the second half of this statement is quite accurate, but the first is not. Both in this correspondence and in the first claim for Donald Allen, I take Snyder to mean only the pre-Japan poems, since it would be a contradiction to say that poems written in Japan are "entirely North American."

Further, while Chinese and Japanese poetic structures are clearly not much of an influence, there does seem to be a grammatical influence from Chinese and Japanese on Snyder's use of English, as in the dropping of articles, the frequency of participles and infinitives, and the use of sentence fragments. Snyder builds in the early poems of *Riprap* a unique syntax, which unavoidably was influenced by his study of the Chinese and Japanese languages. He does not, however, strictly maintain it throughout the volume. Rightfully so, Snyder employs a different syntax for a different kind of poem from one section of *Riprap* to another.[6] Similarly, Snyder only occasionally makes use of the kind of field composition found in *Myths & Texts*. He does, however, tend throughout to use "I" quite sparingly and to practice frequent enjambment, especially in the poems that have very short lines. The enjambment opens up a multiplicity of possible meanings, then, for many words, which depend on whether the reader aligns them with what precedes them or with what follows them and whether or not they can be read as both noun and verb. Often the most fruitful interpretations are those that provide for the simultaneous resonance of the multiple meanings that enjambment enables.

The first poem of *Riprap*, "Mid-August at Sourdough Mountain Lookout" (3), places the speaker atop a mountain far from civilization. The degree to which this isolation has affected him is suggested by the pronoun "I" not appearing until the second of the poem's two stanzas; it appears once again in the same line and that is all, as if self-identification has become a burden. This relative absence of "I" in a first-person poem supports my previous point about linguistic influence on Snyder's style. In both conversational and written Japanese "I" is almost never used, except for emphasis. In English the use of infinitives and participles, as in the eighth and ninth lines of "Mid-August," facilitates such elision.

The opening five-line stanza depicts natural events without emotion or point of view. Then, the second stanza begins with the speaker identifying himself in the first person but only by means of a negation: "I cannot remember things I once read." He recalls that he has friends, but they belong to the far-off cities. This place has caused him to establish a new point of orientation and identification. It has pulled him loose from his past, but not abolished it. As the poem moves toward closure, emphasis is placed on human activity as natural actions, part of the nature of the place, just like the activities depicted in the first stanza.

This understanding occurs in the "high still air," because it is a place for meditation and observation. As Katsunori Yamazato suggests, "the reader feels behind the poem the solitary figure of the young Snyder who . . . is deeply engaged in adjusting the way in which he absorbs the world, his mechanism of perception."[7] The observational condition shifts the emphasis of perception and the focus of the poem from the point of view of the speaker to the point of the speaker's attention, the natural world of the present, which establishes in his mind a contrast with the civilized world of the past.[8]

Timothy Gray points out the complexity of the syntax of this poem, which, through enjambment, prevents a reader from isolating one item or action from another. There is also the effort of the poet to fit into the rhythms of the world as observer-participant, not merely observer: "As the rhythmic landscape of the first stanza implies a gentle series of processes . . . so too does the poet who wishes to connect with it partake in a series of simple processes." Gray contends that this rhythmic relationship signals a significant poetic achievement for Snyder: "By avoiding fixation (the most basic of Zen tenets) and by granting the land its own agency, Snyder distances himself from the egotism and appropriation plaguing most Romantic landscape poetry."[9]

But if the Sourdough summer was a significant period for Snyder learning about himself in relation to the wilderness that he surveyed as fire lookout, the following summer plunged him back into that other world of "cities," alienation, and conflict. The second poem of *Riprap*, "The Late Snow & Lumber Strike of the Summer of Fifty-four" (4-5), also ends with the activity of "looking," but lacks the meditative serenity prompted by Sourdough. Paul observes that "stillness now hovers over an entire landscape, its psychological equivalent is not serenity but quiet desperation."[10] Like virtually all of the poems of *Riprap*, these first two are highly autobiographical. Snyder had gone up to Washington state in 1954 to start work but after only a few days was dismissed because of being blacklisted. As a result, he had to find work as a logger and locating a job was made more difficult by a labor strike.

Snyder opens "Late Snow" with snapshots of conditions in Washington during the strike, depicting himself roaming the state looking for work. In the second stanza, he attempts to get back to the Sourdough experience through a quick climb, but the attempt fails. The effort to achieve a moment of tranquility is suggested by the way the lines of the stanza shorten into a haiku-like structure, reminiscent of *Myths & Texts*. Pines shrouded in fog appear to float, and the drifting speaker reflects that he can find "No place to think or work." These lines remind one of part of "Logging," when the narrator is depicting the mythic character of the dragons clawing the pines. But the reality there of the Cats killing the forests, as with the reality here of not being able to meditate without also being able to work, thwarts the mythic, idyllic impression sought in this moment of "Late Snow."

The speaker, however, does not despair. Instead, in the third stanza, he tries again by climbing Mt. Baker and feels a sense of ecstasy, although only momentarily. While on Sourdough in 1953, employed to observe and wait, Snyder could distance himself from cities and civilization. But on Mt. Baker in 1954 he is reminded that there is no part of the world perceived as wilderness without a civilization around it, so he must descend the mountain to stand in a Seattle unemployment line. In the moment of revelation, as with the first poem, the "I" is finally introduced when recognitions about relationships and mind occur.

After "Late Snow" Snyder leaves the mountains, from which he has been turned away by the economic imperatives of capitalism. He intrudes into the volume a poem he later omitted from *No Nature*. "Praise for Sick Women" (6-7) focuses on a multiplicity of patriarchal cultures and their myths and ritual practices based on perceptions of the menstrual cycle. The word "sick" here becomes complicated in its meanings and misunderstandings.

The first stanza of Part 1 presents the stereotype of a woman as innately closer to nature, therefore more instinctive and intuitive, but the last line renders the image problematic: "A difficult dance to do, but not in mind." Does this last line replicate the anti-intelligence stereotype depicted or does it call that image into question? A favorable interpretation of the poem would be that the difficulty of the dance comes not from a problem with the intelligence of the women but from the constraints of a male-dominated society that fears the power of menstruation. As a result women are required to lead their lives in highly restricted patterns and the identification of women with nature, which ought to be a laudatory recognition of humanity's condition as a part of nature, is in actuality used to justify the domination by men of the wild in both.

The second stanza moves into archetypal imagery that depicts the woman as the cause of male sexuality and the belief that sexuality binds him to the earth and to earthiness. Such a relationship should be a positive result of women's alleged proximity to nature. But as Susan Griffin has demonstrated in *Woman and Nature: The Roaring Inside Her*, such a view has not been the common one throughout most of the history of western culture (nor is the problem limited to the West).[11] From early Christianity through the Enlightenment, one finds the body viewed as a link to mortality, temptation, sin, and defilement. Therefore, man's relationship to woman is a soul-corrupting one. The temptation of sexuality is clearly evident, but what is it in the poem that the man sees? The next single, long stanza reveals that he sees the woman menstruating but that he does not see it for the natural event that it is, part of a natural cycle in which he too participates.

Bob Steuding relates that Snyder explained this poem at a poetry reading in 1969 by remarking that he was trying "to put myself in a place where I could understand the archaic menstrual taboos in regard to the growth and conception of the fetus." And Steuding goes on to explain that Snyder "implies how fear and awe of the procreational process influenced the development of ritual in the hope of controlling the experience."[12] But what also needs to be emphasized is the degree to which such efforts at male control of the female reflect male efforts at control and domination of nature as well.

Crucial to the recognition of the failure of such stereotypes to educate men or women, and to represent reality, is Snyder's repetition of "All women are wounded." This kind of notion denies the natural, cyclical character of the menstrual cycle and sees it as a weakness rather than as a sign of strength and fecundity, likely because men have been frightened by both of those qualities in women. As with his criticism of Chinese and Japanese cultures in *Myths & Texts*, Snyder here criticizes implicitly primary cultures that demonstrate significant ecological awareness and balance between culture and nature but fail to see the balance inherent in menstruation. When he asks, near the end of the poem, where hell is and answers that it is "in the moon" and then "in a bark shack," he is highlighting through juxtaposition the contradiction between humanity's being a part of, and in rhythm with, natural cycles and various cultures' denials of that relationship.

Looking at "Praise for Sick Women" by itself, readers often have trouble discerning that Snyder does not accept the various mythologies and cultural beliefs that he presents in the poem. But by reading it along with other poems in *Riprap*, particularly "Milton by Firelight" and "For a Far-Out Friend," it becomes clear that the myths he upholds, as in *Myths & Texts*, are ones that affirm human physicality and the interconnectedness of mind and body. They are ones that contradict the dualisms that he finds running rampant through the menstrual taboos used to denigrate women. Part of the negative interpretations of this poem may result from readers' knowledge of Snyder's use of myths that place women in passive roles as representatives of the Void, the muse, or other symbols for the working out of male-initiated projects, as in *Myths & Texts* when he refers to "vagina dentata" in "Burning 13."

Because of Snyder's selection process in choosing poems from *Riprap* to include in *No Nature*, I want to treat the poems slightly out of order here and jump ahead to another poem that he omitted from that collection, "For a Far-Out Friend" (13-14). This poem takes the reader back to "Praise for Sick Women" in part because it is the second poem in which women are mentioned in *Riprap* and in part because of the subject of mythological depictions of women and the feminine. Sickness comes up again in this poem, but here it is the sickness of the male speaker, who reveals a lack of sanity resulting from his participation in the male chauvinism of American patriarchal culture and its violence against women. And here is a curious contradiction. The poem presents a recognition of the dangers of idealization at the same time that the speaker engages in idealizing a woman by identifying her with images of Hindu goddesses. The reason for his violence toward her remains unstated, and, while recognizing a certain superiority on her part because she "had calm talk" for him, the speaker wants her to share the blame for the situation.

The first stanza concludes with the speaker thinking back to an earlier time of ecstasy between him and the woman, and he remarks, "I saw you as a Hindu Deva-girl." In the second stanza, he claims that visions of her body made him "high" for weeks. From his idealization and mythological imaging of her "body"—but not her person, apparently—he is pulled down to earth by a sudden recognition:

> And I thought—more grace and love
> In that wild Deva life where you belong
> Than in this dress-and-girdle life
> You'll ever give
> Or get.

What remains unclear at poem's end is the degree to which the speaker recognizes his own complicity. Does he realize that he too has been part of that "dress-and-girdle life" through his violence and through his idealization of her physical attributes as displaying some divine essence? Further, the problem of falling back on mythology to stereotype women, even when stereotypes are allegedly positive and beatific, seems unrecognized.[13] The images employed by Snyder in this poem of the Deva girl may seem part of a positive depiction of women, but they actually feed into the kind of stereotypes that he criticizes in "Praise for Sick Women." In neither poem is a real woman adequately engaged by the speaker. Charlene Spretnak makes an interesting remark in this regard: "I think the full capacity for valuing the radical female voice arose within Gary only at midlife. . . . The women in the early works are often presented as slightly alien creatures who are perceived to be in an adversarial relationship, at some level, to the poet."[14]

One can in the context of *Riprap* as a sequence profitably read this poem as the demonstration, perhaps unintentional, of the limitations of the speaker's developing consciousness. These limitations are manifested in two ways. One, while he has been working out the relationship of humanity to wild nature, he has clearly not learned much about the relationship of human to human when gender and sexuality are involved. Two, he has not figured out how to mediate the contradictions between his budding vision of an appropriate relationship of human to nature and the violent, destructive characteristics of modern American society.[15] They have proven to be generally unsuccessful poems; as a result, it is not surprising to see them omitted from Snyder's selected volume, *No Nature*. Also, to the degree that *Riprap* is a sequence based on work rhythms, neither poem fits in particularly well with that unifying structure.

"Piute Creek" (8) returns to the meditative mood of "Mid-August" and also speaks against dualistic thinking. The speaker here is in the Yosemite high country, which Snyder experienced in 1955, and he is recording his experience of a tremendous awe-filled moment as he is overwhelmed by the natural world in which he is immersed. Part of this awe results from the abundance of nature in its myriad variations and seemingly endless continuation. Besides filling the speaker with awe, this moment also induces a sense of what the poet Robinson Jeffers called, in the Preface to *The Double Axe and Other Poems*, the "transhuman magnificence."[16] Nature includes and surrounds the individual, and in the process of realizing that participatory inclusion, he moves beyond the limitations of being human.

> All the junk that goes with being human
> Drops away, hard rock wavers
> . . . .
> Words and books
> like a small creek off a high ledge
> Gone in the dry air.

The key concepts here are the wavering of the rock and the simile comparing books to evaporating water. In the first instance, the sense of natural entities as solid, static objects—things as resources, inert except for human use—breaks down. They are seen as an interactive, dynamic web of energy transfers, which is self-organizing. In the second instance, the forgetting of that book knowledge, which is irrelevant, trivial, and inaccurate, is depicted as itself a natural process of learning. The behaviors of the creek and the speaker result from the specific conditions of dry summer days in the Sierras.[17] As Gray notes, the lineation of the poem with its multiplicitous enjambments mimics in its cascading structure the image that the lines I have quoted verbally render.[18]

The second stanza of "Piute Creek" pulls back from this immersion to work out the experience as a lesson. And this stanza renders it a different kind of poem from "Mid-August at Sourdough Mountain Lookout." That poem depicted the process of meditation and its implications but drew no specific lessons. What Snyder has learned at Piute Creek is summarized in the first three lines of this second stanza: "A clear, attentive mind / Has no meaning but that / Which sees is truly seen." One's vision is based on one's place when experiencing that vision.

But Snyder has not yet finished the poem. To leave it here would, if only by force of human habit, give the impression that nature still exists for people to use it as they see fit, since it is a person who is doing all of this seeing and using nature to draw moral lessons for other people. But even as one could say that a human looking at Piute Creek is civilized nature studying wild nature, the reverse can occur. Snyder introduces to the poem the belief that wild nature in its various manifestations can and does see and study human nature:

> Back there unseen
> Cold proud eyes
> Of Cougar or Coyote
> Watch me rise and go.

At the end of the poem Snyder remarks on the fact that the speaker is but a visitor to this particular part of wild nature, not a resident of it. It is appropriate, then, that he approach the place not only with awe for the landscape but also with deference to its inhabitants.

"Milton by Firelight" (9–10), the companion poem to "Piute Creek," with the dateline "Piute Creek, August 1955," continues the same process of lesson-learning but does so in the course of attacking some of the myths that make it difficult for humanity to learn the ways of wild nature. The poem begins with a dismal quotation from Milton's *Paradise Lost* and then contrasts it with the portrait of a man utterly in tune with "The vein and cleavage" of the rocks he works with building trails. Looking at this man in place, Snyder concludes, "What use, Milton, a silly story," rejecting in its entirety the Genesis account of Adam and Eve's expulsion from the Garden of Eden.

The next stanza describes an Indian who, like the rock-working trail builder, is in place and hungry for fresh food, including apples. There is no temptation here and no loss of innocence. Being from a different culture, he need not be subjected to Christian mythology. As Thomas Leach suggests, referentiality not symbolism is what concerns the poet at this point: "An apple for Snyder is a real fruit, not a symbol of supernatural knowledge."[19] From the observation of this "chainsaw boy," Snyder is led to an observation about temporality and the relationship of human time to biospheric time. Recognizing that the land surrounding him will eventually dry up to the point where it cannot sustain human life, he concludes that there never was a "paradise" or a "fall." According to Snyder, the acceptance of human mortality and the much greater longevity of the mountains frees humanity from both the desire for paradise—the utopian idealization of the unattainable—and the abhorrence of hell—the demonic idealization of human fallibility.

At the end of this third stanza, the speaker utters the epithet "OH HELL!," but it is only an expression of frustration. Hell may be a state of mind, a sense of damnation that people genuinely experience, but it is not part of the natural world except as nightmare. The final stanza places Milton and the speaker's wrestling with his own words in proper perspective. "Fire down" is a real event, the fading of the campfire, but it may also be a metaphor for the dying down of the kind of Puritanical mind Milton exemplifies. And in the end, the speaker accepts Milton's imaginings and the myth he promotes as part of human participation in the world, no matter how misguided. If humanity's stay in the Sierras is temporary, eventually giving way to the scorpion, then the kind of concerns Milton espouses, and some of the speaker's contemporaries share, must also eventually pass away. Snyder has passed judgment on Milton's beliefs and the Christian myth of the Fall, but his tone changes from anger and frustration to an acceptance of the existence of such beliefs and a recognition of their temporality. The change of tone in "Milton by Firelight" is reminiscent of the tonal changes in "Logging 15."

"Above Pate Valley" and "Water" (11 and 12), the two poems that follow "Milton by Firelight," continue to address the issue of temporality by representing the specific events of two separate summer days. In these poems the direct experience of the thing-in-itself is emphasized, although the contrast of "On their / Own trails. I followed my own / Trail here" makes an implicit thematic statement. Human temporality is depicted in the first poem by the speaker's finding thousands of arrowhead shavings, indicating that Native Americans had camped where the speaker now camps. There is, then, a continuity of human experience but also a recognition of difference. Snyder knows he is not Indian and cannot replicate the life they once lived in this place; rather, he must pursue his own way into the kind of human/nature harmony that he would attribute to them. At the same time, the last line of the poem, "Ten thousand years," which is in no way explicitly linked to the previous part of the poem, seems to honor the presence of a humanity in this place that has known how to act accordingly, leaving little trace and less damage. Continuity and discontinuity, change and permanence abide together in this experience.

"Water" depicts a unique moment. The speaker dunks himself into a fast-flowing mountain stream and with "ears roaring," "Eyes open," and head "aching from the cold," finds himself facing a trout. The suggestion is that of an experience undergone in a state of ecstasy, as implied by the dancing, leaping run of the speaker, mimicked by the lineation and sounds of this single-stanza poem. Here there is total immersion without separate consciousness, both literally through the head dunking and figuratively through the indication that the nature of the place compelled the speaker to act in this manner. He claims that the sun "Whirled" him into his descent while a baby rattlesnake forced him to leap.

But more can be read into this poem if one recalls that in "Mid-August at Sourdough Mountain Lookout" the speaker is "drinking cold snow-water." He has moved from meditation in that poem to a state of ecstatic immersion in nature in this one. That first poem and this one can be seen to frame a certain passage from the beginning of a new level of consciousness about humanity-in-nature to its fulfilled awareness.

The next two poems focus on meeting two people very different from one another, but in both cases Snyder addresses the issue of possibilities and probable futures (one of these "For a Far-Out Friend" I have already discussed). The four poems following these address various topics, but all seem focused on decision-making processes. Like "Piute Creek," they are more about the one seeing than the seen. They are followed by the Japan poems of *Riprap* and one cannot but help think of them in terms of Snyder's biography. The months between the end of the Yosemite work and Snyder's first trip to Japan were ones of preparation for departure. Perhaps most interesting here is the range of tones and the subtle but unmistakable expressions of conflicting emotions in these poems.

"Hay for Horses" (15) is a much simpler poem than "For a Far-Out Friend," which precedes it. Basically, Snyder presents the narrative of an old man who has found himself performing the same work his entire life and being dissatisfied with it the entire time. On the one hand, the poem clearly shows the dangers of being locked in to one thing for life by the necessities of wage labor. In this sense, although tonally much lighter, "Hay for Horses" echoes elements of "The Late Snow." On the other hand, while there is the warning of the danger of being locked into a particular form of work, there is also the crisp, straightforward description in the first half of the poem of the actual process of stacking the hauled hay. The poem radiates with the same type of rhythm that must be established to accomplish such work efficiently, and in the rhythm and his words Snyder clearly shows admiration for doing manual work and doing it well. Although the old man complains of his lot in life, Snyder seems to suggest that he could have done far worse than he has.

"Thin Ice" (16) seems to follow in the same vein of simple representation. Snyder describes an experience in which the figurative language of an old saying, "Like walking on thin ice," is depicted as a literal event, and, as a result, takes on new meaning through concrete experience informing abstract thought. If read in relation to "Hay for Horses," "Thin Ice" can be read as having the same kind of dual message, a warning and an appreciation. As for the warning, in terms of Snyder's life, what if he had decided not to go to Japan but had stayed in California drifting from one temporary job to another or becoming a permanent trail crew member, always just barely getting by—the thin ice of marginal economic subsistence? The poem also suggests that people do not take folk wisdom and myths seriously enough, forgetting that such stories are based on real, and often painful, experience. Beyond this warning there is also the appreciation of the speaker's direct, immediate lesson-learning while out in the mountains "Walking in February." Nature remains the great teacher and such teaching always contains risks.

There is also the common experience of someone knowing something but not really taking it to heart until a significant event alters that person's perspective. "Nooksack Valley" (17) displays this kind of shift in perspective. Gray notes that " 'Nooksack Valley' was composed on a hitchhiking trip Snyder made with Allen Ginsberg in January and February of 1956. . . . Snyder pauses to reflect upon where he is, and where he is going."[20] Staying overnight in an empty "berry-pickers cabin" the speaker is observing the valley around him, but he is not really paying much attention to it. Instead, he is thinking of the near future when he will return to the San Francisco Bay Area and then a few months later depart for Japan. His thoughts do not produce euphoria or even happiness on the eve of this great adventure. The poet looks back with doubt and uncertainty. He realizes how much he loves the land he has come to know intimately through his years as a mountain climber, hiker, fire lookout, and logger, and feels a certain premature nostalgia for the positive aspects of American culture. He also doubts his own development, speaking of "wasted theories," "schools, girls, deals," and writing bad poetry. A sense of transience might very well make the speaker feel that interest in the literary arts is just a fad without much substance.

Ironically, his doubt about poetry and his complaint about "damned memories" and "wasted theories" is expressed in a carefully crafted poem, with close attention to line breaks, phrasing, and the layout of the poem on the page. Although the memories and theories may be "damned" and "wasted," Snyder has ensured that they will be remembered and appreciated through their encapsulation in a published poem that will live on long after his own death. The doubt expressed here, then, is couched in a larger recognition that the speaker is a poet who will in the end imitate the "setter pup," who after turning about in circles settles down to sleep. At a certain point the speaker has to quit worrying and take the next step regardless of the risk it entails, even though the entire project of traveling to Japan involves "walking on thin ice."[21] In the meantime, he may as well get some rest.

Such a conclusion is reinforced by the following poem, "All Through the Rains" (18), which describes the independent behavior of a mare the speaker tries, and fails, to catch and ride. This poem strikes me as one of the least successful in the collection, in that the story it relates does not carry on the surface the same level of interest or quality that one finds in "Hay for Horses," while its potentially symbolic meaning seems to float too far beneath the surface. Read as a counterpoint to "Hay for Horses," "All Through the Rains" could be understood to uphold the independent, element-bearing spirit of this horse in opposition to the man who finds himself trapped in an unwanted life's work. The horse thereby becomes an animal-model to emulate. In contrast, if the horse is imagined as symbolizing the goal of Snyder's quest that is leading him to Japan, then the poem reinforces the ambivalence and self-doubt of "Nooksack Valley."

"Migration of Birds" (19) is clearly a rejoinder to "Nooksack Valley." Here the speaker is resolved and recognizes that different people have different paths to follow, even as birds migrate along their own separate routes. A hummingbird pulls the speaker into the world and out of his book. The "It" that opens the poem may very well be the kind of "trip-stop / Mind-point" found in "Nooksack Valley." This mind-point this time, however, clarifies and crystallizes incipient feelings. The hummingbird causes the speaker to think of other birds, then of another human. Jack Kerouac, who shared Snyder's cabin in Mill Valley just north of San Francisco for a while, is brought into the poem. An interesting contrast is established. Kerouac, who will remain in the United States, although professing an interest in Japan and Buddhism, is reading *The Diamond Sutra*, a Buddhist text, in translation. Snyder, in contrast, according to the poem, has just read *The Migration of Birds* the day before, a book about North American species. The speaker remarks that "Today that big abstraction's at our door," with the abstraction being the book that he has read, which uses words to convey the idea of birds' observable behavior. *The Diamond Sutra* is also an abstraction, being read by Kerouac and treated only as a text rather than a living practice. Snyder will soon be at Buddhism's door, so to speak, arriving in Kobe by ship in late May. Once he reaches Kyoto he will begin an experiential rather than textual study far more intense and directly experienced than his time spent at the Berkeley Buddhist Church. The speaker identifies with the migration of birds that are leaving the Bay Area. He implies that, while the Pacific Northwest is his home, Japan may be an equally appropriate nesting place, at least for a certain season of his life. And that recognition implies, in turn, that his own natural cycle of migration will bring him back to the United States, which shores him up against the sense of loss that he would otherwise feel.

At this point in *Riprap*, then, Japan becomes the focus of attention. And based on the publishing record of his poems, this first year in Japan for Snyder was focused on Buddhist practice rather than on poetry. Although this first trip afforded him a range of experiences and important insights sufficient to keep him returning for nearly twelve years, all of which involved Buddhist study, Snyder provides the reader of *Riprap* with only four poems, and in the *No Nature* selection only two of these are reprinted (there is a similar dearth of poems from this period published in *Left Out in the Rain* as well).[22] Snyder has provided an explanation for this phenomenon. Frequently he has remarked that when he meditates he does not think about poetry, and in Japan the kind of intense Zen study he undertook involved many long hours of meditation. He also had to work on improving his ability to speak Japanese and to engage in the translation and related work expected of him by the First Zen Institute of America, which financially supported his trip.

The Japan poems, although only four in number, do significantly contribute to the volume. "Tōji" (20) depicts the extremely relaxed atmosphere at a Kyoto temple in the mid-1950s. Even though the city is besieged with the tourists, both national and international, who flock to it today, such an atmosphere continues to exist. Unlike the previous poems in which the speaker was clearly a participant, here he is a recently arrived observer, not yet sure of what he sees, as in the line "Cool Bodhisattva—maybe Avalokita." As he concludes that "Nobody bothers you in Tōji," Snyder depicts not only the relaxed behavior of the people in the part of the temple compound open to the public, but also the very different kind of statues of the gods found there. Snyder wants to impart to the reader a sense of freedom and flexibility that he discovered shortly after arrival in Kyoto—one of the few Japanese cities to be spared Allied bombing and the recognized religious center of the country due to the amazing number of shrines and temples standing within its city limits. Sherman Paul believes that the use of "shadow" and "shade" implies that this flexibility relates in particular to an acceptance of the unconscious, which in turn would suggest the less repressed attitude toward sexuality that Snyder associated with the "Cool Bodhisattva" statue.[23]

In the second poem, "Higashi Hongwanji" (21), another temple in Kyoto, Snyder depicts the temple's interior. This time the people receive only a single line and the observer's focus rests instead on a "carved wood panel" high up behind a beam that reminds the speaker of the sexuality found throughout nature. The main point of this poem appears in the final three lines, "The great tile roof sweeps up / & floats a gray shale / Mountain over the town." Here, while still thinking about sexuality and culture as in "Tōji," Snyder seems to be considering the relationship of religion to culture not only in terms of sexual mores but also in terms of what is considered natural. With the temple imaged as a "Mountain" he contemplates the power of

Buddhist beliefs to affect cultural values. Bob Steuding contends that in these two poems "what particularly interests Snyder, in contrast to his Christian experiences, is the complete lack of religiosity and sanctimoniousness in regard to these oriental places of worship."[24] Sanehide Kodama keys in on Snyder's interest in the ancient wood carvings to be found in the temples, noting that Snyder writes to a friend that summer: "I have gotten an unreasonable passion to learn wood-carving now."[25] Kodama, however, agrees with Steuding in that he believes that the interest in wood carving is a means to an end: "But what Gary Snyder was interested in was not the sculpture itself, but 'a love relationship' and 'Bodhisattva relaxation'. . . . He was discovering in the statues and panels the kind of peace of mind he could not find in the Western world."[26]

Sexuality remains an abiding concern for Snyder, especially in terms of the "love relationship" Kodama identifies. The poem that immediately follows "Higashi Hongwaji" in *Riprap* was written some eight or nine months later in March of 1957. Here in "Kyoto: March" sexuality is depicted through the representation of familial ties and multigenerational love. Here human nature and wild nature are intertwined, as are the lovers and their offspring, in a relationship rendered sacred to the speaker by its ordinariness and its repetition. Perhaps, then, the key point here is the recognition of the distinction between "love" and "relationship," in that the latter requires duration and yet must avoid the boredom and indifference that can come with routine.

Three of the remaining seven "Riprap" poems in *Riprap* were dropped when Snyder assembled *No Nature*. One of these is "A Stone Garden" (23-25). Unlike "Kyoto: March," this poem was composed after Snyder had left Japan for his tour on the *Sappa Creek*. As the credit line indicates, Snyder had ample time to reflect on his first year's experience in Japan. Stylistically it is quite a strange poem within this collection, being written in a loosely iambic pentameter with various end rhymes and inverted diction apparently for the sake of the meter, such as "more the sweet." In such lines Snyder fails to make the metrical scheme work smoothly while in others he is quite successful, as in "Leafy sunshine rustling on a man / Chipping a foot-square hinoki beam" where he shortens the first foot for effect. I see three possible explanations for the use of a formal metrical pattern: one, Snyder wants the metrics to reflect his sense of Japanese formality and craftsmanship and his own seriousness in reflecting on this country that has deeply, and troublingly, affected him. Two, he is experimenting with various types of discipline, crossing from the religious discipline of Zen training to the poetic discipline of formal metrics. Three, in contrast to the riprap rhythm of the previous poems in the collection, this metrical formality is more willfully structured and hence more garden-like than wild. Despite the complaints of some critics, this formalism is just as organic as the riprap poetics in the sense that the organization of the poem embodies the orderliness and structured relationships that Snyder finds in his subject matter. Although quite a beautiful poem overall, the language of "A Stone Garden" is somewhat stiff and the phrasing syntactically contorted in too many places for it to succeed completely.

"A Stone Garden" is nevertheless worthy of thematic attention in that it continues to develop the relationship of human and wild nature explored in "Kyoto: March," as well as the theme of loving, multigenerational families. These reflections are particularly poignant given Snyder's circumstances at the time of composition: isolated on an oil tanker, doing monotonous industrial work, divorced and without a relationship, and somewhat ambivalent about his own future in terms of returning to Japan and returning to visit his own family. Snyder initially focuses on his recognition that Japan's highly organized society and well-cultivated nature retain some of the values Snyder had previously found only in the wilderness. The word "stone" in the title connects this poem with the previous trail-building poems of Yosemite and with the final poem "Riprap," but here the poet is pausing on the trail for recollection and reflection.

In the first stanza, Snyder intermingles real and dream images of Japan, reflecting in part his own process of idealizing and dreaming about Japan while in the U.S. and his experiencing its realities firsthand. There is also a sense of historical continuity, the kind of mythic linkages associated with dream time, transmitted through rural agricultural practices. As Paul reads the poem, "the culture that he depicts here gives woman and domestic life a central place. . . . founds itself on *eros* and *ecos*."[27]

The second stanza treats the familial relationships already appreciated in "Kyoto: March." Here they receive the same idealized treatment. Snyder then claims that "time is destroyed." As the lines that follow that expression indicate, "time," in the sense of movement and passage continues. But since it is recognized as more cyclical than linear, the destructive perceptions that people have of aging and dying, perceptions that produce misery, despair and self loathing, are banished. This recognition, however, proves inadequate against the nostalgia and loneliness the speaker feels as a result of remaining an outsider. In the third stanza, in highly stylized rhyming lines, Snyder compares the insignificance of the individual poet trying to fill the silence of his own personal emptiness with words and music when "The noise of living families fills the air." For poetry to have meaning, it must establish or continue a dialogue, a relationship with others.

Lack of such dialogue and relationship is precisely what is regretted at the start of the final stanza of "A Stone Garden." But Snyder turns away from this regret and emphasizes instead the possibility of family based on his observations of its realization in Japan. He concludes this fourth stanza and the poem as a whole with a couplet: "Allowing such distinctions to the mind: / A formal garden made by fire and time." The contemporaneous Japan of the poem did not just arise full-blown out of the sea but was built through both geographic and human forces. The islands formed through the fire of volcanoes and the long, slow, relative stabilization of the land over eons. Families and relationships are not simply realized and stumbled into but are built through passion and patience, with both domesticated and wild features. The speaker must maintain these qualities of passion and patience even in his moments of loneliness and isolation, if he is to be prepared to experience human love in the future. That there is hope for such love has been suggested throughout by imagery and allusion, such as the real girl who opens the second stanza, or the allusions to "Narihira's lover" and the "long-lost hawk." The depiction of the girl reminds the knowledgeable reader of a relationship in the ninth-century Japanese volume, *The Tales of Ise*, while the allusions refer to an eighth-century poem by Yakamochi on falconry which relates the story of a lost falcon that returns, and to Thoreau's comment in *Walden* that he is "still on the trail of a lost turtledove."[28]

The next five poems treat the *Sappa Creek* tanker days, based on the time Snyder spent on that ship working his way back to the United States from Japan in a rather roundabout journey. The first three poems are largely descriptive, showing Snyder orienting himself toward this strange new situation and its quite distinct work rhythms, fully aware of the contrast, as indicated in "At Five A.M.. Off the North Coast of Sumatra" (27), between machine life and plant life. "T-2 Tanker Blues" and "Cartagena" (29-30 and 31) are rich poems similar to "Kyoto: March." In the first of these, Snyder is working through the mythic implications of the seeming contradiction between East and West and between human nature and wild nature. In a response to Robinson Jeffers's doctrine of Inhumanism, which he defined in his 1948 Preface to *The Double Axe and Other Poems* as humanity's moving beyond egocentrism,[29] Snyder states: "I will not cry Inhuman & think that makes us small and nature / great." Here he is clearly expanding on his deepened appreciation for humanity in its diversity that he realized more fully in Japan than in the previous years of his life.

The immersion in immediacy expressed toward the end of "T-2" also suggests an emphasis on the present moment, on the *tathata* or suchness of the world in its Buddhist sense, when he compares "Mind & Matter" with the foam on a glass of beer. Although some critics hear a tone of sadness and depression because of the lines preceding these, these lines are, rather, ones of simple recognition, a letting go of the objects and problems that have earlier possessed and troubled the poet's mind. As Thomas Leach notes, "the mood of nostalgia yields to an air of detachment in which human life becomes simply another facet in the ever-shifting kaleidoscopic pattern of nature."[30]

"Cartagena" seems to share this tone as well. Snyder speaks here of the nearly mindless, frenzied behavior of himself and his fellow seamen on an overnight shore leave. And he recalls a similar experience when he was a seaman that summer after his graduation from high school—thus the dateline of the poem: Colombia 1948—Arabia 1958." Virtually nothing has changed from one event to the other except time and place. Such events occurred and continue to occur, part of the life that can only be studied in the process of experiencing it rather than as a substitute for experiencing it.

Such temporality and contingency prepare the reader for the final, title poem "Riprap" (32), which speaks of how to live as well as how to write and read poetry. Poetry, as a material thing—in the form of the written poem, the performed text—and as a relationship, forms part of the world in which humans find themselves and is a source of clues by which they may interpret that world and their place in it. But place is also a relationship, an activity, a "Game of *Go*" (a Japanese board game for two players emphasizing the strategic positioning of pieces). This poem, while embodying in its theme and form the aesthetic concepts displayed throughout *Riprap*, also embodies a way of learning the world, and a world by which to learn the way. This way is nothing short of "being-in-the-world," a constantly transitory process. It is crucial to realize that the *Riprap* collection ends with an emphasis not on coming to terms with the world but on the recognition that the world constantly changes, and humans must change their perceptions to keep pace.

I want to close with brief attention to the "Cold Mountains Poems," of which Snyder included twenty-four plus an introduction in *Riprap and Cold Mountain Poems*, retaining seventeen of them in *No Nature*, with the result that in that collection the "Riprap" poems and "Cold Mountain Poems" are evenly balanced. That Snyder considers these poems to be something more significant to his overall poetic work than just translations is suggested by the fact that when he edited another collection for inclusion in *No Nature* that contained a section of translations, the poems of Miyazawa Kenji in *The Back Country*, he omitted the translated poems entirely.

It is understandable for a critic such as Gray, with his focus on "Pacific Rim Communitas," to give significant weight to the Han-shan translations in his discussion of Snyder's works. As he argues, referring to the original introduction to the poems in the *Evergreen Review* in 1958, "the tone of Snyder's note suggests that, in a mythologized region where time and distance are fantasmatically collapsed, anyone who cultivates a Zen sensibility may share the greatness of a Han-shan, for to appreciate him is merely to appreciate another contour of one's multiplicitous Pacific Rim identity." More significant, however, I think, is what Gray notes as Snyder's view of translation as a process of "visualization," in which he translates Han-shan's poetry by means of his own experiences in the Sierras.[31] These poems are something more than translations precisely because Snyder renders them as a melding of Han-shan's Chinese Ch'an Buddhist mountain spirit trickster mentality and Snyder's own mountain wilderness meditation and labor activities.

The "Cold Mountain Poems" become a hybrid mentality speaking mostly playfully and paradoxically about a particularly rigorous spiritual practice of "transcendence" in its root meaning of "climbing over." Through climbing over the rocks, boulders, and other obstacles that obscure "The path to Han-shan's place," so that it becomes "laughable" (39), a person can gain release from the tribulations of civilization: "Freely drifting, I prowl the woods and streams," becoming something other than human, since "Men don't get this far into the mountains" (45). It is clearly the case, however, whatever Han-shan himself has achieved in his maturity, that Snyder has not yet reached that place along the way of utter detachment. He closes out the twenty-fourth poem with the quotation: " 'Try and make it to Cold Mountain' " (62), which rings like a challenge to others. Not only does he then still show concern for what others say about his study of Zen and his pilgrimage to Japan, but he also takes a rather stubborn pride in his own achievements along the path of spiritual practice. But then Snyder at age twenty-eight, publishing the translations he has worked on for several years, does not have the same wealth of experience or years of meditational discipline that the old Han-shan has under his belt.

4
Passing and Returning
Passage Through India and The Back Country

As with *He Who Hunted Birds in His Father's Village*, I have chosen to discuss *Passage Through India* in relation to its initial composition rather than its date of book publication because of where it fits in Snyder's evolving sensibilities and poetics. *The Back Country* is the third book-length volume of poetry that Snyder published—*Six Sections from Mountains and Rivers Without End* was published in 1965, but it comprises only a portion of the complete poetic sequence.[1]

Passage Through India

Throughout much of his life Snyder has kept copious journals and has drawn on these journals for a variety of prose publications. His trip with Joanne Kyger to India was no exception. The two of them left Kyoto in early December of 1961 and went to Yokohama where they boarded a French ship, the *Cambodge*, which stopped at various ports until reaching Sri Lanka. From there they ferried to southern India. They stayed in India, spending part of the time traveling with Allen Ginsberg and Peter Orlovsky, until April of 1962 and then returned to Japan. In his foreword to the 1983 book edition, Snyder states that "I wrote this account out of journals and notes, and sent it to my sister," which he did a few months after returning to Japan.[2] He also comments on the original publication of an earlier version of the project, saying that it "was published low-key in an issue of *Caterpillar* in the early seventies and then let be, partly because it seemed the topic of India should be allowed to cool. Now that most of the pilgrims have returned home . . . we might ask ourselves, what was it about. Whatever answers there might be are all within paradox-paradigm" (ix).[3]

It is evident that Snyder was deeply impressed by India, the home of both Hinduism and Buddhism, as

> The spectacle of a high civilization that accomplished art,
> literature, and ceremony without imposing a narrow version of
> itself on every tribe and village. Civilization without centralization

or monoculture. The caste system as a mode of social organization probably made this possible—with some very unattractive side effects. (x)

But he was also ambivalent about the country, and in ways different from how he felt about Japan. It does not seem that he ever felt comfortable there, whereas he could feel comfortable in Japan. Such discomfort is apparent in the opening pages of *Passage*, which are written retrospectively. Snyder emphasizes how drastic a transition he and Kyger felt leaving Japan and entering the ship: "I was immediately uncomfortable because of the warmth of the heated ship when we have just come from unheated Japan" (1). And at opening paragraph's end, he states: "India seeming so remote and scary still" (2).

According to Timothy Gray, Philip Whalen visited Snyder's sister Thea in October of 1962 and, after reading the original version of *Passage* that he had sent to her, mailed a letter to Snyder asking him, "What really did you see?"[4] Indeed, it is hard to imagine that the original journals contain only the kinds of cursory remarks and travel journalism that Snyder has chosen to include. Kyger's journals from the same period are far livelier and questioning. *Passage* as it stands is unlikely to garner much critical attention as a work in its own right and will remain a rarely accessed source of autobiographical information for interpretation of the poetry.

Nevertheless, it remains worthy of some comment. While few overtly critical remarks appear, much can be made of surface-level comments and comparisons. For example, Snyder describes a bus trip in Hong Kong to the border with the People's Republic of China. Unable to cross over, Snyder can only stare into the mist at distant figures. Shortly after this description, he relates the story of a Swiss and Chinese couple who are emigrating. He relates that "they claimed no good had come out of communism. . . . I think they just found life getting dull there" (7). Then at the end of the book he writes of being again on the same ship now heading from Bombay back to Japan and aboard are Chinese men emigrating from India to China. Snyder approaches one: "I ask him, aren't you afraid to go to Communist China? He says yes. But it's China, and my family is there" (98). When a reader thinks of this juxtaposition in light of the emphasis on familial relationships and love represented in "Kyoto: March" and "A Stone Garden," it takes little imagination to appreciate the significance for Snyder of this person's answer.

While *Passage* is strongly outward focused on where the travelers went and what they saw, the trip itself clearly turned Snyder more inward in a self-critical fashion, not only in a religious sense, but also in terms of interactions with his wife, others around him, and other cultures. The effects of this trip on his poetry appear not only in *The Back Country* but also in *Mountains and Rivers Without End*. Not only did he have his own research into the Indian dimensions of Mahayana Buddhism and various Indian subcontinent sects—he had studied Vajrayana, for instance, in Berkeley[5]—but as a result of the trip he now had the kind of experiential knowledge necessary for his best poetry. Even though he makes no mention of his trip to India in "The Making of *Mountains and Rivers Without End*," experiences from this trip do show up in a section such as "The Market."

The Back Country

With the publication of *The Back Country* in its final form, the outward directed and inward directed journeys are synthesized into another loosely structured sequence, like *Riprap*. As Snyder remarked in an interview, "the capacity of communication has many levels and the most fundamental in a sense remains the communication of inward states of being." Snyder then continues by saying that

> there is a direction which is very beautiful, and that's the
> direction of the organism being less and less locked into itself,
> less and less locked into its own body structure and its relatively
> inadequate sense organs, toward a state where the organism
> can actually go out from itself and share itself with others. And
> poetry in language is of the greatest order of that sharing of the
> inner self with the outer, with the non-self. . . . humans can
> share their real feelings with each other.[6]

Certainly *The Back Country* is at least as much about that "communication of inward states of being" as it is a record of Snyder's experiences in the western United States and Asia through 1964, when Snyder returned temporarily to the United States in the fall and remained for about a year. Part of the reason for making such a claim rests with the fact that Snyder does not stick to geographic subtitles for the four main sections of this book. They are "Far West," "Far East," "Kālī," and "Back." Although "Kālī" includes poems from Snyder's visit to India, the majority of them treat memories of Snyder's earlier years in the American Northwest and in Japan. And "Back," although focusing again on the western United States, may also be read as *back from Kālī*. If one thinks of the archetypal quest motif of separation, initiation, return, with the West being the location from which Snyder separates in order to experience initiation in Japan while on his quest for Buddhist enlightenment, then the "Kālī" section parallels the visit to the underworld that so many epic heroes undertake as part of their quest, including certain Buddhas. "Back," then, is the return not only to the West but also to the human world and to responsible immersion in human society.

The Back Country has a somewhat complicated publishing history in that it first began coming together in 1966, with an intermediate version appearing in a 1967 limited edition, and the final version, with its subtitles and translations of Miyazawa Kenji's poems, appearing in 1968. Of the final New Directions version, Snyder told bibliographer Katherine McNeil that "I arranged it very deliberately, section by section, but it's mixed, a very diverse gathering of poems, and some of them are much better than others."[7] Part of that diversity and unevenness in quality reflects the fact that these eighty-six poems plus eighteen translated poems were written over a longer period of time than most of his other lyric collections. "A Berry Feast," for instance was written in 1953 and originally intended for inclusion in *Myths & Texts*, while others were written while he was assembling the volume. Some seventeen poems appear here in print for the first time, but clearly many of them were written much earlier. At the same time, the varied original publication dates indicate the degree to which Snyder has arranged the poems thematically rather than chronologically.

What is most interesting about this collection as a book is that Snyder chose it to mark his permanent return to the United States in 1968. By that time he had a solid reputation and was in the process of writing a series of celebratory poems, as well as preparing to publish a significant prose volume, *Earth House Hold*. Yet, instead of preparing a book of triumph, Snyder marked his return to the United States with a book that records the difficulties, the failures, and the doubts with which he had been dealing during his extended period of overseas Buddhist study. Proclamations of enlightenment and ecstasy would, for the most part, have to wait for the record of his marriage to Masa Uehara in *Regarding Wave*.

As Bob Steuding notes, "the trials and tribulations, the pain and exaltation of [Snyder's] psychic journey, his quest for sanity and wholeness, are recorded" in *The Back Country*.[8] Snyder began to put together this collection following the end of his relationship with

Kyger and before he had clearly determined when he would permanently return to the United States. Although the 1964 trip to the U.S. provides a convenient structuring device for the round-trip character of *The Back Country* journey, he knew very well that it was only a temporary visit. During this assembly process, also, his *roshi* (Buddhist master teacher), with whom he had been in intensive contact for years through one-on-one koan study interviews, died. It is perhaps not surprising, then, that many of the poems he selected for inclusion refer to ended relationships and treat family as a crucial dimension of his life. From this vantage point, the first three sections can be expected to contain grief, nostalgia, self-recrimination, and an emotional range of memories.

"Far West"

"A Berry Feast," which Snyder performed at the famous Six Gallery reading in San Francisco where Allen Ginsberg first performed "Howl," appropriately opens the "Far West" section of *The Back Country* because it is one of Snyder's very early mature poems. Grounded in Native American cultural beliefs, it emphasizes the survival and carnival trickster life of Coyote. It also sets up a parallel with the poem "Oysters," which closes "Back," the final section of the sequence (although the Miyazawa Kenji poems are Part V of the volume, they are not part of Snyder's poetic sequence). Both poems speak of feasts through immersion and gathering in wild nature, with the first set in the mountains and the second set at the ocean's shore. Stylistically, though, the poems are quite distinct.

"A Berry Feast" emphasizes fecundity and sexuality, as well as trickster subversion and the blurring of boundaries established by categories that separate the human from the rest of nature. Such blurring occurs in several ways, but perhaps most noticeably through the interweaving of bear and coyote myths with human stories. In the same way that Han-shan is used elsewhere by Snyder, Coyote partly figures here as a stand-in for the Beat generation.

Like the sequence itself, "A Berry Feast" is organized in four parts. Part "1" introduces in highly humorous and scatological language both Coyote and Bear. The first stanza about Coyote ends with "Bringer of goodies" and the second stanza about Bear begins with "In bearshit find it in August."[10] Snyder makes it clear that Bear is of equally mythic proportions to Coyote through including reference to the mythic text of "The Woman Who Married a Bear." Working in mythic time with Coyote and Bear, Snyder suddenly interjects an obscure two-line stanza: "Somewhere of course there are people / collecting and junking, gibbering all day" (3), which takes on meaning only in relation to the later lines, "sang Coyote. Mating with / humankind—" (3). The implication through the juxtaposition of field composition seems to function on two levels, at least. One, interaction with the nonhuman world that Coyote represents enables people to rise above their "gibbering all day," leading them to function on another level of existence. Two, that other level of existence is precisely the ability to generate myths about the powerful, natural shaping forces of human destiny. But the next part of the stanza makes it amply clear that the availability of myth does not guarantee enlightenment or even understanding. Rather, here the generation of miles upon miles of "Suburban bedrooms" will destroy that larger consciousness that myth represents as the typical suburban home becomes "a box to catch the biped in" (4). Yet part "1" ends with a sense of hope in that the shadow of Coyote and Bear "swings around the tree," continuing to affect the numbed white-collar workers of modern civilization. In "A Berry Feast" Snyder maintains a strong sense of humor demonstrated by frequent use of actual nursery rhymes or lines styled like such rhymes.

Part "2" opens with an image of common cats hunting with "bits of mouse on the tongue" (4), but they are transformed later in this section into "Fat-snout Caterpillar" tractors used in logging operations. In between Snyder establishes a contrast between people trying to return to the wild on the one hand and the long history of domestication of animals in the service of logging on the other. But the image of the nursing mother camping along the river is blurred so that it becomes an intermixture of the mythic wife of bear and a real person—quite likely the Joyce named in the dedication, "For Joyce and Homer Matson" (3). A struggle is on between the civilization that would trap people in boxes and destroy the imagination, as imaged by the shooting of Coyote for bounty, and those people who refuse to separate themselves from wild nature. Snyder ends part "2" by suggesting that time is on nature's side, with an image of huckleberry shoots growing where a forest has been logged off, providing food for Bear to survive.

In part "3" the counterculture is giving birth to a new generation, bound to the earth even as the huckleberries are growing in the once-logged mountain meadows. These huckleberries become the symbol of how the practitioners of the "rucksack revolution" that Snyder will discuss some years later in *Earth House Hold* will proliferate without organization or centralization, as wild and chaotic as any healthy seed dispersal. Such proliferation will be aided and abetted by Coyote, who dominates part "4." After clearing the alienated humans out of the deserts and mountain fastnesses so that humans who are willing to "intermarry" with the animals and attain animal consciousness can flourish there, he will then invade the cities. And in his wake berries will grow, paving the way for the return of Bear.

For all of its lighthearted, countercultural bravado with an utter disdain for the post-war middle American model of the good life as exemplified by tract housing and life in the suburbs, the poem contains a certain, unintentional irony—at least in its original composition (the poet may very well have recognized this irony by the time he assembled this book). While Snyder certainly is attempting to align himself with Coyote as trickster, he also finds himself in the poem in the position of looking on at the relationship of the Matsons, which is mutely and obliquely depicted, so that he seems more the observer than the participant in the life they are living. Further, Snyder is trying to create a sense of self and identity in this poem through the adoption of another culture's beliefs rather than through the kind of synthesis that acknowledges one's own roots as he does in *Myths & Texts*. Finally, what resonates most strongly in this poem, which would not have stood out when read alone, is the emphasis in it on marriage and family, a key issue in *The Back Country*. This emphasis is heightened by the poem that immediately follows "A Berry Feast," "Marin-an" (8). In this poem, the speaker's solitude, simplicity, and leisure are set in contrast to the "thousands of cars / driving men to work." With utter seriousness, then, Snyder reinforces his previous critique of suburbia, the product of American consumerism.

In "Marin-an," despite its critique, the poet still remains an observer rather than a participant. He corrects this distance from nature in the third poem of *The Back Country*, "Six-Month Song in the Foothills" (9). One of Snyder's truly beautiful poems, it is full of alliteration and carefully crafted lines, creating an indelible visual image in the mind. Jody Norton provides a succinct interpretation of this poem: "These seasonal activities take place in a shared home . . . and in the larger shared home of nature. In their home-in-nature neither being interferes with the other, bird and man pursuing separate works, separate ends without destructiveness or hostility."[11] And Charles Altieri emphasizes the anti-transcendent, immanent quality of the poem, in many ways in contradiction to some of the yearning felt in "A Berry Feast": "Man does not have to transcend nature; he has only to recognize how that flux generates meaning."[12] Significantly, the bird in the poem is a swallow, a migrator who will travel far but always return. And although the "shed" with which the poem begins and ends is clearly intended in its literal meaning—the workplace where the action occurs—it can also be seen as a type of haven from the mindless work that Snyder criticizes in the previous poem, as well as being associated with the kind of *shedding* of things and ideas that an *unsui*, a novice monk, would undertake. This impression of *shedding* is encouraged by the powerful use of participles that Altieri aptly notes: "the free interchange of awakening mind and nature is beautifully sustained by Snyder's use of participles in the poem."[13]

The next three poems are in riprap-style and based on outdoor work experiences. The time and place of "The Spring" is unstated, but is likely related to Snyder's work in Yosemite, while the next two are definitely identifiable as such. "The Spring" (10) works internally by contrasting two different kinds of darkness, one that covers things up and one that reveals natural mystery. The poem takes on added resonance by its location at this point in "Far West." The highway here reminds one of the highway in "Marin-an," thus suggesting work that does not conserve the landscape but only facilitates traffic. Snyder, however, suggests that the laborers themselves realize that a different world exists from the one of asphalt and concrete. When readers first see the line, "the foreman said let's get a drink," they are likely to assume that he means getting a beer in a tavern, but Snyder reveals that they have a different kind of thirst. They need to be refreshed, both physically and psychically, by the wild nature surrounding the "rocked in pool / feeding a fern ravine." Through this poem Snyder places his working-class characters on the side of those who appreciate wild nature rather than on the side of those who lay out the suburbs and the highways that connect them. An early notebook draft of the poem in the Snyder Archives indicates that the poem initially was filled with greater detail, including a separate stanza at the end that sets the spring in direct opposition to urban life. That stanza is gone by the next available draft, which shows Snyder trying out varying lines of description about the spring; gradually he reduces these. Too much detail would reduce the level of mystery and difference that he succeeds in evoking with the scaled-back imagery of the published version of the poem.

In "A Walk" (11), Snyder strips the poem almost entirely of any elements that do not contribute to literary depiction of a day's activity on a Sunday break from trail-crew work. The character named Murphy and place names explicitly identify "A Walk" as a Yosemite poem. Michael Castro believes that it "works convincingly as a poem because it accurately registers impressions in a language appropriate to their immediacy and in a form that synthesizes the natural rhythms of voice, sense, and the experience in nature that is the poem's subject."[14] But the title seriously understates this little adventure. It thereby emphasizes what Altieri sees as the crucial relationship between the difficulty of the trek to Benson Lake and the swim and lunch that Snyder enjoys at journey's end before his return to camp. While Altieri emphasizes the meal as "sacramental" along the lines of Christian communion, I would emphasize the swim as the symbolically sacramental aspect, due to the central role that ablutions play in both Japanese Buddhism and Shinto. The purification in water is a well-earned wilderness blessing.

But while that tension is important to the plot of the poem and Altieri's reading does define "A Walk" as "ecological," Altieri ignores the extensive set of human-animal-environmental relationships that Snyder presents. The first few lines establish a parallel among the mules, Murphy, and the speaker, all of whom are relaxing because it is Sunday. Similarly, once Snyder sets out he is immersed in a heavily populated landscape in which everyone, he included, is on the move, skittering, running, shimmering, and wading. Throughout, a sense of mutual respect defines the relationships between the local animals and this visiting human animal. The end of the poem also establishes that Snyder's walk is part of a larger, ongoing, and relatively undisturbing human presence.

But the leisurely walk on Sunday cannot be separated from the rhythms of work, both of which occur in the same locale. "Fire in the Hole" (12-13) describes the dynamiting aspect of trail-crew work but tellingly ends with the recognition that the narrator's "hands and arms and shoulders" have been freed. Exertion leads to liberation in this setting, but actually the freedom is relative, a pause before the resumption of labor. Like purification or enlightenment, freedom does not exist as a place of stasis, but each is part of an ongoing process, like the realm of death and rebirth in this world, which is ecologically universal. Freedom, or rest, and labor are part of the rhythm of ongoing cosmic energy transfer, as suggested by the next poem, "Burning the Small Dead" (13). Jody Norton provides a careful structural reading of this poem, emphasizing the way in which its temporal scope widens out in "quantum leaps" through its five parts.[15]

The power of this poem resides in its ability to be simultaneously metonymic—explicitly literary—and metaphoric—each object a symbol for some dimension of human culture. What is most moving is the way in which Snyder telescopes out from the fire of the burning branches, which he has foraged rather than cut from living trees, to the burning stars in the sky and yet imbues each with a sense of temporality. All is process, and all contains the rest. Everything on the earth, whether dead branches or human beings, has come in its atomic forms from the dust of stars.

Several of the poems that follow could have easily been added to *Riprap*, having been composed at or about the same period of time, but clearly not the closing one of this section. These poems, like the three just discussed, contribute to establishing the speaker's rootedness and experience in the "Far West," with some of them receiving close critical scrutiny. And the diversity of critical choices of which poems to emphasize from this section is in itself quite interesting. Norton reads "Trail Crew Camp at Bear Valley, 9000 feet. Northern Sierra—White Bone and Threads of Snowmelt Water" (14) through the politics of "Marin-an," relying on the implications of a single line, "strippt mountains hundreds of miles." But I think Norton overreads the poem as a result, claiming that a trail can become a highway, without looking at the specificity of the title. Rather, "Trail Crew Camp" seems to be much more of a unity-of-opposites poem, with its theme more fully realized in "The Black-tailed Hare" poem of *Mountains and Rivers Without End*.[16] Like the "threads of snowmelt water" the speaker follows a trail downhill that conforms to the contours of the landscape. And yet at the same time, he is aware of having altered that landscape. This awareness, however, does not elicit a perception of contradiction but of necessary relationship. Water, too, clears obstacles out of its way as it proceeds downhill from 9,000 feet. Such inevitability of change and transformation seems even more so to be the point in relation to the poem that appears on the facing page, "Home from the Sierra" (15), which records the speaker's preparations and travel from the high altitudes "Down to hot plains." While the destination of this trip is San Francisco, the penultimate line's reference to "green tea" invokes an image of Japan.

"Foxtail Pine" (16-17) is a poem about right naming, a subject that Snyder will return to in *No Nature* with several of the new poems published there. Here he seems to be echoing the recognition of the arbitrariness of names and their illusory quality that is a central tenet of *The Diamond Sutra*, where it is stated that "as to any Truth-declaring system, Truth is undeclarable; so 'an enunciation of Truth' is just the name given to it."[17] In an act of humility, he recognizes the limitations of human knowledge and the lack of the world's need to conform to what people know or think they know. Relating instances of scientific classification of conifers, their use as food, their exploitation for commercial products, and their role in ancient myths, Snyder comments early in the poem that "nobody knows what they are" and later questions himself, "—what am I doing saying 'foxtail pine'?" In the end, the speaker recognizes that the names are his because of the associations generated by his own perception, which is always "sort of" precise and imprecise simultaneously.

As with "Trail Crew Camp" and "Home from the Sierra," the two facing poems, "A Heiffer Clambers Up" (18) and "August on Sourdough, A Visit from Dick Brewer" (19), are best read in relation to one another. "A Heiffer" depicts a utopian vision of what the world could be like if countries and creatures would "cease their wars" and celebrate "with the baby happy land." But Snyder knew very well that no such world existed in the midst of the Cold War, and hence the sad tone of "August on Sourdough." As Timothy Gray notes in relation to this poem, Snyder remarked in his essay "North Beach" written in 1973 that "in the spiritual and political loneliness of America of the fifties you'd hitch a thousand miles to meet a friend."[18] Gray goes on to comment that "Snyder sees fit to stay on his western peak. Indeed, by claiming proud residence in the 'far, far, west,' Snyder implies . . . that his positionality is sufficient for his artistic ends,"[19] but I do not see any direct connection being made in this poem to "artistic ends." Rather, read in conjunction with "A Heiffer Clambers Up," a tone of dystopian isolation can more easily be read into the conclusion of the poem, particularly with the earlier line, "Waving a last goodbye." If New York, where Dick Brewer is headed, serves as a synecdoche for American culture, then Snyder recognizes that he himself has moved beyond the margins of the culture. This Sourdough poem brings in the other side, the loneliness and self-doubt, of the separation and isolation from others, which "Mid-August" in *Riprap* omitted. It should also be noted that, whereas in the later *Riprap* poems Snyder has the speaker being explicit about plans to travel to Japan, no such foreshadowing has so far appeared in "Far West."

Rather, the next two poems of this section place the speaker at sea. Instead of emphasizing a sense of journeying, they are work-related poems that emphasize the dystopian counterpoint to "A Heiffer Clambers Up." Of the two, only "Oil" (20) is relatively successful, while "The Wipers Secret" (21) seems insufficient for the issue it attempts to address. Charles Molesworth in *Gary Snyder's Vision* comments on "Oil," but provides an excessively serious reading of the poem that causes him to distort the implications of much of the description. Here as in "The Spring," Snyder has sympathy for the workers on board the tanker; he also expresses respect for the organic way in which the machinery of the ship seems to maintain its own sense of direction and movement—an appreciation expressed in other poems in later years, as in *Axe Handles*.[20] But the main point of the poem is contained in the final stanza, where Snyder depicts "steel plates and / long injections of pure oil" not only as a problem of addiction, as Molesworth notes, but also as the Christian communion sacrament of unleavened bread and wine.[21] Molesworth is so intent on the serious issues raised by Snyder's work that he overlooks the humor and satire that is often coursing mole-like just beneath the surface.

Several of the remainder of the poems in "Far West" emphasize a sense of community in contradistinction to the isolation of "Sourdough Mountain" and the speaker's separateness depicted in "Oil." One of these poems, "After Work" (22), is highly problematical, however, from a gender perspective. This point may be highlighted through contrasting readings of this poem by two different male critics. Sherman Paul, in "From Lookout to Ashram," writes of "After Work":

> Love here is a prized part of a steady continuum of living whose sensations the poet fully savors and deeply appreciates. . . . for the poet who transfers the rhythm of his experience to the poem knows the values of relation and contrast, the care of the husbandman, and is as confident of the pleasures of love, as of other goods of life, the food to come, the wine, the enveloping warmth and darkness.[22]

Paul unwittingly reveals the fundamental problem with this poem in that series, in which "love" is defined as one of the "goods of life," as if it were an object on a par with food or wine. Such defining renders the woman who apparently provides these "goods" as also an object to be possessed by the man. Gray in comparing this poem with "Logging 9," notes in contrast to Paul's analysis that

> Within "After Work," however, there exists a more overdetermined distinction between gender roles. . . . woman is confused with hearth, the surface of her body a sensual substitute for the stove's warmth. . . . His work is done before hers, yet he immediately seeks to transform her delegated work space into his lair of leisure before her work is done. . . . This distinction between female work and male leisure, a distinction which is routinely fixed yet conveniently obfuscated throughout Beat literature, will reappear often as Snyder encounters and writes about women in "The Back Country."[23]

"How to Make Stew in the Pinacate Desert Recipe for Locke & Drum" (28-29) reflects the sense of community Snyder felt in the Bay Area in 1964, the year the poem was written. Locke McCorkle practiced carpentry and had the cabin in Mill Valley where Snyder lived for a while before leaving for Japan. Drummond Hadley is a rancher and fellow poet who studied at Berkeley in 1964, where Snyder was lecturing at the time.[24] In a rather detailed analysis of this and other similar poems in "Recipes, Catalogues, Open Form Poetics: Gary Snyder's Archetypal Voice," Robert Kern argues that "How to Make a Stew" is an extremely important poem for understanding Snyder's poetics. He states that

> Yet it is precisely the possibility of reproducing a valuable experience (such as a meal) that the recipe as a form holds out, and Snyder deliberately emphasizes the implicit contrast here between the impersonal, unlimited nature of recipe rhetoric and the temporal limits of the actual personal experience that he nevertheless insists on including. . . . Such a method enables him to utilize his own experience without having to claim it as his own, to be aware of it as human possibility rather than binding personal fact.[25]

The several poems emphasizing the Beat sense of community are followed by "Sather" (30), which reminds readers that community has to be grounded in a personal sense of place, and yet similar places exist in relation to one another around the world. As a result, a Norwegian named Sather can find himself at home in the mountains of the Pacific Northwest. Although the speaker of the poem only refers to himself in the opening line, there is a sense throughout of a feeling of camaraderie as he and Sather exchange stories on a long bus ride north from California. Such a feeling will be shattered at the close of the section with the very different tone of the final poem.

"For the Boy Who Was Dodger Point Lookout Fifteen Years Ago" (31) was not written until 1965, well after most of the other poems in "Far West." As Snyder indicates in a prefatory note, it is about a backpacking trip he took with his first wife, Alison Gass, about 1950, while they were both enrolled at Reed College. As Paul notes, "the poem is also for the *boy* Snyder was fifteen years ago."[24] His description of Alison as "Swan Maiden" clarifies the nostalgic stance of the poem, idealizing her, and idealizing this brief moment of utter tranquility. It also alludes to the myth that he studied for his undergraduate thesis, which is especially poignant in that he ended his 1978 preface to the book version with the following words: "In scholarship we often don't understand ourselves well enough to know why we *really* do something. The one dimension of the myth 'He Who Hunted Birds in His Father's Village' that I somehow didn't clearly state, was that it's a story of lost love."[25] In this poem Snyder expresses a sense of loss and a feeling of self-pity for the way he has perhaps too easily *shed* his relationships with others. By the time of his writing this poem, Snyder had already gone through two marriages and the lost relationship with Robin Collins.

Following his feminist discussion of "After Work," Gray concludes an analysis of "Dodger Point" with these remarks:

> The intersection of women, landscape and memory in "Dodger Point" takes on added resonance in the "Far East" and "Kālī" sections. . . . As he faces the challenges of acculturation and the rigors of philosophic training, Snyder discovers yet again that the presence of women facilitates his understanding of himself and his place. Toward this end, Snyder continues to make mysterious women the centerpieces of *The Back Country*'s cultural geography.[26]

To the degree that *The Back Country* can be said to have the subtheme of "lost love," which Snyder has indicated as a concern of his from the time of writing his B.A. thesis, the reasons for such losses are revealed in many of the poems depicting women. But with the exception of "To Hell With Your Fertility Cult" in the "Kālī" section, the reader's understanding of these reasons exceeds that of the poet's, whose tendency is to render women as objects of male attention rather than as mutual subjects.

"Far East"

"Yase: September" (35), the first poem of "Far East," strongly shifts tone, suggesting overall that the Japan years to be depicted are an overwhelmingly positive experience. This poem and the four that follow reveal a strong sense of dislocation but also a growing feeling of relation and integration. "Yase" describes what Snyder learned from his Kyoto landlady who, as she managed to cut weeds and pick flowers simultaneously, taught him about the relationship between work and art. As Katsunori Yamazato notes, "the implied admiration for her act arises from his perception that, for her, there exists no separation between aestheticism and daily life and work."[29]

"Pine River" (36) and "Vapor Trails" (37), which follow "Yase: September," function as polar opposites. The first poem finds Snyder working through the continuities and discontinuities of Japan's past and present and feeling the tranquility arising from the lookout's viewpoint while visiting Matsue castle. But such tranquility is shattered in "Vapor Trails" by American jets screaming overhead. In "Pine River" he could lose himself, but in "Vapor Trails" he has to affirm his own existence, and his personal commitment to the Buddhism he has been intensively practicing, in the face of young American pilots skilled in the craft of war: "I stumble on the cobble rockpath." Here he must concentrate on finding the design of "two-leaf pine" for the same reason that he called upon the memory of the Dodger Point moment—to grope for sanity amidst the civilized world's madness.

But the differences between that familiar Western landscape and Japan are emphasized by his realizations in "Mt. Hiei" (38). In this poem, he cannot do what he would normally do if he were back home. In recalling what his behavior had been when a lookout—mistaking "Aldebaran / for fire"—he admits that he has confused Japan with someplace else. But as "Out West" (39) warns us, Japan is not even what it once was, much less the idealized dream of a young American. What Snyder has found distressing in the United States threatens to destroy, by means of westernization, all that he hoped to find in Japan. Here the new machinery and "that straw hat shaped like a stetson" and the boy's "blue jeans" represent a far more devastating invasion of traditional culture than the jets overhead in "Vapor Trails."

These two poems are followed by "Ami 24.XII.62" (40), which seems to be placed here to provide a segue between the two previous poems, in which Japanese culture is the object of Snyder's attention, and the next poem, "The Public Bath," in which Snyder is the object of Japanese attention. But "Ami" is, finally, not a successful poem because the poet does not seem to be fully conscious of his own emotional reactions to the ostensible topic indicated by the title. The poem opens celebrating Snyder's friend Ami's having given birth to a baby boy. Then the second stanza shifts to the empty house—presumably Ami has given birth to the child in another location—and the father's having gone off to teach; the third stanza continues to focus on the father with the speaker wondering if he has learned yet about his new son, since he is away at work. But inexplicably the fourth stanza, rather than returning to the mother and closing the family circle, focuses on the family dog who is tied up outside in the rain and "shivering." It would seem that the poet's identification with the dog implies a feeling of his being left out of participation in this sense of family, even though the date in the title indicates that Snyder was married to Kyger at the time.

Drafts of this poem available in the Snyder Archives indicate that Snyder shifted the focus of the poem as it underwent several drafts. Initially, much more detail is given over to Ami and her giving birth in a hospital, and the poem concludes with the garden crops that Snyder later moved to an earlier point in the poem. Subsequent drafts show Snyder eliminating the names of his friends from the poem, except in the title, reducing the lines given to Ami while increasing the lines given to "the father," and moving the dog to the end of the poem and increasing the emphasis on "shivering." The published version of the poem, then, fails for me, because the ostensible female subject becomes merely an object for the representation of the poet's feeling of separation or isolation as represented by the dog. In contrast, "Asleep on the Train" (46) succeeds in maintaining its focus on the female white-collar worker and the extension of the poet's empathy to this woman as a subject. He recognizes that she, like the other professionals on the train who all look alike because of the uniform way they dress, has her own life beyond the formal image she presents.

Unlike the problem of the point of attention in "Ami," the shift in focus at the end of "The Public Bath" (41-42) works quite well. This poem shows the poet not only immersed in warm water but also in the daily life of common people. Yet he cannot lose his sense of differential identity; he is not Japanese. Recognition of the racial differences seems mostly a result of curiosity on the part of the "bath-girl." But the history of World War II that separates Snyder and his fellow bathers, gruesomely recalled at poem's end, cannot be so easily dismissed. To reinforce for his readers this historical sense of responsibility, Snyder pairs "The Public Bath," originally published in 1963, with another poem first published in 1966, "A Volcano in Kyushu" (43). Yamazato points out that these are from two different periods of Snyder's years in Japan; theme rather than chronology links them. In the second poem, Snyder, on Mount Aso, initially thinks of the history of place and geological time that displays a universal interconnectedness of mountains around the world. But an individual's appearance, "a noseless, shiny, / mouth-twisted middle aged man," interrupts this universalizing nostalgia and shifts Snyder's attention to a more immediate and particular memory: "J. Robert Oppenheimer: / twenty years ago / watching the bulldozers / tearing down pines / at Los Alamos." Nagasaki, one of the two atom bomb targets in World War II, is on Kyushu. The man, like the pines, is a victim of America's destructive might. The Japanese appreciate the "bare rock" created by volcanic power; but the "bare rock" that Oppenheimer helped create can only be abhorred.

Memories of the United States remained strong apparently throughout at least Snyder's first few stays in Japan, as suggested by "Four Poems for Robin" (47-49). The first poem combines the memory of an undergraduate backpacking trip with his life now in Japan. It may be the case that Robin here is a composite portrait of his college girlfriend, as well as Alison and, by this time, Joanne, and perhaps others. What comes through is not his desire for a particular life-style but his sense of loneliness when he is not in an emotionally intense sexual relationship. This theme is reiterated in the second poem. A ghostly vision of Robin has appeared to Snyder while in Kyoto, significantly in the Spring, but his describing it by means of an episode from the well-known Japanese tale of Genji shows Snyder identifying himself more strongly with Japan than with the Pacific Northwest of the first poem.

By Autumn in the third poem, this ghostly apparition has become more fierce and bitter. Snyder's remark that he awakened ashamed and angry, remembering "The pointless wars of the heart" (48), suggests that he is perhaps learning the lesson of his nightmare in terms of his own limitations as a partner. He does not speak this time of her body, but only of their hearts. And by December, Snyder has worked through the nightmares and come to some understanding of what has driven these two "star-crossed" lovers apart forever. According to Yamazato, the plan with which Snyder says he is obsessed is to build a Buddhist meditation hall in the United States.[30] And such a plan, in his own mind, meant he must "make it alone." At the poem's end Snyder knows what he has accomplished, but remains unsure if he has chosen wisely.[31]

Before he closes out the "Far East" section of *The Back Country* with a major mini-sequence, Snyder includes four poems, two of them about cats. Then "The Firing" (51) pays tribute to two friends he knew in Japan, one already dead. The emphasis here on their work as potters demonstrates the cross-cultural possibilities of art and the ability of the poet to create a linguistic artifact similar to their material artifact. As with any other poetic elegy if successful, this one both works to immortalize the subject and the author. While "The Firing," then, could be said to be artistry matching artistry, "Work To Do Toward Town" (52) is physical work matching intellectual work in importance and function. This poem compares the work of farm women bringing crops to market with the speaker's work of bringing intellectual products, in the form of books, to town. Since "all roads descend toward town," both food and thought contribute to the development of culture.

While Snyder pauses to look back in the "Four Poems for Robin," and the final poem of "Far East," as well as several others in between, he nevertheless knows that he must move on. The thirteen-section "Six Years" (54-69) records his movement through Japan up through 1964. "January" establishes a setting and a tone through the depiction of a balanced Japanese landscape. "February" then places him in that landscape. Yamazato notes an important distinction about the use of Japanese words in this poem as compared to others. Here they name aspects of a normal household and everyday life rather than being allusions to Buddhist mythology and literature. As such they demonstrate Snyder's "record of actually trying to enter into the whole taste and flavor of the country and culture."[32] A curious moment occurs, though, in the midst of his meticulous labor, when after observing that "all the different animals are persons," he asks, "what will I do about Liberation" (55). In an interview, Snyder explained this kind of descriptive poem by saying that "if I am sweeping the floor and thinking about sweeping the floor, I am all one."[33] Apparently here, his oneness is momentarily interrupted by his compassion for other creatures. But the stray metaphysical question arises and floats free rather than being latched onto by the conscious mind. In a sense, the close of the poem serves as a koan, with the answer to the question about liberation being "charcoal. black. the fire part red / the ash pure white" (55).

"March" and "April" record two very different experiences of community eating and entertaining and show Snyder alive and immersed in both secular Japanese company and Buddhist monastic company. But in both cases, Snyder identifies and associates with the lowly and the common, not the elite, whether intellectuals or priests. "May" takes him out to the Japanese countryside where he works through a series of associations between Japan and the American Northwest. In contrast, "June" records Snyder's experience in 1961 of having to teach English as a second language after he left the Zen institute. Against this experience he contrasts in "July" a trip to the beach and his observations of the relaxed behavior of the people there. "August" goes a step further, with Snyder recounting an experience of sharing in the labors of a fishing village one evening. And in "September" he records one of the many trips he and Kyger took, but in this one they follow Japanese tradition by staying at an inn, rather than camping out.

The tension felt at the beginning of "Far East" regarding Snyder's differences due to race and history have completely fallen away to the point where he can feel comfortable being simply silly in the pronouncements and sloganeering of "October." "November" and "December" place him back at temple work and engaging in the eight-day December Sesshin, an intensive meditation session. The key idea here is that of "a far bell coming closer" (67, 68), which introduces and ends the poem. At the literal level, this describes the practice during *sesshin* of awakening the participants at 3:30 A.M. by having a monk run toward the *zendo* (meditation hall) ringing a hand-held bell. This image can also be interpreted as Snyder deepening his understanding of Buddhism. Yamazato believes that this poem is based primarily on Snyder's first experience of such a *sesshin* in 1960. But the placement of the poem in the volume also allows the "far bell" to serve as an image of Snyder readying himself to return to the United States in 1964. The "Envoy to Six Years" places Snyder aboard ship. The last line, with him in the bowels of the ship, allies this "envoy" with other sea poems that identify work in the engine room as a descent to the underworld. It can also be interpreted here as an allusion to the biblical Jonah in the belly of the whale. Both images work in relationship to the "Kālī" section of *The Back Country* in that it symbolically represents a heroic descent to gain knowledge and an emotional descent and self-examination, similar to Jonah's anguish.

"Kālī"

The subtitle page for this section contains a rather terrifying description of the goddess laughing over a beheaded corpse. It is followed by an epigraph consisting of four rhymed lines in which the speaker testifies to death and loss, and is listed as one of Snyder's poems in the table of contents (it also appears in *No Nature*, but is no longer listed as a separate poem). These two devices establish both a clear image and a decisive tone for the section. The poems published over a ten-year period that Snyder selects for inclusion here tend to record more pain than delight. The time span is important for realizing that the "Kālī" section cannot be read solely as Snyder's reaction to India. Rather, India made him conscious of certain aspects of his own life and mind that he had not previously recognized.

The first two poems of "Kālī" are "Alysoun" and "To Hell with Your Fertility Cult" (73). The first line of "Alysoun," "My mother called you Robin," has caused some critics to think that Robin and Alison Gass (Alysoun being an alternate spelling of her name that probably alludes to a medieval English love poem identifying the speaker's love for "Alisoun" with the return of Spring[34]), Snyder's first wife, are the same person. They are not. This line pertains to mistaken identity, which may arise not only from an individual's confusion but also from a split between the conscious and the unconscious as symbolized by the character Alysoun's "evil dreams." Their camping in the poem takes place "by dark," so that the experience fits symbolically into the quest motif of "Kālī" as descent to the underworld.

In "To Hell with Your Fertility Cult" Snyder assumes the viewpoint of the woman, who pelts the male character with a fertilized egg, while the "your" and "he" of the poem could very well be Snyder himself. In fact, Snyder changed the pronouns during the drafting of the poem, to render it a first-person rather than third-person narrative. In this way, by letting the woman speak from her point of view, Snyder is able to atone for his error of objectifying the woman without making himself the focus of the poem. At the same time, the title alludes implicitly to the goddess Kālī, who is, among other things, the goddess of fertility and death. Snyder had not published this poem before its appearance in *The Back Country* and he has chosen to omit it from *No Nature*, which is unfortunate, in that it stands as one of the few instances up through 1968, along with "Another for the Same," when a woman is made the speaking subject rather than the object of Snyder's poetic attention.

Seven poems emphasizing lost relationships or sex without such relationships, many of them written in the 1950s, follow "To Hell With Your Fertility Cult." The mythic is invoked in three of them, but not in the positive, ecstatic manner found in other poems. In "For a Stone Girl at Sanchi" (74), the poet is half-dreaming at night about the smallness of the world spinning through space and through all human time people loving each other. But the poem ends: "this dream pops. it was real: / and it lasted forever." The "it" remains unclear, with the reader unsure of whether "loving" is to be taken as the real or if it is the dream of loving that has been real and lasting, even though, then, not actually fulfilling. Such ambiguity seems productive for a reading of the next poem, "Robin" (75), in which Snyder reflects on "How many times I've / hitchhiked away" from the ones he purports to love. It in turn is reinforced by "North Beach Alba" on the same page, in which he drives away from "a strange pad," implicitly after a night of sexual activity.

"Could She See the Whole Real World with Her Ghost Breast Eyes Shut Under a Blouse Lid?" and "Another for the Same" (76, 79) invoke mythic images, but do so to undercut or critique their use as a substitution for direct encounter with the female Other as a living human being, another individual. In "Could She See" the "Goldwire soft short-haired girl" insists on talking and thereby interrupting the poet's mythic fantasies. The poem ends with a curious quotation: "'Once a bear gets hooked on garbage there's no cure.'" While a literal statement, no doubt, its being included here as a quotation not attributable in style or tone to the girl opens it up for interpretation as a comment on the poet himself. The conclusion, then, would be that the bear-poet has become addicted to garbage-myth at the expense of direct human contact. Similarly, "Another for the Same" juxtaposes mythical and literary images to the demands of a strange woman who accuses the poet of creating loneliness by his behavior. Although it is difficult in this poem to attribute lines to particular characters, it seems likely that the female speaker is in the accusatory role and the male speaker in the defensive role.

In between "Could She See" and "Another for the Same" are positioned "Night" (77) and "A Dry Day Just Before the Rainy Season" (78). Most of "Night" is an extended response to the opening three-line stanza about how night "rights the hearts & tongues of men / and makes the cheerful dawn." But the long description of sexual activity and the chaos of the room at night's end does not actually demonstrate the existence of love or of lasting relationships but more implies a fleeting and escapist character for such activity. "A Day" depicts a hung over speaker who is in the midst of a multi-day drinking binge yet trying to use the activity of nature to sober himself up. The speaker seems unsure at poem's end of what kind of impression he has made on other people.

But Snyder does not allow reflections on his personal relationships to overwhelm this section or to be isolated from the rest of humanity's problems. After nine poems, seven of which focus on relationships, Snyder places "This Tokyo" (80-81), originally written in December, 1956. Here Snyder views the entire world as burning with the flames of negative, destructive desires. One of his most pessimistic poems, it perhaps reflects a bitter response to a recognition that he had idealized Japan and Buddhism while he was in the United States. This is certainly no liberating recognition of the impermanence of material forms. Rather, it is a pessimistic appraisal of the possibilities for the kind of change that he hoped an American Buddhism could bring about. It is followed by "Kyoto Footnote" (81), which records the traumatic life of an impoverished Japanese prostitute. Like "This Tokyo," it also indicates Snyder's complicity, through his solicitation of the prostitute, in the degradation of women and the debasement of the culture of which she is a part, thereby reinforcing his self-critique on this score in the previous poem.[35]

"The Manichaeans" (82-83), which is dedicated to Kyger, serves as a counterpoint both to the earlier poems about relationships and to the despair of "This Tokyo." But an element of desperation appears here as well, insofar as love seems to exist only as fulfilling a need to "keep back the cold" of India and of death. The title names a sect that epitomizes the extreme dualistic thinking against which the anti-dualistic act of passionate embracing is designed to respond. But the tone remains uncertain, as if the energies of death remain stronger here than those of life. It would seem that overall such is the case throughout the India poems, as exemplified in "Circumambulating Arunachala" (96). Here the vibrancy of life that flower-carrying little girls represent is muffled by the knowledge that "they die or sicken in a year." From a Buddhist standpoint, Snyder's emphasis rests on the recognition of suffering as a given in the world—part of the going around in a circle—rather than on the compassion that can ameliorate it. Snyder does not accept this dying as simply part of the impermanence of the world but feels that modern society has exacerbated the suffering. Such an indictment is expressed with particular anger and bitterness in "Xrist" (86), which does not just attack Christianity but numerous cultures with destructive religious practices.

"Kālī" continues through many poems that reiterate basic themes established up through "The Manichaeans." In "Artemis" and "Madly Whirling Downhill" (84, 85), the poet seems to rebel momentarily against his own self-criticism, rendering Artemis and "THE WITCH" as destructive female forces arrayed against innocent men. At the same time, however, "Artemis" can be read in the opposite direction as the attitude of Actaeon that causes his death—a failure to acknowledge the power and strength of the goddess and an underestimation of the significance of sexual liaisons. There may then be a link between this poem and "Mother of the Buddhas, Queen of Heaven, Mother of the Sun; Marici, Goddess of the Dawn" (92). Initially the beatific title seems to be in contradiction to the poem's description of an "old sow in the mud," but then as the poem proceeds the social mistreatment of the people who tend and eat pigs is raised. Then, at the end of the poem there is contact between the poet and the pig as she turns her gaze upon him. A very oblique poem, this one implies through the dialectics of title and text that the goddess may appear in the most despised and unassuming aspects of nature, and that wherever she is found, and in whatever form, she should be respected and attended.

Snyder soon leaves the mythic realm of the poems just mentioned and returns to his own personal recognitions, as in "Nanao Knows" and "Lying in Bed on a Late Morning" (98, 99). In the first of these, he calls himself up short for making universal remarks about all women. He does so because this attitude distracts him from the recognition of the new way of life that Nanao Sakaki and his followers are pursuing, which is described in the first and third stanzas. In the second, he admits to his own hypocrisy in having sex with one woman when he is really longing for another one.

Despite the recordings of pessimism, despair, doubt, rejection, and failure, Snyder does not end "Kālī" on any of these notes. "Go Round" (105) presents a Zen resolution of the contradictions of India by seeing them as part of the wheel of life, death, and rebirth, which must be accepted and engaged. Through a pubescent girl's recognition of sexuality and her mother's knowing gaze that she will soon lose her daughter in marriage, Snyder implies that the loss of innocence in exchange for the knowledge of experience is an inevitable process. Enlightenment comes through engagement with *samsara*, the illusory realm of the phenomenal world, not through disengagement or avoidance. In line with the Tantric orientation of the next poem, sexuality can be a path to enlightenment. The last poem of "Kālī," "[After Ramprasad Sen]" (106), reinforces this stance by presenting rebirth as a positive rather than negative event, since it provides the opportunity to "dance" once again. As Bert Almon notes, this poem is in imitation of the eighteenth-century Indian poet named in the bracketed title and utilizes a Tantric philosophical position that teaches that "the suffering of the passions can be turned into joy."[36]

"Back"

Charles Molesworth concludes that " 'Back' resolves the negative tones that threaten to dominate all of the volume and does so by turning to figures of sensual completion and harmony, for which the epitome is the figure of graceful movement or dance,"[37] which is prefigured in the last poem of "Kālī." Readers see this reversal of tone prominently in "Nature   Green Shit" (110), in which the poet celebrates gardening and his own finite place amidst the world of death and rebirth. The poem closes with a note of surprise as the speaker sees his cat "Coming home" in the early dawn, suggesting a sense of homecoming for the speaker as well.

"For the West" (115-17) uses the imagery of women, from Europa through white American women to a "little girl," to suggest that some deeper fundamental activity of procreativity and movement charts the future for humanity in contrast to the technology and consumerism that seem to drive the Western world. Europe and the United States in their present form are an aberration, a "flowery glistening oil blossom," but one fated to disappear so that the poet can "see down again through clear water." The poet realizes that change is so dynamic and far-reaching that it can never be intellectually measured, plotted, and predicted, even in terms of his own life: "I did not mean to come this far" (119), he states in "Twelve Hours out of New York After Twenty-Five Days at Sea." Here his reading about gardens hearkens back to his experience with them in "Nature   Green Shit," while his memory of having sailed this same coast sixteen years earlier evokes memories of Kyoto. In both instances, he is reflecting on the changes that have shaped his life.

Part of the process of accepting such changes involves adapting and realigning one's vision. In "Across Lamarck Col" (120), he tries to come to terms with the end of a relationship. The style of this poem is awkward and stilted, and purposefully so to suggest the difficulty of expressing these feelings. Here Snyder is trying to realign his vision, but having great difficulty in doing so. It is not surprising, then, that this poem is paired with "Hop, Skip, and Jump" (121), in which Snyder tries to adapt to the intricate steps of a child's game on the beach. Here he seems not only able to adapt to the circumstances but also to realign his vision in terms of marriage and family now that his relationship with Kyger has ended. The self-criticism of the previous poem in which he labels himself "stony granite face," is replaced by his joyful participation in a game that requires a person to maintain his balance.

In order to perceive the change and flow of personal relationships and the larger ones of cultural and social dynamics presented in the preceding poems in "Back," a person has to rely on intuition and sensation: "What 'is' within not known" ("Beneath My Hand and Eye the Distant Hills, Your Body," 123). But such intuition cannot be simply attained. "Through the Smoke Hole" indicates that it comes through cultivating deep cultural and spiritual practices, such as that of the kiva rituals practiced by Southwestern Indians, beginning with the Hohokam precursors of the Anasazi and Hopi. But the kiva is a model only for emulation.[38] The concluding point, that "plain men / come out of the ground" (127), emphasizes humanity's origin as well as its ongoing relationship with the earth. To be able to affirm rebirth and societal vision one must be grounded, physically and culturally, in place and practice. And despite whatever Japanese Buddhism would have to offer the United States, the cultural practices already in place here for thousands of years will also have to be taken into account, learned from, and brought forward. It is also fitting that the "smoke hole" imagery is employed here, toward the end of *The Back Country*, because it clearly signals that the poet has safely returned from a psychic/spiritual underworld. As Gray notes, this return depends heavily on an erotic, feminine depiction of the American landscape, not only in the poems I have mentioned above, but also in "Across Lamarck Col" and "The Plum Blossom Poem" (120, 124).[39]

"The Back Country" four-part series of poems ends with a deceptively simple poem, "Oysters" (128). The key line, repeated and emphasized by Snyder, is "ALL WE WANTED," but what exactly constitutes "all" remains more implied than stated. For the characters in the poem it means feeding on the wild natural plenitude the planet has available for human habitation. Altieri draws this conclusion about the poem: "Only when one learns to control the desire for plenitude by a sense of the simple necessities whose satisfaction constitutes one mode of that plenitude will one free the dream and the dreamer from the bitter disillusionment that often torments self-consciousness."[40] In terms of the volume as a whole, then, Snyder has freed himself from certain expectations and idealizations of Japan and Buddhism, fears and repressions of his own unconscious, and recriminations about his own past failures, particularly in relationships. And he has done so by going through these experiences and stages of awareness rather than withdrawing from them. The sequence ends, then, with a tone of tranquility and peace, as well as a sense of place in the larger flux of universal energy exchange.

"Miyazawa Kenji"

Appended to *The Back Country* are Snyder's translations of the poems by Miyazawa Kenji, who lived from 1896 to 1933. One can see affinities between Snyder's poetry and these poems, which Hisao Kanaseki has clearly outlined.[41] But they do not add to an understanding of Snyder or his poetics. They are not part of the British edition of *The Back Country*, since they had already appeared in *A Range of Poems* the year before. When New Directions published its edition, this section was added because the poems had not yet appeared in the United States.

Snyder's reason for being interested in Miyazawa, however, is readily apparent from a reading of these poems. Many of them contain vivid nature imagery of a wild, mountainous region of Japan, while "Spring and the Ashura" (132) has Miyazawa defining himself as "one of the Ashuras." Snyder explains in a note as follows: "*Ashura* is a Sanskrit Buddhist term for beings inhabiting one of the six realms of existence. They are malevolent giants in constant strife. . . . The ashura realm is the warring, contentious, hostile area of the mind" (133). It is likely Snyder saw an affinity here between Miyazawa's self-description and his own feelings as author of many of *The Back Country* poems, especially ones in the "Kālī" section. Even more so, however, he might want to imagine himself as the character in the final translated poem, "Thief" (150), who finally stopped "And listened to the humming of his mind."[42]

Even without the translations, *The Back Country* is a large collection and one of uneven quality. Of the books included in *No Nature*, only *Left Out in the Rain*, a miscellaneous volume to begin with, had more poems omitted in the selection process. And within *The Back Country* it is the "Kālī" section that is most reduced in scope. Nevertheless, it should be recognized as a major contemporary volume of American poetry. In the early 1970s, fellow poet Alan Williamson paid respectful tribute to Snyder, commenting that his short poems seemed "subtler" and "more intellectually suggestive" than those of his contemporaries. And as for the more ambitious poems of *The Back Country*, Williamson claims that they are "remarkable" both "for their historical insight and for the canny humor and daring that spring from Snyder's essential mystic's disbelief in history."[43]

5

The Waves of Household and Marriage
Earth House Hold and Regarding Wave

Earth House Hold

Snyder's first published prose volume, *Earth House Hold: Technical Notes & Queries to Fellow Dharma Revolutionaries* (1969), is similar to *The Back Country* in that it collects pieces written and published over a sixteen-year period, 1952-1968. At first glance it may seem a miscellany, consisting of a mixture of journals, reviews, translations, and essays. Snyder did, however, carefully select the materials, omitting some prose pieces and arranging items in roughly chronological order. Some of them had also been revised various times over the years, such as "Buddhism and the Coming Revolution."[1] As he explains it, "the way of putting all the pieces in Earth House Hold together is in a sense a poetic rather than a prosodic composition, in an essentially field perception manner. . . . they are miscellaneous, but they touch base with a lot of what I think are important points of my own education."[2]

There are two fundamentally different, even though complementary, ways to read this volume: one, the most common, is to use it as a reference work to interpret the poetry, particularly in order to emphasize the autobiographical dimensions of the verse; two, is to read it as a work standing on its own, designed to educate people in the United States at a particular moment in history. *Earth House Hold* can be profitably read as a reference work alongside virtually any of Snyder's poetry written up through 1968. Readers who take this approach, however, tend to overlook the book's integrity as an aesthetic artifact. They also tend to forget that, when it was published in a first printing of ten thousand copies, many people read the book without having read any of Snyder's other work and so were not reading it to learn about his poems. As the subtitle suggests, the book was oriented toward a specific audience in the United States. Such "Dharma revolutionaries" would be reading *Earth House Hold* to see what Snyder had to say about ecological change, spiritual transformation, and social revolution.

The Back Country outlines a circular journey that takes Snyder from the western United States to Japan and then India and back to the

West. *Earth House Hold* brings the reader forward in time to Snyder's marriage to Masa Uehara. His permanent return to the back country of the western United States is here firmly anchored in ecological practice and the responsibilities of marriage and householding. Much of the volume comprises a primer on Snyder's own spiritual education; it also contains his positions on the direction for ecological and spiritual practice in the United States at the beginning of the 1970s.

Many of the entries teach by example, with this method reinforced particularly by Snyder's "Record of the Life of the Ch'an Master Po-chang Huai-Hai." Translated without commentary, this essay provides an argument about the need for discipline, for training, and for a specific spiritual practice: Ch'an Buddhism, called Zen in Japan (Po-chang lived prior to the division of Ch'an [Zen] into two major schools: Ts'ao T'ung [Soto] and Lin-chi [Rinzai]). Most significant here is the final section, "The Regulations of the Ch'an Line," emphasizing discipline, community, and comradery. Such practices are necessary to insure the flourishing of the Dharma and the transmission of the "three inheritances": "if the three inheritances (word, deed, and thought) are not good, men cannot live together."[3] As Snyder remarked in a 1985 interview, "Buddhism is not just a religion or practice of personal, psychological self-knowledge and enlightenment, but is also a practice of actualizing personal insights in the real world."[4]

The five items included in *Earth House Hold* that precede the Po-chang translation cover the years 1952-1958, roughly the same period treated in *Riprap*. The first entry, "Lookout's Journal," records Snyder's work in the summers of 1952 and 1953 on Crater Mountain and Sourdough Mountain respectively. Sherman Paul's long essay, "From Lookout to Ashram," devotes considerable attention to "Lookout's Journal," comparing it favorably with Thoreau's *Walden*. According to Paul, "changing one's point of view (adjusting the mechanism of perception) is the revolutionary issue; only a discipline as radical as that undertaken by Snyder will, he believes, create an ecological conscience."[5] The second item consists of two 1954 reviews of Indian legends of the Pacific Northwest and Indian tales. By including them Snyder emphasizes that his education comes from Native American as well as Asian sources.

In "Lookout's Journal," readers get a glimpse of the variety of activities and reading that Snyder undertakes during his stints as a fire lookout first on Crater Mountain and then Sourdough Mountain. Not only does he engage in reading Chinese and Japanese materials, such as the sutra of Hui Neng, but also English and American poetry, which leads him at one point to question the inhumanist philosophy of Robinson Jeffers (2, 4). He is also engaged in various Japanese arts and Buddhist religious activities, such as "moon-watching" and putting up prayer flags (2, 8). Snyder is also thinking about the craft of poetry in relation to his own writing, as when he writes that "form— leaving things out at the right spot / ellipse, is emptiness" (5). One also finds various sources for *Myths & Texts* as well as *Riprap*, as when he describes the "Vaux Swifts" who will appear in "Hunting" (8). Finally, many instances appear of what Paul refers to as "adjusting the mechanism of perception," from both an observation-of-the-phenomenal-world orientation and from a religious-philosophical orientation, which are frequently combined. For instance, in noting how important radio contact becomes for the lookouts isolated on their separate mountains, Snyder concludes that "in this yuga, the moral imperative is to COMMUNICATE" (9; a yuga is one of the four ages of human history in Hinduism). Later, he comments on "the usefulness of hair on the legs" in terms of warning people of the arrival of mosquitoes and deerflies and then in the next paragraph writes: "(an empty water glass is no less empty than a universe full of nothing)—the desk is under the pencil" (19), thereby inverting the usual gestalt of phenomenal relationships.

The third entry is from journals kept during his first trip to Japan in 1957-58. Although generally less intense and far sketchier than "Lookout's Journal," "Japan First Time Around" records realizations significant for the poet's intellectual development. These entries open with Snyder's recognition of the interrelationship and geological transformations of mountains and waters, with the line "Marine limestone in the Himalaya at 20,000 feet" (31). Also Snyder's recognition of the connections among Zen, Avatamsaka, and Tantra suggest the need for people to develop a syncretic rather than dogmatic or separatist spiritual path in the present (34). This syncretism will be reflected in his own practice more than twenty years later in the United States in setting up the Ring of Bone Zendo in California. Further, Snyder recognizes, and promotes, affiliations between Zen and "the subtle steady single-beat of oldest American-Asian shamanism" (35). And perhaps his best-known statement from this journal: "Comes a time when the poet must choose: either to step deep in the stream of his people, history, tradition, folding and folding himself in wealth of persons and pasts; philosophy, humanity, to become richly foundationed and great and sane and ordered. Or, to step beyond the bound onto the way out, into horrors and angels . . . possible enlightened return, possible ignominious wormish perishing" (39).

"Spring Sesshin at Shokoku-Ji" records Snyder's experience of intensive Zen practice. Whereas the Japan journals present what Snyder thought about his Buddhist studies and experience of living in Japan, this passage describes his actual practice during one of the annual intensive meditation periods at the temple compound. "Tanker Notes" follows with another kind of practice, that of being a seaman working his way from Japan back to the United States via the Middle East and the South Pacific. The Po-chang translation is followed by a brief excerpt describing the early-1960s trip with Joanne Kyger to India.

Having established the authority to speak through the presentation of his personal practice in these formative years and the spiritual traditions in which that practice is taking place, Snyder then focuses on his perceptions of the implementation of such practice in North America in the mid- 1960s. He does this with "Buddhism and the Coming Revolution" (written in 1961, revised 1967), "Passage to More than India," "Why Tribe," "Poetry and the Primitive," and "Dharma Queries" (all written in 1967), interrupted by a 1965 journal of a summer in the mountains, reminding readers of Snyder's continuous grounding in wilderness. Throughout these essays, Snyder intimately connects ecological activism and Buddhism. For example, he writes: "The soil, the forests and all animal life are being consumed by these cancerous collectivities. . . . The joyous and voluntary poverty of Buddhism becomes a positive force. The traditional harmlessness and refusal to take life in any form has nation-shaking implications" (91).

Perhaps most to the point in terms of Snyder's own practice are his relatively newfound emphases on "tribe" and "family," both of which elaborate on his general remarks about "community." Snyder is not satisfied merely with a negative critique of America's ills but sees the need to offer alternatives. "We use the term Tribe," he writes, "because it suggests the type of new society now emerging within the industrial nations" (113). In a 1977 interview, Snyder remarked that "the natural unit of practice is the family. The natural unit of the play of practice is the community."[6] Interestingly enough, Snyder ends the collection with another illustration of practice. "Suwa-no-se Island and the Banyan Ashram" describes Snyder and Masa Uehara's wedding and concludes on an optimistic note, appropriate for newlyweds, and consonant with the general attitude of those in the United States at the end of the 1960s that revolution was in the air and a new culture on the verge of being born.

Even though these essays were written over the course of a decade, the publication of *Earth House Hold* as a single volume very much reflects the late-1960s milieu in which Snyder found himself when he returned to the San Francisco Bay Area temporarily in 1964 and early 1967, and then permanently in 1968. He was surrounded by the hippie and drug cultures of the period on the one hand and the intensifying anti-war and American minority resistance movements on the other hand. The rise of the ecology movement was only on the horizon as such, but was easily imagined as coexistent with hippie values. While *Earth House Hold* is directed at a specific audience, the tone and style suggest that Snyder did not have a very clear sense of what most of the United States was like or what the attitudes were of most Americans outside of the rather special and circumscribed society in which he was moving. Such distance should not be surprising, however, given that he spent the majority of the decade in Japan, did not follow popular media, and would have been as susceptible as anyone else to the euphoric revolution-in-the-wind mentality that pervaded the counterculture at the time. The irony that arises from this phenomenon, however, is that this excessively optimistic perception of the possibility of swift cultural change is very American and very non-Buddhist. At the same time, the later essays in *Earth House Hold* also demonstrate that Snyder had then—as he continues to have at the end of the millennium—a very detailed, long-range vision for the future of an American society that if it were to come into being would not be recognizably American to most of the nation's citizens today. That much of what he had to say at that time still holds relevance in his mind for the future can be seen by his decision to include nearly two-thirds of *Earth House Hold* in *The Gary Snyder Reader* published in the summer of 1999.

Regarding Wave

Given the tremendously optimistic conclusion to *Earth House Hold*, it comes as little surprise that within two months of its appearance Snyder published an extremely celebratory collection of poems and songs. *Regarding Wave* was initially published in a limited edition by Windhover Press of Iowa City in conjunction with a poetry reading given at the University of Iowa.[7] Sixteen months later New Directions brought out an enlarged edition of *Regarding Wave*.[8] The first three parts, "Regarding Wave I," "Regarding Wave II," and "Regarding Wave III," are identical to the text of the Windhover edition. To these, Snyder added two sections: "Long Hair," containing twenty-one poems, and "Target Practice," comprising fifteen mostly brief and playful poems.

"Regarding Wave I"

The celebration of *Regarding Wave* never becomes escape from reality. Instead, it often serves to widen radically reader perception of what should be recognized as real. Such is the case in the collection's second poem, "Seed Pods," an ecstatic meditation that connects the poet's own experience of sexual intercourse with a variety of other transmissions of life-building matter, such as the seeds "caught and carried in the fur" (4). "By the Tama River at the North End of the Plain in April" (7) situates Gary and Masa as lovers within a human community in the larger natural community. Bob Steuding sums it up in this way: "In *Regarding Wave*, energy manifestations—or fields such as mind (consciousness), language (voice), and food (meat and plants)—combine and are given expression in terms of Snyder's domestic situation that is made symbolic."[9]

But not all is celebration. The last two poems of "Regarding Wave I" speak of the Vietnam War and its life-destroying effects. Contrasting with the previous poems celebrating life-affirming fertility and sexual activity, "In the House of the Rising Sun" emphasizes "burned-off jungles" and "new Asian strains of clap" (9). The poem's title alludes to a song by Eric Burden and the Animals (appropriately enough), in which the first-person speaker is trapped in a house of prostitution in New Orleans. Clearly, Snyder is stating that the Vietnam War is destroying not only those who fight in that war, but the nation as well. And "White Devils" depicts American urbanization's rape of nature, vividly imaged by a still-living, gutted wolf (10). Snyder presents here Buddhist recognitions that suffering is a given in the world and that compassion is the proper response to such suffering. In "Rising Sun" there may also be the implication that the death of the United States as an imperialist nation would be an act of compassion in relation to the rest of the world.

These are not the poems, however, that have attracted the most attention in "Regarding Wave I." "Wave," the opening poem, has received as much commentary as any other in the entire volume. And critics often turn to Snyder himself for assistance in interpretation, citing a brief section of "Poetry and the Primitive" in *Earth House Hold* subtitled "The Voice as a Girl" (123-26). There Snyder theorizes that "Poetry is voice, and according to Indian tradition, voice, vak (vox)—is a Goddess. Vāk is also called Sarasvati. . . . As Vāk is wife to Brahma ('wife' means 'wave' means 'vibrator' in Indo-European etymology) so the voice, in everyone, is a mirror of his own deepest self. The voice rises to meet an inner need" (124-25). The poem "Wave" (3), then, is about the woman to whom the volume is dedicated: Masa.

She is the "wave" who answers Snyder's "inner need." But one also sees in this formulation a dangerous objectification in that the "wave" cannot function as a distinct person in her own right, but must serve as "a mirror" of the poet's "own deepest self."

Some critics believe that the first stanza of "Wave" treats "disparate objects," but actually these are related. On one level, as Bert Almon notes, "Physics and Mahayana Buddhism would agree that there are no stable objects, merely the illusion of stability."[10] Snyder observes in "The Voice as a Girl" that "the conch shell is an ancient symbol of the sense of hearing, and of the female; the vulva and the fruitful womb" (125). The waves of the clam shell are reflected in the striations of rock, trees, sand dunes, and lava flows. Both inorganic and organic manifestations of the nonhuman form part of the earth, which is mythically rendered as Gaia, the Earth Mother. Since Snyder himself tends to conceptualize the Earth as female and to associate fertility with both women and nature, it comes as no surprise that Masa can take on in his imagination all of these manifestations of the cosmic and the sacred, while remaining physical and sensual.

It is important not to forget that this and other poems in the three "Regarding Wave" sections are not only metaphorical but also metonymic, not just symbolic but also literal. At least in part this poem, as well as the one that concludes "Regarding Wave III," is about a real person, with whom he was married for more than twenty years, inspiring Snyder's life to the point that he images her as a goddess. "Wave" is not just a metaphor for relationships but also narrates the story of energy transfers throughout the universe. The phrase in the poem "every grain a wave" accurately depicts the wave/particle relationship of matter, as well as images a Buddhist conception of human life as a particular turbulence in the energy flow. Voice is a wave produced by vibrations. Love is also a wave produced by the couple's shared psychic and physical vibrations.

"Regarding Wave II"

"Regarding Wave II" comprises seven poems. In March 1968 in *Poetry* magazine, Snyder published six of these along with "Wave" at the end and "The Rabbit" at the beginning as "Eight Songs of Clouds and Water." Steuding believed that "The Rabbit" was intended for *Mountains and Rivers Without End*, and so was not reprinted in *Regarding Wave* (It does not, however, appear there, perhaps being superseded by one of the other rabbit poems that is included). Snyder places at the end here a poem not previously published, "Archaic Round and Keyhole Tombs." This arrangement of poems suggests that it makes sense to read "Regarding Wave II" as a set following "Wave." There may very well be a rather elaborate pun involved with the "Clouds and Water" title in that the Zen term for a monk is *unsui* (cloud water), although one would not know this from the book version alone.

In a footnote in *Earth House Hold*, Snyder states that "the term is literally 'cloud, water'—taken from a line of an old Chinese poem, 'To drift like clouds and flow like water.' . . . One takes no formal vows upon becoming an Unsui. . . . After becoming temple priests . . . the great majority of Zen monks marry and raise families" (44). One can easily see here the relationship between the literal meaning of *unsui* and the imagery of "Wave," as well as the relationship of the poems to the phases of Snyder's own life.

In "Song of the Cloud" (13), while emphasizing the drifting movement of clouds, Snyder also alludes to temple life in terms of the activity of sweeping. In the second stanza, the breakdown between subject and object, human and nonhuman, becomes more explicit as the speaker identifies himself as a cloud. Snyder also approvingly notes the ecological diversity of cloud formations. In the closing lines, he may very well be alluding to the kind of "moving elsewhere" described above; that is, monks marrying and raising families, undertaking a new phase of spiritual practice. Such practice, however, moves one closer to Tantra than to Zen, as suggested by "Song of the Tangle" (14) and its explicit sexuality. Specifically, Snyder seems to be depicting an act of "yab-yum," a Tibetan form of coitus-meditation. Steuding believes that this poem depicts Gary and Masa engaging in such a ritual at a Japanese shrine.[11]

"Song of the Slip" (15) continues this sexual imagery but moves from the particular to the general and shifts from cloud to water imagery. The poem ends on an obvious pun, with such word play continuing in "Song of the View" (16). These two poems could be understood as songs to celebrate the event described in "Song of the Tangle," continuing the emphasis on coitus as sacramental. "Song of the Taste" (17), however, moves beyond this human emphasis, placing sexuality in the context of all natural fertility and the interrelatedness of food chains. Snyder has commented in some detail about this poem:

> If you think of eating and killing plants or animals to eat as an unfortunate quirk in the nature of the universe, then you cut yourself off from connecting with the sacramental energy-exchange, evolutionary mutual-sharing aspect of life. And if we talk about evolution of consciousness, we also have to

> talk about evolution of bodies, which takes place by that sharing
> of energies . . . which is done by literally eating each other. And
> that's what communion is.[12]

"Kyoto Born in Spring Song" (18-19) moves to the results of the sexuality already celebrated and the other side of the process of eating each other, which is producing each other, giving birth. Katsunori Yamazato points out that, just as in the previous poem, Snyder erases the "differentiating line" between human and animal by calling all of the offspring "children" and "babies." This erasure is underlined by Snyder's use of several Japanese folk tales, which tell stories of human children being born of a melon, a bamboo, a plum, and a bird.[13] Snyder ends by universalizing the primal character of such nondifferentiation.

The final poem of "Regarding Wave II" seems to suggest that Snyder views his songs as part of a representation of an archetypal awareness beneath and beyond consciousness. The shape of the tombs identified in the title "Archaic Round and Keyhole Tombs" (20), but which are nowhere mentioned in the poem, represent the efforts of many cultures to depict the tomb as also the womb. Examples of both of these styles can be found in Japan and Okinawa, the latter Masa Uehara's place of birth. The poem fits with the basic imagery of the set, with water represented by the pond and clouds figured by the final line, "Coast out of sight," which parallels the phrase in the first poem of the set, "moving elsewhere."

"Regarding Wave III"

"Regarding Wave III" takes the couple from marriage through the conception and birth of their first child and on to the continuation of their relationship after that event, realizing the promise of "Wave" with reflection and meditation—the "Regarding" component—as well as continued ecstasy. David Robbins has provided an excellent reading of Snyder's epithalamion, or marriage poem, "Burning Island" (23-24).[14] Robbins makes the overall point that "the great action behind the island cycle is the ancient ritual of marriage as a cosmogonic event, signifying creation's renewal" (92). And he goes on to point out that "the poem's surface is thus a field of shifting tones and references without a governing perspective. . . . Students who have difficulty with this poem, I've found, collide instructively with this feature of it" (92). Snyder works to break down the normal distinction between subject and object. The speaker is not seeking to observe but to participate in the cosmic communion of which the sacrament of marriage is but one component. Again, to quote Robbins: "the personal request," which is to "All / Gods" to bless the marriage, "has had to wait upon the larger quest, not only because of the diplomacy of ritual supplication but because the prayer for marital blessing must emerge from a balanced, living relation to the surrounding world if it is to be effective" (104).

And one can see this quest for balance working throughout the poem, as Snyder addresses the gods of the four elements: water ("Wave God"), fire ("Volcano Belly Keeper"), air ("Sky Gods"), and earth ("Earth Mother"). In keeping with the heterosexuality of the marriage, Snyder images the first three sets of gods as male and the final one as female. Balance is also represented through interpenetration, such as the liquid lava being solidified by the water and the creation of the land providing a home for the fish. To some extent Snyder maintains this emphasis on balance, in particular between the cosmic and the specific and between the ecstatic and the mundane throughout "Regarding Wave III." After the ecstatic, richly allusive, aesthetically complex "Burning Island," Snyder places "Roots" (25), a very simple yet subtle poem with obvious symbolism. Then he presents the reader with "Rainbow Body" (26-27), a poem stylistically midway between the previous two. It has the literary complexity of "Burning Island" but limits the language to literal, factual descriptions rather than mythic, symbolic ones. Yet the ecstatic and the spiritual hover in the background, implied through such phrasing as "great drone" and "dazzled ears." The balance of this poem arises from the nondifferentiation of various states of being. As Tom Lavazzi reads it, "the entire poem performs like a living, breathing organism."[15]

Two poems in the midst of "Regarding Wave III" turn from Snyder and Masa's relationship to the larger community experienced on Suwanose. In "Everybody Lying on Their Stomachs, Head Toward the Candle, Reading, Sleeping, Drawing" (28), the title emphasizes the proximity of human community and the sharing of the light in its literal sense. But in the poem proper the light that is being shared is not so much a physical as a metaphysical one. The lightning in the poem is not only a magnified version of the candle light, but also a conduit between visual images in the retina and envisioned images of the spiritual energy flow of the universe in the mind, as indicated by the closing line: "Half-open   on eternity" (28). "Shark Meat" (29) refrains from the metaphysical visions of the preceding poem but enlarges the circle of community by bringing the shark that becomes dinner into the circuits of energy flow and transfer. As Snyder reflects on the process by which the shark has built up its own flesh through

"Thousands of days," he also reflects on the process by which he built up his own flesh on this day by eating the shark. As is frequently the case in his writing throughout the years, eating as a sacrament is presented here with the recognition of the ultimately necessary and accidental interdependence of all living things.

The four selections that precede the poem "Regarding Wave" focus on Masa's pregnancy and her giving birth to Kai. "It Was When" (30-31) speculates on the moment of conception. The most important line is "new power in your breath called its place." Here, Snyder attributes the mystery and vitality of voice as arising within Masa, within the woman. Previously he had emphasized such power in relation to his own inspiration, to the role of the poet. But as implied in the final lines of "Wave," he recognizes here that creative inspiration co-originates in male and female, spiritual birth and physical birth.

"The Bed in the Sky" (32) finds Snyder focusing on himself in terms of his changing responsibilities and behaviors in relation to the event celebrated in "It Was When." Yamazato argues that "this is a crucial moment in which the poet emerges out of the world of The Back Country, a world permeated, as in Snyder's quotation from Bashō on the dedication page, with wandering spirit."[16] As Yamazato notes, two lines near the end of the poem, which describe the desire to remain alone at night outdoors, echo a haiku by Bashō in which the poet does stay out all night. But Snyder says "ought" and does the opposite. He surrenders the fleeting desire of his younger "wandering spirit" and accepts the warmth, companionship, and pleasure, as well as responsibilities, of marriage.

"Kai, Today" (33), the next poem, presents this marriage as if it were fated, through recalling a series of Snyder's and Masa's memories of events that led them to each other. (This poem provides a stunning contrast to "Logging 15" of *Myths & Texts*, in which the speaker recalls a sterile relationship as he fatalistically prepares for the apocalypse at the end of the kalpa cycle.) As for "Not Leaving the House" (34), Steuding observes that "in this poem we can clearly see that Snyder, too, is reborn: the birth of Kai energizes him by drawing something from deep inside him which he may not have known existed."[17] Timothy Gray, however, has a somewhat different take on the situation:

> "Kai, Today" reports on the child's birth from his mother's 'sea.'
> Like the Pacific, Uehara's 'sea' is a fecund realm that nevertheless
> suggests a sublime void. . . . A child born out of the sea
> embodies this roiling sublimity, and is thus a key representative
> for those who want to promote original forms of community

while resisting arbitrary boundaries. Kai's very name suggests this originary connection. As Snyder has told me, 'Kai' is the Sino-Japanese word for 'open,' 'beginning,' or 'founding.'[18]

In the poem "Regarding Wave" (35), Snyder brings together Buddhism, ecology, the living interpenetration of the entire world, and marriage. In the final lines he reaffirms his relationship with Masa, who continues to be an inspiration as wife, mother, and lover. At the bottom of the page are printed the three seed syllables of a Buddhist mantra. Julia Martin argues that here "the Dharma (the law, the way things are, the teachings of the Buddha) is articulated . . . in the pattern of this all-pervading energy." She finds Vāk's presence in the sound of the "shimmering bell" and suggests that the poem's ending with a mantra "is very appropriate, since Snyder's sources consider mantra to be the closest human articulation of Vāk; . . . the poem invites the audience to participate, not only in ideas about Vāk, the interconnectedness of phenomena, of 'self' and 'universe,' but also in the direct experience of union which reciting the mystic syllables is believed to evoke."[19]

"Long Hair"

The title of this section of *Regarding Wave* allies Snyder with the hippie movement of the 1960s and his major audience for *Earth House Hold*, released the previous year. It suggests that these poems will be more socially and politically oriented than those of the three "Regarding Wave" sections. Charles Molesworth notes that "Snyder speaks in *Earth House Hold* of long hair as a symbol of the acceptance of appetite and change, a willingness to go through the powers of nature."[20] Appropriately enough, the first poem is "Revolution in the Revolution in the Revolution" (39), the title a play on a Trotskyist slogan. Snyder begins with an axiom of the Maoist theory of guerrilla warfare in the first line and then extends it philosophically in the second. Here "back country" takes on the multiple resonances developed in Snyder's volume of that name, particularly its meaning of collective unconscious. In the second stanza, Snyder steps beyond all versions of Marxist theory by breaking with the anthropocentrism of revolutionary movements and positing that the environment has been far more exploited than any class of people. He then integrates in the third stanza the positions taken in the first two, and puts forward his ideal of "true Communionism" in opposition to both communism and capitalism. The poem ends by invoking the spiritual power of Buddhism.

In the title "It" (42-43), Snyder probably alludes to a book of the same name written by Alan Watts about the immanent spirituality that he found pervading the alternative culture/youth movement in the United States. In part, the point of Watts's book was to encourage people to stop worrying about defining and intellectualizing what was happening to them and society, to go out and experience "it" for themselves, and to go with the flow that "it" produces. Snyder indicates in a parenthetical statement that this poem came to him while reading Blake in a typhoon. William Blake, the most mystical and visionary of the British Romantic poets, also heavily emphasized experiencing spiritual states of being and wrote numerous poems concerned with the need to reintegrate the conscious and unconscious dimensions of the human psyche. Snyder begins by attempting to express the experience through language and comments at the end of the first stanza that "fields follow the laws of waves." In the next section of the poem, Snyder switches attention from the tropical storm to the book in hand and the movement of language between author and reader. Just as his immersion in the storm is participatory, so too is his immersion in the text, "mind-fronts"—like weather fronts that cause typhoons—"bite back at each other." Through this line Snyder links himself with the "puppy" mentioned in the first stanza. Both are responding to "storms," one the typhoon and the other Blake's poetry. The two experiences, physical and psychic, meld in the final stanza into a single energizing event, much in the same way that "myth" and "text" meld together at the end of Snyder's *Myths & Texts*. "It" remains undefined, experiential, and all-encompassing, rather than intellectualized and limited.

Some of the poems in this section, however, do not bear any specific connection with the "Long Hair" movement as such, as can be seen with "Running Water Music" and "Sours of the Hills" (44, 45), which are typical wilderness poems. The first emphasizes the benefits of simple living alongside water, but contains the enigmatic line, "*beyond wounds*," which has nothing in the poem to clarify its appearance. "Sours of the Hills" emphasizes, as Snyder does in other poems, the various ways by which nature accomplishes seed dispersal. Here, however, the role of humans in facilitating such dispersal is depicted in the second half of the poem. Not only is such activity the result of seeking berries growing in the wild, but also aligns the participating individual with natural processes.

"To Fire" (48-49) is a poem about Snyder's burning up old poems, letters, and useless belongings, celebrating through mythic imagery the joy of voluntary poverty. The poem is humorous in many ways but also thematically hortatory. The ecstasy of the speaker is expected to rub off on the reader and the religious significance of the poem—it is not merely a literary use of myth—is made plain in the final lines. There the poet clarifies that the burning of these external objects symbolizes the burning away of material desires and attachments within the speaker's mind.

Another poem that suggests a certain kind of cleansing and simplification is "Love" (50), which is one of the Suwanose Island poems. The *"obon"* named in the poem is the Japanese festival for the dead held in late August. The spirits of ancestors are welcomed among the living and then sent back to the spirit world by means of dancing and song. Here Snyder emphasizes the power of the older women who lead the dancing and through their songs about love knit the community together even "On the wind-washed lonely islands."

"Meeting the Mountains" (60) may at first seem neither social nor political but merely a raw reportage of the infantile behavior of Snyder's son, Kai. It represents, however, another form of the kind of teaching by example practiced in *Earth House Hold*. Snyder captures the instinctive behavior of a baby, which when broken down into its separate components can be viewed as a type of ritual. The baby without consciousness greets the mountains and the waters in a ritualistic, reverential fashion. Perhaps most important about this behavior is that like some forms of baptism it requires immersion in the element itself.

In contrast, and more overtly political, "Before the Stuff Comes Down" (61) presents an unusual voice for Snyder, one that is smug and dismissive about the transiency of late capitalism in the United States. While the previous poem contains a sense of permanence and itself has lasting interest thematically and aesthetically, the same cannot be said for "Before the Stuff Comes Down." Rather, it stands as a poem primarily of historical interest exemplary of the kind of revolution-around-the-corner optimism that suffused the 1960s counterculture. In the past twenty years, the "big E," a discount store, has survived with less difficulty than the "Turkey Buzzard" in overpopulated California.

In some ways, the poem "Long Hair" (65-66) combines the best of "Meeting the Mountains" and "Before the Stuff Comes Down." While it maintains the spirit of optimism of the second poem, humor replaces smugness and a commitment to long-term transformation replaces a mentality of instant revolution. This poem begins by telling a story of inversion in which deer allow themselves to be hunted and eaten in order to transform human beings. Such a deer is similar to the spirit-deer depicted in *Myths & Texts*. Here, though, the deer are depicted in terms of their ability to survive human expansion through circumvention and adaptation. At poem's end Snyder celebrates their wildness and lays claim to their spirit. The deer can "bound through" his hair because it is long, with that length symbolizing his countercultural status.

"Target Practice"
The brief poems of "Target Practice" have not received much critical attention, and if the volume ended with these it would be an unsatisfactory tapering off of the intensity of much of the rest of *Regarding Wave*. But Snyder saves a significant salvo for the last page, titled "Civilization" (84). Here he clearly sets forth his place and practice in the United States as an integrated opposition to the current aberration of human society called civilization. As he has remarked elsewhere, on his 40,000-year time-line of civilized human inhabitation of the planet, current social structures are a new and anomalous form of existence. In contrast to what he sees as a brief interlude of imbalance and disharmony in human evolution, Snyder affirms the inhabitory and archaic values that he outlined in *Earth House Hold* when he writes "Fetch me my feathers and amber." In the second stanza of "Civilization," suggesting that he is writing this poem while organizing "Regarding Wave II" or "Eight Songs of Clouds and Water," he depicts himself as being pulled out of cultural/intellectual immersion into natural/experiential immersion through beholding a cricket. He concludes by delineating his ongoing individual practice as both poetic and physical, writing poems and heaping stones. His responsibilities to community, to family, and to place require both activities. In this poem, "the interrelatedness of work and culture," according to Molesworth, "is represented by the common image of a riverbed. . . . Poetry and the real work are both seen as ways of nourishing the community."[21]

Molesworth's observation needs to be amended by noting that Snyder does not view these actions dualistically. Poetry is also a form of "real work," but circumstances determine what kinds of work are more appropriate at a given moment. To pursue poetry when a flood is imminent would be acting irresponsibly in relation to family and community; to build a stone wall when a marriage ceremony needed a song would be equally irresponsible. "Civilization," like the rest of *Regarding Wave*, integrates these responsibilities and emphasizes especially seizing the opportunities to sing of achievements, events, and "miracles," such as birth, love, and marriage.

6
Reinhabiting the Land
Turtle Island

By the beginning of the 1970s, Snyder had a solid body of poetry and prose in print and had clearly established his reputation among a sector of the American public. As his decision not to distribute the chapbook *Manzanita* east of the Rockies suggests,[1] however, Snyder was mainly established on the West Coast. But his 1974 volume *Turtle Island*, particularly when it received the Pulitzer Prize for Poetry in 1975, ended the regionalism of his reputation.

More than any of his previous collections, *Turtle Island* delineates Snyder as an inhabitant of the North American continent, someone digging in to build the kind of earth-house-hold he had recommended in his 1960s prose. The poems in *Turtle Island* were written between 1969 and 1974, after his permanent return to the United States. As Katsunori Yamazato sees it, " 'how to be' is the central question that Snyder asks and tries to answer throughout *Turtle Island*."[2] And Sherman Paul views inhabitation as Snyder's "climax of consciousness."[3]

Some critics have suggested that this volume should be understood as a post-Buddhist work, but that opinion overstates the case. The primary focus of *Turtle Island* is reinhabitation, but Buddhism remains an integral aspect of Snyder's understanding and practice of a comprehensive philosophy of "how to be." In *Turtle Island*, the focus narrows in the sense that Snyder is primarily concerned with how to be in *North America*, which he conceptually represents in terms of an ancient Native American name, Turtle Island. As he says in the "Introductory Note": "the old/new name for the continent, based on many creation myths of the people who have been living here for millennia. . . . The 'U.S.A.' and its states and counties are arbitrary and inaccurate impositions on what is really here."[4] Here Snyder reaffirms his attitude toward the unreality of nation-states that he developed in his youth and affirms that Native American cultures remain a significant influence on his life. He renewed contact with Native Americans and resumed his study of their cultures as soon as he returned to California from Japan, and by 1970 he had formulated his conception of North America as Turtle Island.[5]

Charles Molesworth, who approaches Snyder's work from a concern with his sociopolitical ideas, claims that "Snyder's vision largely ignores the social issues—that is, the mechanisms of daily life and such mundane concerns as urban experiences and bureaucratized work schemes—in favor of the political, such as the question of our relation to the environment, the blindness engendered by loyalty to the nation-state, and our allegiance to ideological systems based on domination and waste."[6] True, Snyder does not focus on "urbanization" and "work schemes," not because he ignores the mundane but because he includes a vision of an alternative, life-affirming mundane. And, after all, he has addressed various issues of wage labor in his earlier volumes, from the contradictions of working as a logger to the redundancy of wiper work aboard a tanker.

"Manzanita"

To develop an alternative vision of a balanced, sane daily life based on the history of this continent's inhabitants, Snyder initiates the "Manzanita" section of *Turtle Island* with "Anasazi" (3). This poem depicts the ecologically balanced life of the Native Americans who preceded the Hopi. Snyder follows this with "The Way West, Underground" (4-5), outlining the dimensions of the circumpolar bear cult in terms of its ancient origins and its alleged continuations in the present. This poem, in turn, is followed by "Without" (6). Here Snyder claims that "the path is whatever passes"; it is not an "end in itself." These two poems are followed by another two relating specific practice in the present. In "The Dead by the Side of the Road" (7-8), Snyder emphasizes the tradition of using every part of an animal that has been killed and especially making use of road kills—animals that have been hit by cars and trucks—as a modern adaptation of traditional practice. Such practice stands in direct contrast to the debased use and waste of animals practiced by modern agribusiness (which is criticized in "Steak" [10]) and sport hunting.

"I Went into the Maverick Bar" (9), the fifth poem, is one that has received considerable attention, both positive and negative. In it Snyder recognizes that his own heritage is the same as that of the people he encounters here (this topic is addressed again in "Dusty Braces" [75]). In the end, however, he emphasizes the difference between him and them: he denounces that cultural heritage because it has become destructive, xenophobic, and repressive. The speaker realizes that his responsibility to Turtle Island and to these people requires that he continue to promote his alternative vision. That this vision involves nothing short of complete social transformation is suggested by his defining the "real work" in terms of " 'What is to be done,' " the title of a major theoretical work by V. I. Lenin on the necessity of a Marxist revolution in Russia at the turn of the century.

If readers link these five poems rather than treating them separately, they can see a pattern in which "Anasazi" depicts a specific path in a particular place and time, a historical example of appropriate inhabitation. "The Way West, Underground," then, links Native American experience, through the bear cult archetype, with other peoples and their related beliefs around the globe. These links provide the possibility for a new "underground" that may transform human relationships with the earth worldwide. This poem specifically embodies Snyder's call at the end of the "Introductory Note" to "hark again to those roots, to see our ancient solidarity, and then to the work of being together on Turtle Island." The connection between the Anasazi people and the other cultures identified in "The Way West" is reinforced through the latter poem's last line, "underground," echoing the image in the former poem of "sinking deeper and deeper in earth" (3), and the earth here is identified with the sacred.

While "Anasazi" depicts a specific historical practice and "The Way West" extends such practice globally, "Without" treats the issue of proper inhabitation in abstract terms heavily indebted to Buddhism and shamanism. The crucial Buddhist perception behind this poem is that of total interdependence and mutual co-creation of all entities in the world. In the universal process of co-creation an individual's vantage point is not a fixed, static position but a momentary node in the ongoing transformation of energy. As a result, determining the proper forms of right practice requires attention to localized specifics—"the path is whatever passes"—because diversity is a crucial feature of any healthy ecosystem.

Any practice, then, to be right must be attuned to the features of the local processes in which it will take place. One such right practice is depicted by Snyder in "The Dead by the Side of the Road." This practice, though, seems somewhat out of time and not necessarily specific to its location because of the generality of the actions depicted. "I Went into the Maverick Bar" brings all of these connections explicitly home. It takes the speaker into the immediacy of the present, the problems and the promise of responsible behavior here on Turtle Island.

"Steak" (10), in contrast, addresses irresponsible behavior. At the same time it extends Buddhist compassion to the cattle being raised for slaughter. A key statement in this poem is" slowly thinking / with the rhythm of their / breathing," which reminds readers that all animals are sentient. Mind, then, is not the sole attribute or possession of human beings. Rather, as "No Matter, Never Mind" claims (11), "Mind" or consciousness arises from the dynamic processes of the material world. This poem is reminiscent of the remark that "matter seeks consciousness," with the corollary reminder that the earth has generated human beings and not the other way around. At the same time, the title's use of negatives produces a Buddhist joke in that both matter and mind are part of the illusory world of *samsara*, the world of appearances rather than "essential nature." Here, then, Snyder returns to the ideas expressed in the sutra of Hui Neng that descriptions are only labels rather than the thing-in-itself. In terms of *Turtle Island* as a whole, this poem can be seen as one of the mythic celebrations of the phenomenal world that Snyder includes here and in his next poetry volume, *Axe Handles*.

In "The Bath" (12-14), Snyder returns to one of the themes dominating *Regarding Wave* and evident earlier as one of his concerns in the Japan poems in *Riprap*: harmonious family life. If family is the practice hall, as he has remarked, then his vision of a new, more harmonious, ecologically balanced culture for North America must include a functional family. "The Bath" accomplishes that inclusion. As Julia Martin notes, "to give this attention to bathing indicates a deliberate making of community, and a definition of family-as-energy-network that is radically different from the familiar nuclear structure. The model of interrelationships which this offers extends in other poems to 'The Great Family,' to include those who are not necessarily blood-relations, and may even be non-human"[7] (Martin is referring here to "Prayer for the Great Family" [24-25]). The interrelationship consists of both social and ecological harmony, in process through time since the family will change as the children grow and as each person's body ages. Here and in "Prayer for the Great Family" there should also be noted the religious, sacramental quality of the activity and the tone of each poem. Snyder makes this explicit through the refrain about "our body," which echoes the language of the Catholic communion service but renders it plural: each body is our body through mutual co-creation and interdependence.

"Spell Against Demons," reprinted from *The Fudo Trilogy* chapbook (1973), displays a different dimension of Snyder's religious concerns in *Turtle Island*. Very different from the verse that has preceded it in the volume, "Spell Against Demons" is, as Yamazato explains it, "a poem that attempts to exorcize the demonic forces inside the civilization by introducing a powerful figure from Buddhism,

'ACHALA the Immovable' (*Fudōmyō-ō*, in Japanese)." Interestingly enough, Snyder derived his knowledge of this Shingon Buddhist deity by way of Shugendo, which "originally was a nature-worship religion that borrowed its theoretical basis from Shingon."[8] At the end of the poem is a Buddhist mantra attributed to Fudōmyō-ō, which is translated in the "Smokey the Bear Sutra" by Snyder as meaning "I dedicate myself to the universal diamond be this raging fury destroyed."[9] Snyder here both seriously and playfully adapts and updates the Buddhist mantra to emphasize the interrelationship of the spiritual and social dimensions of his vision for a new way of life.

That the spiritual is not adequate unto itself Snyder makes explicit through the next two poems. In "Front Lines" (18), the forest is depicted as a victim threatened by contemporary America. The third stanza displays an angry reaction by the speaker to jets overhead because they represent the entire economic empire with its military might that threatens the trees and the land. To emphasize this point, Snyder spells out the enemy as "Amerika," a popular epithet during the 1960s used to identify the U.S. with fascism. He combines this name with an organic metaphor that likens the U.S. economy to an obese man with cholesterol-clogged arteries. The fifth stanza then combines with the end of the third to sandwich this image of decadence between two depictions of the "rape" of Mother Earth.

In "Front Lines" the individual working the bulldozer is not treated as the "enemy." Here, rather, Snyder's wrath is reserved for the man from the city, who is engineering this destruction without having any direct contact with the environment that he is having razed for financial gain. Snyder demands of himself and readers that they take a stand, here and now, against further devastation of the natural world. For Snyder, defense of the forests is both a planetary issue, in relation to the decimation of the rain forests and their potential impact on the greenhouse effect, and a local one. His area of California borders the Tahoe National Forest, and that part of the country has been badly damaged in the past by both hydraulic gold mining and clear-cutting of forests. The poem, then, reflects not only a general political stance but also a specific one speaking to the local defense of nature in which he and his neighbors have been engaged. Snyder remarked in a mid-1970s interview that "it's the eternal moment. I think in those terms, but I also think in terms of organic evolution, and from that standpoint we have a critical time now in which decisions are being made which will have long reaching effects on the survival of many forms of life."[10]

"Control Burn" (19) continues the issue of forestry practices, but here the literal is secondary to the figurative. Snyder depicts actual

Indian behavior in California; he does so, not so much to teach readers about the native activity of controlled burns, but in order to use it as an image for the kind of purgation that American culture requires. In effect, he argues that American society has become cluttered with too much "logging slash" and secondary growth that renders the entire ecosystem vulnerable to catastrophe. "A hot clean / burn," a sudden upheaval or revolutionary social transformation, would clear away all of this tangled undergrowth that obscures vision and threatens the "tall and clear" stands of trees normal to a mature forest.

"The Call of the Wild" (21-23) addresses the issue of human beings threatening nature, as did "Front Lines." But here the tone is more sorrowful than wrathful as Snyder expresses concern more for what the next generation will lose than for what his own may suffer. Each section consists of a mini-narrative. The first focuses on the life of an old man who has been a "native" but clearly has never become an inhabitant. He refuses to hear the coyotes "singing," and so he will have them killed by the "Government / Trapper." The old man will never realize his loss, but Snyder's children will: "My sons will lose this / Music they have just started / To love." Snyder also indicates that establishing a harmonious relationship with one's environment is not automatic. The sons are only just starting to learn, but it is not simply a matter of time or else the old man would also share that love. It is, instead, a matter of attitude, attention, and interdependence.

The second section tells the story of hippies who move to the countryside as a result of a psychedelic religious impulse rather than out of a commitment to nature and inhabitation.[11] They commit acts as destructive as the old man's and they too fear the coyote, because, as Snyder implies, they fear the unconscious—"the wild"—inside themselves. In the third section Snyder expands his mournful critique from individuals to government. He develops an analogy between the Vietnam War and the modern scientific, technological attack on the earth through pesticides, chemical fertilizers, synthetics, and sterile, artificial housing. This "war against earth" will not only destroy the ecology but will also result in "no place / A Coyote could hide." Snyder's capitalization clarifies that he is not speaking here of one animal but that he is using Coyote symbolically to represent the wild or trickster spirit within people that connects humans with all other sentient beings.

The "envoy" of the poem stresses in an elegiac tone that nothing guarantees the survival of the human-animal spirit. By implication, those who would seek to preserve that spirit must act to defend Coyote and his habitat. L. Edwin Folsom's observation about the volume as a whole seems relevant here: "Snyder announces the opening of the frontier again and attempts to push it eastward, to reverse America's historical process, to urge the wilderness to grow back into civilization to release the stored energy from layers below us."[12]

Clearly, the middle poems of the "Manzanita" section of *Turtle Island* take on a tone that, if not apocalyptic, certainly registers a sense of impending crisis. But the section does not end on that note. Snyder circles back to the more long-range kind of perception suggested in the first several poems as he approaches the section's close. "Prayer for the Great Family" emphasizes human, ecological, and cosmic interdependent harmony and hearkens back again to the old ways of Turtle Island's original inhabitants. "Source" (26) begins to suggest that the activist who left the "Maverick Bar" to resume his real work should learn to imitate the manzanita, a second-growth bush that proliferates rapidly in mined-off and clear-cut land. At the end, Snyder also suggests that the plant proliferates because it has learned to grow not only with sunlight but also with "that black light" of the night stars. If one associates this image with the political notion of the "underground" implied in "The Way West," Snyder can be seen to be recommending that the proponents of the new culture work in darkness, in quiet, in out-of-the-way places, as they build strength, extend their communities, and deepen their roots.

In the poem that provides the title for the "Manzanita" section, Snyder suggests that the manzanita plant itself can serve as part of the healing magic necessary for reinhabitation. This magic will allow him and others to realize the true size of the many little signs by which the Earth can be seen to be regenerating itself. Looking at "Manzanita" along with "Charms" (27 and 28), Molesworth argues that these two poems "show how the reinhabitation of the land will be aided by songs of knowledge and community."[13] These are precisely the kinds of poems that Snyder has arranged into the second part of Turtle Island, "Magpie's Song." This section contains thirty-one poems displaying a much greater diversity of styles, tones, lengths, and content than to be found in "Manzanita."

"Magpie's Song"

Although this section contains many powerful poems, it begins with a surprisingly unpoetic one, "Facts" (31), which provides data pertinent to Snyder's overall theme in *Turtle Island*. The information is presented so prosaically and with so little framing that it is unlikely to affect anyone not already sympathetic with Snyder's position. The next two poems, however, are quite effective. Both "The Real Work" and "Pine Tree Tops" (32, 33) depend on very specific experiences to make their points. The first emphasizes the degree to which all animal, including human, energy is expended on just "sliding by," in the sense of surviving from one day to the next. And yet, the reality is that all beings necessarily fail to survive in part because their deaths enable others to survive.

The second poem, set at night in the woods, concludes with an ambiguous statement: "what do we know." This line can be read in two initially contradictory, but finally complementary, ways. One, the poet out in the night, paying attention to the trees and the animals attentively enough to spot rabbit and deer tracks, is doing what it takes to really get to know Turtle Island. What we know depends on how we have learned, and the poet has learned a great deal. Two, no matter how much time is spent alone in the woods, the natural world remains a mystery; what we know is actually very little compared to all that goes on. These two interpretations become complementary when readers realize that one of the things the poet has learned, and that he wishes his readers to learn, is that wisdom is born out of the recognition of one's own ignorance. The poem that follows this one, "For Nothing" (34), however, reminds readers that the world exists in itself; it is not the responsibility of wild nature to educate people, to be a thing-for-us, but it is our responsibility to educate ourselves, to learn from whence all existence arises.

"Night Herons" (35-36) addresses in some detail ideas present in several poems that precede it. Snyder, on a walk with friends down by the wharf area, meditates on the presence of the "night herons" in San Francisco. As he notes the machinery of modern life, he also gradually realizes the continuous presence of animals who are managing to inhabit this area, just as the people do. As he wonders about the herons' return, he suddenly realizes that their return is no more peculiar than his own and that he enjoys being here amidst the machinery of the city. Part of the "joy" he feels, which he assumes the other animals feel, comes from the experience of surviving. As Timothy Gray notes, "by the late twentieth century the San Francisco Bay Area may have become an industrial eyesore, full of smoke stacks, stationary boilers and steam turbine pumps, but apparently its living creatures will not give up their habitats so easily."[14] Here Snyder feels a sense of self-renewal of humans and other animals in a mutually sustaining community.

In "The Egg" (37-38), the poet celebrates the ways in which that mutually sustaining community comes together in the production of the human embryo. And here he does not only include the molecular activity of cell division, but also the way that the experience of the forefathers and foremothers of each child leave an imprint on that person's life and destiny. They do so in terms of who they are genetically, what they do in their life practice, and what they say in their formative interactions. This poem was clearly initiated by a family experience in which it appears that Snyder is bringing his mother to visit Kai, his son and her grandson, as an infant.

Along with "The Egg," "The Uses of Light" (39) shifts from the meditative mode into a playful, rhyming kind of poetry. Yamazato believes that in this poem Snyder extends compassion for other beings to include the inanimate as well as the animate. The poem's indebtedness to Buddhism is evident because "the principal Buddha in the Avatamsaka Sutra is Vairocana (the Sun Buddha), who is depicted in that sutra as the center of the universe"; and, further, " 'stones,' 'trees,' 'moth,' 'deer,' and people in this world are all interrelated and constitute a harmonious whole while illumined by the spiritual light that emanates from the Sun Buddha."[15]

But it is not necessary to conceptualize the poem in these terms to determine the importance of "light." The last point made in "Facts" is that "our primary source of food is the sun" (31). In terms of the function of photosynthesis in the food chain, the human as well as many other animals' need for sunlight to exist, and the necessity of solar radiation for the composition of the Earth's atmosphere, it could be said from the viewpoint of basic ecological science that everything on the planet is interrelated. But the point of the first four stanzas of "The Uses of Light" is not simply to get readers to appreciate the role of sunlight. The fifth stanza is based on an old Chinese saying about expanding one's perceptual horizons and suggests that a slight readjustment can lead to a significantly expanded awareness. The rhymes about light, then, serve primarily to get readers to reconceptualize the mundane in terms of its complex interconnections from multiple points of view.

Snyder expands on this issue of reperception in "By Frazier Creek Falls" (41). Snyder attempts to immerse readers in the image of nature he portrays so that they will not learn from the poem itself but will imitate it by gaining direct experience. For the second half of the poem to mean anything to readers, they would have had to have experienced the equivalent of the first half of the poem. In this second half Snyder lectures against the kind of transcendence of the physical found in so many American religions as well as in its romantic and idealist philosophies. "We *are* it" insists on not just recognizing interrelatedness but on making that the central fact of existence.

A person who has assimilated the messages of such poems as "Without," "The Uses of Light," and "By Frazier Creek Falls" should have no problem espousing the attitude found in "It Pleases" (44). As the dateline indicates, Snyder wrote this poem on a visit to Washington, D.C., in November 1973. As in "Night Herons," Snyder finds the bird flying overhead the most solidly real aspect of the scene before him. Emblematic of wild nature, it soars over what human society has imagined to be the center of world power. But Snyder declares that "The center of power is nothing!" because "The World does what it pleases." Wild nature goes on about its own business, indifferent to the halls of civil power. Washington, D.C., in effect, is merely a form into which people infuse power through their allegiances.

For many critics, "Mother Earth: Her Whales" (47-49) is Snyder's most grandly accomplished poem in this section. As Hwa Yol Jung and Petee Jung have noted, Snyder wrote this poem about a month after he attended the United Nations conference on the human environment in Stockholm and published it in the *New York Times* (July 13, 1972): "It began with a terse foreword in which he said that everyone came to Stockholm not to give but rather to take, not to save the planet but to argue about how to divide it up. . . . The poem meant to defend all the creatures of the earth."[16] The last sentence sums up the poem's theme, but its structure and style are also worth analyzing.

The opening stanza of "Mother Earth: Her Whales" describes activity without a designated narrator and ends with the participle "watching," which while specific to the sparrow may apply to the owl and lizard as well, all of which appear in these four lines. Any or all of them, then, may be the speaker of the next stanza, which consists of a reverential chant that could serve as a grace before meals. The third stanza provides a sharp contrast to this reverential, nurturing prayer of interpenetrating existence and is clearly presented from the viewpoint of a human narrator. The "Brazil" that is named does not identify a bioregional or ecological entity but stands only for the imposition of arbitrary human boundaries on the Amazon watershed. The government spokesman displays a nature-as-resource mentality that goes hand-in-hand with such boundaries and which the narrator obviously abhors. These first three stanzas focus on the land and its inhabitants.

The fourth and fifth stanzas turn to the oceans and the island nation of Japan. The fourth, paralleling the first two stanzas of the poem, describes the behavior of whales with respect and awe. In contrast, the fifth stanza condemns Japan, as the third did Brazil, for its slaughter of whales and its pollution of the sea. The sixth and seventh stanzas replicate this pattern, this time attending to the river watersheds of eastern Asia. Snyder here adds a historical dimension to indicate that species extermination and agricultural degradation of bioregions are not simply twentieth-century phenomena. It is also worth noting that he attacks in the seventh stanza the basic concept of anthropocentrism that guides the philosophies of virtually all of modern culture. The eighth stanza includes the United States and Canada in its circle of condemnation.

At the ninth stanza, the negative critique is suddenly interrupted by a declaration of solidarity. "The People," consonant with Native American beliefs, means here all animals living together, not just humans. With that cry for solidarity, Snyder returns in the next stanza to his attack on all of the "civilized" governments represented in Stockholm, all of whom failed to "speak for the green of the leaf" (48).[17] Snyder then conflates the image of governmental resource managers as "vultures" with an old English ballad in which the birds pluck out the eyes of a "slain knight" (47). This overlay of imagery implies that no honor and no respect for others exist among the representatives of civilization. The ballad describes not animal but human behavior as rapacious and devouring. Snyder concludes on a note of hope by returning to the owl, the lizard, the whales, i.e., the community of other peoples, who are the "wild" with which he will identify himself. When the poet beholds civilization he is repulsed and disgusted; fortunately, if "It Pleases" is accurate, civilization is not the main thing going on anyway.

"Straight-Creek-Great Burn" (52-53) continues this positive identification with the wild even as it hearkens back to earlier poems. Paul finds it a particularly compelling poem not only for what it does in its own right but also for the ways in which it demonstrates Snyder's maturity and growth. Paul thinks of it not so much in relation to the rest of *Turtle Island* as in relation to the numerous other poems that Snyder has written about the advent of spring. As he sees it, Snyder is "more meditative now, and not solitary . . . his attention—*watching* is now the primary activity of participation (one of the ways he is teaching his sons)—is both remarkably close and wide, aware."[18] As many of the poems that have preceded it in *Turtle Island* suggest, "watching" becomes an extremely significant form of action, if the person so engaged opens him or herself up to changed perception.

There is also a significant political theme developed in this poem, which does not come clear until almost the end: "never a leader, / all of one swift / / empty / dancing mind" (53). Nature contains a high degree of complex organization and interaction and people are introduced as "resting" and "watching" this complexity. That introduction is followed by the last four stanzas on the intricate, interactive flight of a flock of birds. They too are highly organized and complex, but their leadership consists of "mind" rather than governmental structures, civilizations, psychological strictures, or other trappings of the modern nation-state. That readers should establish such an identification between the people and the birds is suggested by the parallel of the last two lines: "they settle down. / end of poem" (53). Both the action of the birds and that of the poet culminate simultaneously.

Snyder makes the point in an interview that "if we talk about the evolution of consciousness, we also have to talk about evolution of bodies . . . which is done by literally eating each other. And that's what communion is."[19] Sharon Jaeger, in her dissertation, provides a valuable commentary on this concept, when she remarks that the "sacramental aspect of eating—a respect for other living beings—becomes, Snyder suggests, one way that human beings deal with the predatory aspects of eating, which primarily has survival value but partakes as well in the pleasure principle."[20] Several of the poems in the "Magpie's Song" section of *Turtle Island* focus on this issue. For instance, "The Hudsonian Curlew" (54) emphasizes the proper way to clean, treat, and eat a curlew felled by Snyder's companion. It is followed by "Two Fawns That Didn't See the Light This Spring" (58). In this poem the first dead fawn results from "A friend in a tipi" who accidentally shot a doe thinking it was a buck and discovered it was carrying a fawn when he butchered her. The second dead fawn results from a car accident and is also discovered during the butchering process. In the first stanza, the hunter is a male and in the second stanza the driver is a female. Both are responsible for the inadvertent death of a fawn, but there is no condemnation or recrimination; rather, compassion is registered throughout on the part of the two responsible parties and on the part of the poet. The meat of the mothers will be eaten and appreciated, while the deaths of the fawns will be mourned, not because they would never be the target of human consumption but because their deaths cannot be salvaged through eating.

Snyder has been criticized, particularly by other Buddhists, for writing poems about eating meat and killing animals, with their criticism based on the principle of *ahimsa*, which is to avoid causing harm to others. Poems such as the two just discussed and others, though, do not extol or promote hunting. I read them as saying that if a person is going to hunt and is going to eat meat, there is a right way to go about it and there are wrong ways. There is another element to this issue, which is the importance of avoiding being too quick to judge others who find themselves in different circumstances. In "Magpie's Song," two poems in particular address this point. The first is "Why Log Truck Drivers Rise Earlier Than Students of Zen" (63). And the second is "'One Should Not Talk to a Skilled Hunter about What is Forbidden by the Buddha'" (66). In both, most of the poem is devoted to straight description, while each ends with an abstract statement. In the former, the close suggests that such truck drivers know no other way to earn a living and so participate in the destruction of the forests. In the latter, the complexities of predation throughout the animal world are "secret," not fully fathomed.

"Bedrock" (64) is much simpler than some of the other poems from "Magpie's Song"; nevertheless, it is an important part of this section. Snyder has so far been emphasizing that true learning comes from the rest of nature, particularly wild nature. But here he turns back to other humans for education, specifically his wife Masa, to whom the poem is dedicated. The first stanza emphasizes their general satisfaction and their breaking free from intellectualizing and rationalizing thought. In this context, Snyder asks: "teach me to be tender" (64). If the poem ended with their having tea, we might consider it simply sentimental, but it does not. It ends by admitting that they "laugh" and "grieve." In the midst, then, of his denunciations of the failures of civilization and his wisdom-figure teaching of his readers to learn from wild nature, he pauses to admit his own weaknesses and to suggest that everyone must continue learning, especially learning to love each other better. The title of the poem, then, can be read as a double pun: one, "bed-rock" meaning foundation, with love playing that role here; two, bedrock as rocky bed, meaning the difficulties of marriage. "The Dazzle" (65) functions as something of a postscript to "Bedrock," celebrating the mysteries of birth that result from the heterosexual love idealized in that poem.

The poem "Magpie's Song" (69) would make little sense if it appeared any earlier in *Turtle Island*. By this point, though, it resonates strongly with the poems that precede it and effectively summarizes this second section of the volume. The initial stanza sets the scene: the speaker in the desert at sunup, sitting by railroad tracks and listening to the coyotes singing. Magpie then sings a song, which begins by identifying human and bird as brothers and invoking a magical stone, turquoise, the symbolism of which Snyder had already developed in "The Blue Sky," published in *Six Sections from Mountains and Rivers Without End, Plus One.*[21] The breeze that Magpie calls on the human to smell may be said to represent the "wave" function of wisdom as it is passed on from being to being—the last line of "Ethnobotany" is instructive in this regard: "Taste all, and hand the knowledge down" (51). But most important is the assurance provided by this representative of wild nature that the speaker need not fear "what's ahead" (69). Snyder suggests that as long as one keeps the wisdom of wild nature firmly in mind, there is no need to fear the future.

As Michael Castro sees it, "the capitalized 'Mind' in the next to the last line suggests the 'original' or 'biomass' mind. The poem itself should be seen as a modern attempt at a 'shaman song' that tries to put us into contact with that 'Mind.' It brings back from the mystical experience the voice of the nonhuman or extrahuman and shares it with the community."[22] "Magpie's Song" reinforces the overall positive and confident tone of this section, and, through the inclusion of Coyote, counters the pessimistic tone sounded in "The Call of the Wild." At the same time, it demonstrates Snyder's increasingly self-conscious assumption of the role of a white shaman for modern Turtle Island.

"For the Children"

In "For the Children," the third section of *Turtle Island*, Snyder assumes the function of a shaman to a greater degree than in the earlier parts, here passing on wisdom and reassurance. This section begins with "0 Waters" (73), which is another of the many ritualized prayer-poems of the volume. It calls on the waters to "wash us, me" as the speaker observes the way in which the mountains and the waters of the world are moving and flowing, following the wave function of the interdependent energy-transfer network. The poem ends by defining this network as a "sangha" (Buddhist fellowship) of the entire planet.

"Tomorrow's Song" (77), after announcing that "The USA slowly lost its mandate" because it failed to include the nonhuman in its definition of democracy, attempts to prepare its readers for the future. Snyder predicates this future upon the continent's return to its status as Turtle Island through people adopting some kind of inhabitory culture. Snyder implies that the future will be built on the basis of a post-industrial, post-fossil-fuel economy that adapts many of the labor and cultural practices of the continent's original inhabitants. People will be capable of building this future Turtle Island because they will have established a set of nature-based values serving "wilderness" and the Earth as mother.

But to be able to participate in preparing for such a rebuilding, the future citizens of Turtle Island will need to know the history of this land they seek to re-inhabit. To that end, Snyder provides the poem "What Happened Here Before" (78-81), which recapitulates the history of the western slope of Turtle Island starting 300 million years ago. The first stanza concerns the continent's earliest geological history; the second describes the formation of the western mountains and the sedimentation of gold there; the third tells of the formation of the waters that make up some of the major rivers of the watershed around the Nevada City area.

Then, at the forty-thousand-year mark, Snyder claims people began to appear, the first human inhabitants of a land already heavily populated by other animals. According to Snyder; "the white man" really only arrived in the area with the gold rush, a last-second smudge on the region's timeline. In contrast to the stanza on the first natives, this stanza makes it very clear that the "white man" did not come to adapt himself to the land and its inhabitants, but to make all else adapt to him.

Only in the final stanzas does Snyder indicate what generated this complex explanation of the history of the land he inhabits. He and his sons have apparently been out camping and they ask, no doubt quite innocently, "who are we?" The poem emphatically declares that that question cannot be answered without also answering "where are we?" And for Snyder, the state of being an inhabitant is what determines the state of one's being, as he declares in emphatic capitals: "WE SHALL SEE WHO KNOWS HOW TO BE." The final line, "Bluejay screeches from a pine," suggests that the bird rather than, or as well as, the human is the one announcing that challenge in response to the "military jets" overhead. As Castro understands it, the poem is written from the continent's point of view, and this would accord with the ambiguity as to whether the bluejay or the poet is the speaker of that militant challenge. Further, Castro claims that "Turtle Island is thus presented to us as a vital thing, vaster and longer-lived than many or any of its species. When we achieve an understanding and an appreciation of the depth and scope of its life, the poem's implicit message states, we can begin to come into proper relationship to our land."[23]

"Toward Climax" (82-85), which follows thematically from "What Happened Here Before," begins to answer the question of "who knows how to be." It does so by contrasting the way of life of the culture that has produced the military jets with the way of life of the inhabitory peoples, human and nonhuman, of the "old/new" Turtle Island. The

contrast is presented most starkly in part four, in which the practice
of mass slaughter, mainly by aerial bombardment, is juxtaposed to a
primitive perception of "virgin / Forest." In this poem, Snyder looks
at human evolution and the development of social organization, with
both its positive and negative aspects, by means of a rich language of
stunningly concise images. And while the fourth part is the most
overtly political, the third part lays out the major and most difficult
task at hand: "stop and think."

As with the other sections of this volume, Snyder shifts into an
optimistic and virtually utopian mood at the end of "For the Children,"
with the poem by that title and "As for Poets." "For the Children"
(86) is a poem that implies far more than it states. The initial stanza
would seem to be describing a mountain hike except for a single word,
"statistics," introduced in the second line. Here human consumption
is the only thing on the rise, while humanity declines as a result of
such consumption. A crisis is imminent in the relatively short time
span of one or two centuries, but the crisis itself will be short-lived.
On the other side, those who understand "how to be" "can meet there
in peace / if we make it." But for now, those who would side with the
earth and the possibility of humanity's recovery of its kinship with
the rest of nature must prepare for difficult times. Snyder offers a
word to those generations who must live through the coming troubles:
"stay together / learn the flowers / go light."

For those unsympathetic to any kind of back-to-nature movement
such a slogan no doubt sounds hopelessly simplistic and naive. And
yet, precisely because of its apparent simplicity this stanza has become
a rallying cry for many environmentalists and bioregionalists and has
remained one of the most frequently quoted sets of lines from Snyder's
poetry. Those sympathetic to Snyder's project know quite well that
there is nothing simple about these words. To remain united is itself a
daunting task. Learning the names of plants is no easy task either; it
is, however, a major step in reorienting people's attention toward the
natural world. And, finally, being able to "go light" in the age of
cellular phones and home-shopping on the worldwide web is virtually
impossible. Nevertheless, the end of the century is witnessing a variety
of efforts on the part of Americans to simplify their lives, reduce their
consumption, and adopt voluntary simplicity even as the efforts to
seduce them to consume beyond their means electronically intensify.

"As for Poets" (87-88) closes out the poetry sections of *Turtle Island*
and speaks to the role of the imagination and of vision in enabling
the kind of understanding to move beyond present-day American
culture. Having worked through the four classic elements of earth,

air, fire, and water, Snyder then adds space and mind. In the spirit of Zen paradox, the final stanza suggests that the mind is both full and empty simultaneously and that the world in all its multidimensionality is one great poem; and by extension, all poems are part of one great world.

"Plain Talk"

Despite the diversity of styles and tones displayed in *Turtle Island*, what stays in the mind of many readers is a note of urgency and a political activism never so overt in Snyder's previous writing. This immediacy is reflected particularly in the fourth part of the volume. The most significant of these five prose pieces is the first one, "Four Changes." This essay had already been read widely prior to its publication here. The original version was distributed in photocopy form in early 1969. Later that year, *Earth Read Out*, a Berkeley environmental newsletter, printed a revised version. Then again that same year, Robert Shapiro in association with Alan Watts printed fifty thousand copies of the essay in broadside form and distributed it without charge nationwide. Eventually, another eleven thousand copies were printed.[24] Nearly sixty thousand copies of this essay, then, were in circulation prior to its book publication. What Snyder has reprinted in *Turtle Island* consists of the 1969 revised version with more recent comments interpolated.

Snyder presents in this essay a clear, concise overview of his social philosophy. The other essays continue in this same vein. The very brief " 'Energy Is Eternal Delight' " (the title comes from the Romantic poet William Blake) deals with the energy crisis and Native American resistance to uranium mining in the Southwest. "The Wilderness" continues with a focus on Native American ways, serving as a sort of prelude to the essays in *The Old Ways* (originally published in 1977; five of its six essays are reprinted in *A Place in Space*). Snyder's main concern here is with getting "what the Sioux Indians called the creeping people, and the standing people, and the flying people, and the swimming people—into the councils of government" (108).

The last two essays are more explicitly linked to the poetry of the volume. "What's Meant By 'Here' " provides a prose explanation of the present condition of the land depicted in "What Happened Here Before." And the final essay, "On 'As for Poets,' " explains the function of poetry in relation to Snyder's own beliefs and commitments, taking the reader back to "Four Changes." In the introduction to that first essay, Snyder makes a remark that emphasizes once again the relationship between immediate action and ongoing practice: "My Teacher once said to me, —become one with the knot itself, til it dissolves away.—sweep the garden.—any size" (91). He confirms that Zen practice continues to guide his way in the world. Later in the essay he defines the garden and the sweeping: "no transformation without our feet on the ground. Stewardship means, for most of us, find your place on the planet, dig in, and take responsibility from there. . . . Get a sense of workable territory, learn about it, and start acting point by point" (101). And one form of such acting is writing poems, which Snyder links with the issues of energy and community: "Poetry is for all men and women. The power within—the more you give, the more you have to give—will still be our source when coal and oil are long gone, and atoms are left to spin in peace" (114). As with the volume as a whole, "Plain Talk" emphasizes cautionary essays that warn of impending crises, and yet closes on remarks of optimism and hope.

While critics such as Charles Altieri have expressed dissatisfaction with *Turtle Island* as a weakening of Snyder's aesthetic strengths because of its privileging of politics and prophecy,[25] Molesworth claims that "taken together, and with the remarkable prose essays as well, the three sections of poetry in *Turtle Island* form a whole that advances Snyder's work well beyond the objectivist poetics of the early books and the political suppositions of *Earth House Hold*."[26] Paul seems to respond to some of the complaints about *Turtle Island* when he concludes that "political action, in fact, may be the most significant measure of [Snyder's] love because learning to love has taught him what to defend. . . . This political book is remarkably joyous, and serene; hence, its authenticity."[27] Finally, the Jungs conclude their study of Snyder's ecopiety with a remark that seems eminently suited to summing up *Turtle Island*: "The political mandate of Snyder's ecopoetry is Communionism. . . . Communionism is first and foremost the way of seeking a deep sense of communion with myriads of natural things on earth, who are also called 'peoples,' without any facile dualism and unnecessary hierarchism of any kind."[28] Overall, critical reception of *Turtle Island* has been far more favorable than unfavorable. It stands as a bioregional manifesto that draws on Native American history and myth to educate and inspire future natives of the content, not to replace native peoples but to live alongside of them. As Snyder explained it, responding to a question from the audience at a 1992 New York City poetry reading,

Anyone is a Native American who chooses, consciously and deliberately, to live on this continent, this North American continent, with a full spirit for the future, and for how to live on it right, with the consciousness that says, 'Yeah, my great-great-grandchildren and all will be here for thousands of years to come. We're not going on to some new frontier, we're here now.' In that spirit, African-Americans, Euro-Americans, Asian-Americans, come together as Native Americans. And then you know that those continents that your ancestors came from are great places to visit, but they're not home. Home is here.[29]

7

Handing Down the Practice
Axe Handles and Left Out in the Rain

Axe Handles

After the success of *Turtle Island*, it probably came as a surprise to many readers of Snyder's poetry that he waited nearly ten years before publishing another full-length collection. In 1983, Snyder produced *Axe Handles*, with a new publisher, North Point Press of San Francisco, and with a new tone. While Charles Molesworth in a review rightly claims that "the central tension here is the same that animated *Turtle Island* (1974): how can we carry on the meaningful transmission of community and culture against the threatening background of ecological perversity and vast geological and cosmic processes," it does not seem entirely accurate to speak of "tension" so much as of continuing concern.[1] One does not hear in *Axe Handles* the same urgency expressed in *Turtle Island*. Rather, as Snyder remarked in an interview in 1983, *Axe Handles* "is more concerned with the metaphor of communication and transmission. It is more concerned with cultural values . . . in the larger sense of the carrying on of cultural sanity." And in another interview in 1998, he commented that "*Axe Handles* is a description . . . of coming into the community and coming into the place in many subtle ways."[2] It is perhaps no coincidence that a year before the publication of *Axe Handles*, Snyder participated in the construction of a "community-built Zendo" (meditation hall).[3]

Teaching, as a form of acting in the world, also takes on a more important function in Snyder's poems. One could argue that Snyder has gone beyond the feeling of apocalyptic crisis since the mid-1970s. At the end of the 1960s he and many others in the United States believed that revolution was in the air and that a major social transformation was on the horizon.[4] Such people felt a tremendous letdown in the 1970s when no such revolution materialized. Most of the *Turtle Island* poems came out of that period. With *Axe Handles* Snyder shows that he has gained a clearer sense of the long cycles of cultural and ecological change. He had entered his fifties by the time it was published, and he takes to heart in this collection the message he reports in one of the poems: "teach the children about the cycles."[5]

"Loops"

Part One of *Axe Handles* is titled "Loops" and comprises twenty-five poems, with the title poem placed first. As Julia Martin notes, "Snyder has frequently used the idea of 'looping back' to indicate a recursive sense of history and tradition. The metaphor implies at many levels a reconnection with origins, 'the old ways,' and a recognition of continuity with ancient tradition."[6] Martin's claims are certainly implied in the epigraph to the volume and restated without ambiguity in the poem "Axe Handles." But to understand this poem, one needs first to consider its epigraph.

If the dedication, "This book is for San Juan Ridge," can be said to emphasize place, then the epigraph can be said to emphasize time, specifically the transmission of culture down through generations. Snyder identifies his epigraph as "a folk song from the Pin area [of China], 5th c. B.C." Rather than "high" literature, he draws on popular tradition, orally transmitted. The opening two lines indicate that the new is crafted on the basis of the old and that such transmission of knowledge requires models. This lesson is then applied to marriage, so that craft and culture, as well as the older generation, the present generation, and the one yet to come are all implicated in custom and ritual. The "go-between" is literally a marriage broker. In a broader cultural sense, however, one could say it is also the artist or poet who, through his or her role as a communicator, brings different people together and educates them about each other. Snyder has explained that "*Axe Handles* goes back to being very close to the functional origins of poetry in terms of folksong and folklore. It's not for nothing that the whole poem, the whole book, the title and the lead poem is out of the Book of Song, the Odes. I am looking back to the Book of Odes as a model for that book of verse, to its simple poems about planting fields and getting together for feasts—real early agricultural community poetry."[7]

Robert Schultz and David Wyatt comment that "instruction is at the heart of this book, emphasized in its beginning and returned to frequently."[8] In essence, "Axe Handles" (5-6) provides a contemporary version of the epigraph's lesson, emphasizing generational communication. The "hatchet-head" lies dormant, awaiting a handle, until the poet's son Kai remembers it and wants to own a hatchet in imitation of his father. We could think of Kai as also being a hatchet-head, full of potential for useful labor but lacking the vehicle for translating that promise into practice. As Snyder shapes the hatchet handle, he is serving as a handle of knowledge that Kai can grab in order to use the hatchet properly when it comes his turn to labor.

Snyder makes this point through his own recollection of Pound and the saying that Pound derived from the ancient Chinese, that when making an axe the model is close at hand.[9] Snyder, in his youth, served as a hatchet-head in need of a handle and found his handle in the poet Ezra Pound, the essayist Lu Ji, and the college professor Shih-hsiang Chen, as the poem indicates. At the same time, Snyder is shaping Kai so that he will also become a handle, as indicated near the end of the poem.

Snyder does not call Pound or Chen either a hatchet-head or a handle but calls each an "axe," because in their lives they joined together the potential of the head and the knowledge of the handle in poetic and educational practice. Snyder in his fifties has also become an "axe," complete in both functions as a "model" and as an instrument in the service of the "craft of culture" (6), and he appears confident that Kai will become an "axe" as well. As Katsunori Yamazato succinctly explains it, "Snyder's commitment to the wild territory and the subsequent inhabitory life leads him to understand a cycle of culture—flowing from Pound, Chen, the poet himself, and to his son Kai—in which one is both 'shaped' and 'shaping,' a cycle preserving and transmitting 'craft of culture.' "[10] The end of the poem emphasizes a positive sense of the continuity of culture that includes internal change, rather than the cultural rupture emphasized in some of the *Turtle Island* poems. There a monolithic national culture needed to be criticized and challenged. Here, Snyder has moved beyond national culture to a larger sense of culture as the multigenerational force of positive human shaping that works simultaneously on entire societies and on one person at a time across nations and across centuries.

The next poem in "Loops," "For/From Lew" (7), continues the emphasis on serving as a teacher. The poem depicts a dream vision in which Snyder's dead friend Lew Welch speaks to him. The first two lines echo the song "Joe Hill," about a hero of the American Left. Snyder implies by this allusion that Welch should also be seen as a working-class kind of hero, one who serves in this poem as a "go-between" attempting to marry the worlds of the living and the dead. Welch instructs Snyder in his responsibilities as a poet in the 1980s: "teach the children about the cycles"; i.e., the cycles of all entities on the planet, which would necessarily include teaching them about death as well as life.

"River in the Valley" (8-9) embodies the practicing of this task in Snyder's role as a teacher to his sons.[11] The poem also shows the fine attention to specific details that recurs throughout *Axe Handles*. The first stanza establishes a set of relationships: through numerical difference, between the human "we" and the "thousands of swallows"; by means of an abandoned "overhead / roadway," between the humans who have created but cannot utilize it and the swallows who are able to adapt it to their own purposes; and through the solid-fluid dichotomy, between the river/creek of flowing water and the road/bridge of seemingly static concrete. The next section treats the behavior of the three humans in the presence of the nesting swallows. Gen imitates the flock's swirling flight, while Kai focuses on tracking a single bird. Their games mimic the two simultaneous forms of energy: wave and particle, as well as two different types of hunting. Meanwhile, the swallows' flight mimics the action of fish, as they flow in and out under the bridge. And as for Snyder? He is busy removing grass seeds that have stuck to his socks. As the swallows engage in a pattern replicated elsewhere in nature, so too the humans participate in such patterns, linking animal and human together. Even Snyder unwittingly finds himself participating in wild seed dispersal, since the plant has used his socks to give its seeds a free ride to another location. This action duplicates his function as father and provides him with the same role as numerous other animals, such as bears and birds, who contribute to the flourishing of plant life by moving seeds as part of their eating patterns.

As the three of them move on, from the abandoned causeway through the town of Colusa and out toward the mountains, "One boy asks, 'where do rivers start?' " (9). Snyder provides a factual answer that quickly becomes metaphysical in its implications. The cycles of planetary life are treated as "One" cycle, just as it is "One boy" who speaks rather than a named individual. Snyder moves out from the particular to the universal, and a qualitative change occurs at the point at which "threads" of water coalesce to form a river; and the river itself comprises a whole more than the volume of individual molecules, more than the sum of its parts. Like the river, the world does not consist of isolated locations, independent atoms, but is "all flowing at once."

The sophistication of this poem arises not just from the philosophical complexity of its conclusion but also from its form, which is structured to replicate the phases of that final stanza. The beginning of "River in the Valley" consists of details and questions, perception without understanding. The second section depicts a deepening of perception through identification of humanity and nature. The third enlarges the context of the poem in terms of both land and community. The fourth fills out the rest of the watershed and provides the people with the vision necessary to encompass the entire land of which they comprise an integral part. As Yamazato observes in regard to the poem's conclusion: "this is the kind of answer that comes from an inhabitory poet who has deeply meditated on 'the whole network,' or 'Gaia,' always focusing his attention on 'the Whole Self.' He rejects the prevalent dissecting mode of knowledge, and instead teaches the sons (and the readers) to see the interpenetrating whole all one place.' "[12]

Several other poems in "Loops" need to be discussed briefly before turning to the next section of *Axe Handles*. "Among" (10), for instance, seems at first to be a descriptive poem. It tells of "a Douglas fir" growing amidst a stand of "Ponderosa Pine." While "River in the Valley," can be read metaphysically, "Among" can be read as a political allegory, embodying the old Wobbly slogan about the new society forming within the shell of the old. That slogan, however, is based on the idea that the old society will eventually be overthrown and replaced by the new. In contrast, Snyder seems to be speaking not of *succession* in this poem but rather coexistence. The kind of inhabitory life-styles that Snyder embraces and practices can individually survive and flourish while being surrounded by the dominant society. If social succession, like arboreal succession, is to take place, it will be more evolutionary than revolutionary according to this allegory.

"Berry Territory" (12-13) results from Snyder's friendship with Wendell Berry, another ecologically focused writer. Unlike Snyder, Berry makes his home in Kentucky and writes out of a Southern Protestant agrarian background and ethics. Snyder, in effect, pays tribute to the differences between them and their territories and to the ways in which Berry has sought to integrate himself with his particular place, much like the tortoise of the first stanza. "Berry Territory" comments on the importance of continent-wide networks and sharing mutual concerns while retaining differences appropriate to one's own locale—a fundamental premise of bioregional politics.

"Painting the North San Juan School" (21-22) turns back to the kind of teaching called for in "For/From Lew," while at the same time having obvious connections with "Among." "Painting" focuses on community while maintaining attention on generational responsibility for handing down the culture. Even as Snyder describes the painting of the school house, he manages to engage in teaching the readers about the knowledge the Ridge community has and shares. This knowledge the adult members of the community intend to teach their children in the face of the opposing values found in mainstream American culture. This conflict of values is first expressed through the juxtaposition of the logging trucks that shake the school in the first stanza and the local practices of grafting, planting, and growing trees in the next one. Snyder then expresses the conflict through the contradictions between a bioregional sense of history that includes the original inhabitants of the area and one based exclusively on the practices of the ruling culture of only the past three centuries. The fragility of what the Ridge community is attempting to do is suggested by the poem's closing image: "Ladders resting on the shaky porch."

Clearly, many of these poems can be understood in terms of "loops," historical, generational, cultural, and regional. Woody Rehanek suggests that "Soy Sauce" (30-31) addresses another type: "man identifying with, representing, and finally becoming a totem animal. This experience transcends intellectual rapport and becomes a total affinity with the nonhuman. . . . A vital aspect of shamanism is this ability to become one with the animal."[13] While "Soy Sauce," then, focuses on the human-animal relationship, it also includes Snyder's looping back to Japan, invoking a strong memory of his life there even after his years away. "Delicate Criss-crossing Beetle Trails Left in the Sand" (32-33) is written from the experience of his family's visit there in 1981. Here the loop is completely literal rather than metaphoric in that the village where Masa takes her husband is a place he has visited once before. While his "trails" do indeed crisscross, the question remains as to their purpose. But as Yamazato suggests, means and ends, experiences and purposes, are equally interpenetrating and impermanent: "From a Buddhist-ecologist view, all that is endowed with life is engaged in impermanent activities, traveling, as it were, on a dusty road to the final dispersal into the permanent cycles of things in this universe."[14]

As with "Delicate Criss-crossing Beetle Trails," "Walking Through Myoshin-ji" (34) depicts another place to which Snyder returns in his 1981 visit: Kyoto. He reflects on the history of civilization in this ancient city, the trade and commerce that went into its construction, and the continuity of human presence in terms of both buildings and religious activities. But then, in the final stanza, he turns from these to "the pine trees" that underpin such human presence. And although he refers to them as "the Ancient Ones," he notes their anonymity, their use, and their impermanence. The poem ends with the word "ash," which literally refers to the burning of trees for fuel but also echoes the biblical phrase, "from ashes to ashes." When Snyder first came to Kyoto, twenty-five years prior to the writing of this poem, he was seeking tradition, continuity, and an alternative culture to the one of his homeland. Ironically, however, through immersion in the continuity represented by a place like Myoshin-ji, he has come to recognize that even the most ancient entities of the world, whether naturally engendered or humanly produced, are all transient. What takes this poem beyond merely an imagistic rendering of a fundamental tenet of Buddhism is its varied tone. "Walking Through Myoshin-ji" contains a mixture of pleasant remembering, awe-filled historical envisioning, and nostalgic sadness.

Two poems in this section return to an image first presented in *Turtle Island*: military jets screaming through the sky. "Fishing Catching Nothing off the Breakwater near the Airport, Naha Harbor, Okinawa" (35) is set on that island, which is part of Japan but home to several U.S. military bases. "Strategic Air Command" (37), as the signature line indicates, was written in the Sierra Nevada. In "Fishing Catching Nothing" Snyder seems to be comparing the activity of the jet practice flights with his unsuccessful fishing, which both criticizes militarism and places it in perspective. And "Strategic Air Command" concludes that the land is enduring while militarism is transitory. In both instances, the observers are implicitly presented as superior to what is being observed because they have the proper perspective from which to evaluate the other's place. At the same time, their positions are rendered as basically passive, waiting out this period of aberrant human history.

Another two poems in this section emphasize the philosophical importance of practical knowledge: "Working on the '58 Willys Pickup" (39-40) and "Getting in the Wood" (41-42). In "Working" Snyder reflects on the fact that when this truck was made he was studying Buddhism in Kyoto, learning seemingly esoteric rather than practical knowledge. But in the "now" of the poem's writing, he finds himself beneath the Willys repairing it and admiring its "solidness." He ends the long second stanza with a phrase that he has since come to regret, "Thinking a truck like this / would please Chairman Mao." Clearly, Mao is not so much the actual individual as the symbol for a revolutionary spirit that builds goods for their use-value rather than their exchange-value, and hence would build them to be long-lived, useful, and practical. The third stanza belies the initial stanza's separation of the esoteric and the practical by observing that Snyder has learned his auto mechanic skills from others who have also studied "the Classics." The fourth stanza then aligns the complementarity of the esoteric and the practical with cross-cultural intellectual fertilization. In the final two lines, the practicality of all knowledge and the value of the process of handing it down is reiterated. The poem's internal structure relies on a series of loops that move from contradiction to complement to unity. "Getting in the Wood" continues the same emphases as "Working" but with more concern about precision and accuracy in the handing-down process. Here Snyder introduces the complementarity and unity of life and death with the multigenerational group of men felling the "elderly oak," with the elders training the youth, and with labor in the dead of winter providing fuel for life-sustaining fire.

Schultz and Wyatt argue that "True Night" (44-45) is the strongest poem in *Axe Handles,* and several other critics concur. According to Schultz and Wyatt, it "beautifully captures the tension between the urge to be out and away and the need to settle and stay"; Yamazato believes that "this is one of the best poems in *Axe Handles,* depicting Snyder's directions and life's commitment to a place."[15] The poem begins with a narrative of simple events: Snyder, awakened from sleep, chases two raccoons out of his kitchen. But suddenly the poet, Antaeus-like with bare feet touching the gravel, is transformed into a figure epitomizing millennia of human-animal interaction, and the world pours into him: "I am alive to the night." The next stanza records his observations of that night, followed by his return to the house. Here the meditational part of the poem begins as he identifies himself with dandelions and sea anemones who have also opened themselves to the world. His sleeping family, however, draws him back from this totemic immersion as he ruefully concludes that a person cannot stay awake for too long in such darkness.

After this turning point, Snyder speaks of the sleep he needs to prepare for "the waking that comes" with each new dawn. The reader can understand this waking in several ways. One, in the light of day the poet's connections to the rest of humanity are more self-evident; two, there is the waking to responsibilities that Snyder must renew as a member of his community; three, there is the sense of personal obligation to the future, to the "dawn" of that better culture he is attempting to assist into being. To remain in the dark too long, to be carried away permanently into the wilderness of the land and of his own mind, would be to renege on the various promises he has made in his life and his poetry. One of those promises is to reverence Gaia, which Snyder has defined elsewhere as "the whole network."[16]

"Little Songs for Gaia"

The "Little Songs for Gaia" section works best when read as a single unit, and Snyder published it in 1979 as a Copper Canyon Press chapbook. This section is, as Schultz and Wyatt note, "made of glimpses—heightened moments of perception or feeling—

communicating an intimacy of contact with things which spices and sustains the life of the poet."[17] And Martin provides a cogent argument for its being placed in the middle of *Axe Handles*: "a net is made of loops, while it is mythically the work of the goddess to weave the disparate threads of the net or web together."[18] Snyder's concept of Gaia is partially based here on both the Gaia hypothesis that he discussed in *The Old Ways* and the Buddhist-Avatamsaka notion of Indra's jeweled net and the interpenetration and co-origination of all aspects of the universe. When Snyder invokes the term Gaia he also invokes a sense of spirituality and religious awe that philosophical and scientific terms lack. If all aspects of Gaia are alive and co-originating, then Gaia too must be living, and each experience of this entity provides access to its total mystery.

This sense of religious awe permeates the "Little Songs" section as instanced by the opening lines in which Snyder observes and meditates on the wonders of the particularities of San Francisco Bay, which is a "slow-paced / system" within other systems (49). Part of his awe is induced by the recognition that the area's time frame far exceeds the abilities of human consciousness to comprehend it. This difference in time frames and perception is reiterated throughout the section, perhaps most eloquently when Snyder compares the relationships of crickets to humans, with humans to trees, with trees "to the rocks and the hills" (51). This set of ratios is immediately followed by a poem about "Corn Maidens," a dream vision similar to "For/From Lew" that heightens the sense of spirituality, here in terms of a Native American shamanist symbol. At the end of "Little Songs," Snyder addresses Gaia directly as the owner of a house he has broken into seeking wisdom in "the library." He writes to apologize for the mess he made while there but in effect is offering an apology for all of humanity's despoliation and degradation of Earth's environment.

While Snyder wields Gaia imagery with sincerity, humility, and reverence, there remains the problem of sex-typing the planet through the use of such mythic symbols.[19] Martin highlights this difficulty: "As metaphor, Gaia represents a perspective that is clearly of a higher logical type than those which either welcome or bemoan an identification of the 'feminine' with 'nature,' and represent the goddess as the reverse image of the 'masculine,' 'patriarchal' god." Nevertheless, the dangers of sexism and the continued identification of woman and nature that has meant the degradation of both in Western cultures remains a problem. In terms of Snyder's use, Martin notes that "although I do find Gaia an effective metaphor; I think that the poetry shows very little self-criticism on this subject, and little sense of the problems inherent in making such connections."[20] Elsewhere Snyder has shown some sense of this problem, particularly in his championing of gender equality among American Buddhists and in his response to Paul's study of his poetry: "Remove the question of gender. . . . 'Patriarchal values' are values of hierarchy, domination, and centralization."[21]

"Nets"

If the first part of *Axe Handles* deploys twenty-five poems to establish a set of thematic loops, then the third part, according to Martin, uses another twenty-six poems to weave those loops into four nets of relationships. Rehanek concurs with this orientation, but takes it a step further in terms of analyzing the reason for the section's subdivisions: "The four parts of 'Nets' are roughly equivalent to four layers of healing songs defined in 'Poetry, Community & Climax,' the final chapter of *The Real Work*." He goes on to define these as: unity with nature; humanity with others outside one's own group; speaking as a voice for the unconscious; and treating a state of mind analogous to the "climax" condition of forests, which Snyder defined in *Turtle Island*.[22]

As with the "Little Songs" section, in "Nets I" there are several poems focused almost entirely on specific details that remind the poet of the spiritual presence of Gaia. In the first poem, "Walked Two Days in Snow, Then It Cleared for Five" (63-64), this evocation becomes apparent when Snyder shifts from the description of different animals sharing the land through which he is walking to direct address in the final line. "Geese Gone Beyond" (65-66) continues in this vein by treating the hunting of geese as an action deserving the respect of ritual behavior. Snyder indicates such behavior in the third stanza by explaining that he is kneeling in the bow of the canoe, and then he identifies his kneeling with that practiced in Japanese ceremonies.

The most sacred moment of "Nets I" comes with the poem "24:IV:40075, 3:30 PM, n. of Coaldale, Nevada, A Glimpse through a Break in the Storm of the Summit of the White Mountains" (71). The title establishes with absolute precision the moment, place, and cause for the composition of this prayer. The poem can be analyzed formally and appreciated for the mastery of its technique, but it is more appropriate to respect the religious sensibility with which Snyder has imbued it by means of a meditative reading rather than a formal explication.

If "Nets I" engages the sacred, then clearly "Nets II" engages the profane world of political and cultural ideologies. "The Grand Entry"

(77-78) takes a critical but whimsical look at the attachment of national allegiance to the rodeo. The next several poems treat Snyder's experience of serving on the California Arts Council. "What Have I Learned" (85) returns Snyder to the basic point introduced at the beginning of the volume as he concludes that when a person gets something right "you pass it on."

"Nets III" finds Snyder writing about the place where he lives, San Juan Ridge, and about Alaska and the Australian outback, both of which he has visited in order to learn from the native peoples and more recent inhabitants. The two poems on Alaska are sandwiched between two poems from the Ridge that focus on tools. The first, "A Maul for Bill and Cindy's Wedding" (89), speaks of the proper handling of the tool, letting oneself go with the flow and momentum of the maul, and the way in which, if handled properly, it will cleanly split wood. Marriage may also be seen as a tool because its function when properly wielded is to join together what is separate and distinct. The second, "Removing the Plate of the Pump on the Hydraulic System of the Backhoe" (93), shows Snyder appreciating a high-technology machine. Here he consciously writes against the naive view that some of his readers have that to learn to live the "old ways" means to forsake all technology. Instead, Snyder repeatedly emphasizes the idea of appropriate technology. He remarks in his letter to David Foreman: "As the ecologist Sterling Bunnell says, bulldozers are funny latter-day elephants, which if used in right time and place would do for the plant communities what elephants used to do around the globe—namely step climax succession back a few phases to increase biomass, by opening the canopy."[23]

"Alaska" (90) and "Dillingham, Alaska, the Willow Tree Bar" (91-92), then, are placed within the context of work on the Ridge. In the first poem, Snyder joins others in looking at the Alaskan pipeline and a graffito that has been spray painted on it: "Where will it all end?" Snyder knows that he shares the concern of the anonymous author, but also that he is complicitous to some extent with that which he opposes. The next stanza begins with "drive back," and the following stanza begins "And then fly on." For Snyder to participate in efforts to determine appropriate human inhabitation of Alaska, he must utilize one of the products that constantly threatens Alaska's ecosystem: oil. The final line suggests that he has not resolved this dilemma but continues working through it. The second poem addresses complicity again, but in a more overtly critical fashion. Snyder is among the oil workers in a bar, and he notes the ways in which these men are subjected to the totalizing sameness of identically designed franchise operations found around the world. At poem's end, Snyder makes clear that he is condemning the economic system, not the men themselves.

Snyder ends "Nets III" with the longest poem in the volume, "Uluru Wild Fig Song" (95-98), which upholds the integrity of the "old ways" of inhabiting the world as practiced by the natives of Australia. Through the ancient yet continuing practices he portrays, Snyder is able to return from the profane world of politics and capitalist economics to the sacred world of interpenetration of human and nature. And through the rituals outlined in shadowy detail and the central image of the wild fig, Snyder encourages readers to recognize that this interpenetration has to occur on both the conscious and unconscious levels, the cultivated and the wild parts of both nature and mind.

"Nets IV" includes a mixture of poems, playful and serious, that circle around the themes raised earlier in the volume. In "Money Goes Upstream" (101-102), Snyder reaffirms his conviction that the current state of culture is a short-lived aberration, while the power into which he has tapped will endure. The experiences recorded in "Uluru Wild Fig Song" enable him to maintain his optimism and his grounding even when he is trapped in boring meetings held in sterile buildings. As Schultz and Wyatt see it, "against this insidious influence Snyder poses his own ability to summon the corrective presence of nature. . . . This power is two-fold: Snyder's firsthand knowledge of nature . . . and his ability to summon what is not present keeps him ever close to the natural law from which he borrows his authority."[24]

"Breasts" (103-14) treats the miraculous way that mammary glands can filter out toxins accumulating within a female body so that the mother's milk is safe for the infant to drink. Playfully, Snyder compares "breasts" with philosophers who temporarily shield the young from the poisons of the world. He then goes on to claim that "For the real self to be" adults must work "to then burn the poison away." While ending on a joyous note celebrating survival into old age, the poem has a deadly serious undertone as readers reflect on various amounts of information available to them. For instance, among populations exposed to certain kinds of environmental pollution mother's milk is actually unsafe to drink; and breast cancer is one of the leading killers of women in the world today.

In a poem that seems to prefigure the title of his selected poems, *No Nature*, Snyder reminds readers that nature has a violent side to it that is part of the natural process. "Old Woman Nature" (108-109) is a poem written in response to Snyder's watching a Kabuki performance in Tokyo, the title of which he translates as "Demoness." Nature is both "sweet" and deadly, since "Old Woman Nature / naturally has a bag of bones" hidden away. This poem hearkens back to the influence of Robert Graves's *The White Goddess* on Snyder in college and its concept of the "triple goddess," one of whose manifestations is the crone or old hag. Snyder uses this image to upset the benign impression of the earth as Gaia, the nurturing mother, that he has invoked in earlier poems. "Old Woman Nature," then, deconstructs the romantic or pastoral impression that readers may have been developing while reading "Little Songs for Gaia." It also inverts the gender imagery of the Gaia trope as well in that, although the image of nature here is initially depicted as a woman, the location line reveals that characterization as illusory. *"Seeing Ichikawa Ennosuke in 'Kurozuka'—'Demoness'—at the Kabuki-za in Tokyo"* (109) informs the reader that the actor playing "Old Woman Nature" is really a male impersonator, since Kabuki uses an all-male cast.

While "Old Woman Nature" addresses violence and death in nature rather playfully, other poems in this section do so with greater seriousness. In the case of "The Canyon Wren" (111), Snyder records a last experience of a part of nature that has literally been submerged by human engineering—in this case, the construction of a reservoir. The song of the wren will remain, Snyder contends, "To purify our ears." It will inspire him to continue to build a different culture here on Turtle Island, one that will not drown the wren for the sake of another reservoir. Here the singing of the bird can be compared to the writing of poetry, in the sense that an artistic activity perpetuates the memory of, and appreciation for, events and places no longer present to the listener/reader. Snyder has chosen to include "The Canyon Wren" as part of *Mountains and Rivers Without End*, and in the context of its reprinting there, Leonard Scigaj observes in it the relationship of labor to enlightenment. Placing the poem in the context of Dōgen's "Mountains and Waters Sutra"—one of the key Buddhist texts undergirding the sequence—Scigaj comments that "Reading Dōgen in the late seventies reconfirmed for Snyder the emphasis on labor and practice as a vehicle for purification and enlightenment realization. Phrases in . . . 'The Canyon Wren' . . . suggest that Snyder may have experienced the . . . state of highest enlightenment . . . when he integrated the canyon wren's downward song into his consciousness as he shot down California's Stanislaus River rapids in 1981. Naturally he quoted Dōgen on dragon vision."[25]

Readers will respond extremely differently to Snyder's last poem in *Axe Handles*, depending on their overall attitude toward the way of life and the beliefs that he has espoused in the previous poems. The first half of "For All" (113-14) relishes the beauty of the everyday details of "fording a stream" and listening to its music and the parallel music inside the speaker's body. The second half is a parody of the United States national anthem. Snyder pledges allegiance not to the United States but to Turtle Island, not to a government but to an ecosystem. And in the final line, "With joyful interpenetration for all," he clarifies the title. Unlike national anthems, which focus on governments and peoples, Snyder's poem focuses on an ecosystem and all its inhabitants, including people, animals, plants, and spirits.

Certainly, as Molesworth claims, *Axe Handles* continues and extends the concerns of *Turtle Island* and confronts the same problems and evils, but it is quite a different book and frequently exhibits a different kind of poetry. Those readers who were looking for the militancy of *Turtle Island* were no doubt disappointed. Those looking for formal innovation may or may not have appreciated the sophistication of much of Snyder's apparent simplicity. Andrew Schelling, in comparing various critics' castigation of *Axe Handles* for its popularity (it sold 30,000 copies in six months, a phenomenal figure for a book of poems), draws this conclusion: "As he defers to an audience more interested in botany and politics than literature, Snyder has introduced numerous explanatory digressions—a practice poetically suspect to those who have cut their teeth on Modernist texts, but indisputably useful for the retention and transmission of certain sorts of information."[26]

Left Out in the Rain

In 1986 Snyder published another poetry volume with North Point Press, one unlike any other he had produced before. *Left Out in the Rain: New Poems 1947-1985* brings together poems that Snyder had written over his entire poetic career but had never previously included in a book or chapbook. The reasons for their exclusion are many, including concerns over quality and seriousness. While *Left Out in the Rain* contains some excellent and interesting poems, it is unlikely that this volume will gain as much attention as any of the others he has published to date. Rather, it will be read primarily by those already familiar with Snyder's work who want to fill in gaps, read comprehensively, learn more about Snyder's biography, or study the development of his poetics. Perhaps this situation has something to do with his decision to include sixteen of the poems in *The Gary Snyder Reader*, since there they are more likely to receive critical attention in terms of their literary merits more so than in terms of their biographical usefulness.

If one has already read Snyder's other volumes, echoes of those poems reverberate throughout *Left Out in the Rain*. But it is important to remember that the poems of this recent collection often were written first. Many of them are examples of poetic experiments more successfully realized elsewhere. As Jack Hicks claims, based on conversations with Snyder, the poet's "intent was to bring the poems into print faithful to the original texts, with little revision."[27] The first two poems were written when Snyder was seventeen and the most recent when he was fifty-three. The volume contains, then, 154 poems written over a forty-year time span.

The first two poems, "Elk Trails" and " 'Out of the Soil and Rock,' " which comprise the "Introduction" to the volume, are informative in terms of the clarity of Snyder's position on nature versus the city at an early age.[28] In "Elk Trails" he defines "Instinct" as the "ancient, coarse-haired, / Thin-flanked God" of these trails, which is to say a consciousness that is not rational or logical but is also not ignorant. He also displays a recognition that understanding and following the trails is not the same as finding or becoming the Elk. While "Elk Trails" is set in a mountain wilderness, " 'Out of the Soil and Rock' " is set in the city. The youthful, western, wilderness-oriented Snyder optimistically dismisses the apparent solidity of New York City as an illusion of permanence when contrasted with the web of natural generation that he outlines.

Part Two consists of nineteen poems written while Snyder was attending Reed College. Most of these appear to be exercises in preparation for writing *Myths & Texts*, particularly the poems that treat shamanism, such as "Message from Outside" (15) and "Birth of the Shaman" (19). Ten of these belong to a sequence titled "Atthis" about a love affair, showing Snyder's desire to work in sequential and extended poetic forms. Most are relatively weak.

Part Three comprises another seventeen poems from the years between college and Japan. Some of these would have been written at the same time as the early *Riprap* poems. Obvious here is the influence of other poets from whom Snyder was learning his craft, such as Walt Whitman, Ezra Pound, and Robinson Jeffers. Also, the cultural influences of Native American tribes, Japanese literature, and Hindu myths begin to appear. "Poem Left in Sourdough Mountain Lookout" (42) is a nine-line poem ending in a couplet. Not very interesting aesthetically, it does, however, reflect Snyder's efforts at combining Buddhism, geology, and wild nature in his claim that "every Lookout sees" the mountains moving and subsiding in a process that takes millions of years, as well as weather patterns and wild animals, such as the deer and the eagle. "Geological Meditation" (43-44) is a somber poem reflecting the influence of Robinson Jeffers aesthetically and philosophically. "Fording the Flooded Golden River" (45), the next poem, in turn, shows the influence of John Muir. The most interesting poem in this section from a biographical perspective is "Makings" (56), written in Marin at the same time as the middle poems in *Riprap*. Snyder reflects on his Depression-era childhood and then observes that he has chosen in the prosperous 1950s to maintain a life of poverty because it provides a certain freedom.

Part Four contains fourteen poems from the first years in Japan and the time he spent working on the *Sappa Creek*. "Longitude 170° West, Latitude 35° North" (59-60), is dedicated to Ruth Sasaki, without whom Snyder might not have made it to Japan when he did. Written aboard ship, it depicts Snyder reflecting on his choice to travel to Japan to study Buddhism. Snyder had been at sea before and so his awe at the immensity of the ocean is more metaphorical than literal, as indicated by the closing lines where he writes of "oceans of truth and seas of doctrine." Interestingly enough, Snyder follows this poem with one emphasizing the time just before he left California. In "For Example" (61), he humorously raises doubts about his need to go to Japan, observing at poem's end that one can practice Buddhism anywhere in the world. The placement and theme of this poem suggest that Snyder knew very well that his reasons for going to Japan were far more complicated than a desire to study Buddhism there.

"Bomb Test" (63), written in Kyoto, reveals his continuing concern with nuclear proliferation, while "Dullness in February: Japan" (64-65) expresses his skepticism about the sincerity of Japanese Buddhists. Yamazato points out that this is the first poem that Snyder has published in which he explicitly registers that skepticism.[29] More significant, though, is his clear intent at poem's end to hold on to his own commitment to Zen and to practice it as a wandering monk in the United States. "Feathered Robes" (68-69) is also an interesting poem in that it links the myth on which the "*Nō play 'Hagoromo'* " is based—which Snyder probably saw in Kyoto or Tokyo—with the Swan Maiden myth that was the subject of his undergraduate thesis.

Part Five covers the ten-year period from his second return to Japan until he, Masa, and Kai came to settle in California. "One Year" (85-87) has been mined by Snyder with some of its lines ending up in other poems. The next two poems, "Housecleaning in Kyoto" and "Seeing the Ox" (88, 89) emphasize in the former the serendipitous character of experience and in the latter the intrusion of the mundane into the esoteric. In "Seeing the Ox" Snyder focuses on a "Brown ox" that defecates "right by Daitoku temple," where Snyder is studying Buddhist scriptures and practicing meditation. There are various interpretations possible, including the implicit parallelism between Buddhist doctrine and the "dung pile" described in the second stanza of the poem; there is also the koan-like character of the "seeing" here, in which the ability to see the world before his eyes in which ox dung and temples are equally real and of equal importance is a step toward spiritual enlightenment.

"Three Poems for Joanne" (91-93) are the most interesting in this section, along with "Crash" (97-98). The first of "Three Poems" is titled "Loving Words" and seems to record an early moment in Kyger and Snyder's relationship, emphasizing their mutual commitment to poetry and a strong sense of optimism. The second, "The Heart of the Wood," records Snyder's belief in the intensity and depth of their love. The third, "Joanne My Wife," abruptly depicts the decay of their relationship. In "Joanne My Wife," the depiction is realistic rather than idealized; and it comes as no surprise that the optimism is gone. In "Crash," Snyder recounts having an accident in which he collided on his motorcycle with a Japanese man on a bicycle. The strength of this poem comes from the way Snyder focuses on the relationship between mind and body, consciousness and behavior. The fifth line reveals that he is "distracted or intense"; by the twenty-second line he wonders "Where was my mind"; and, by the thirtieth line, in meditation at the temple, he recognizes the potentially disastrous consequences of "my inattention." The poem shifts from a description of events to a meditation on the importance of "attention" to one's own actions in the world.

In "English Lessons at the Boiler Company" (105), Snyder relates one of the experiences he had teaching English in Japan after he quit his position at the First Zen Institute of American in Kyoto. Snyder emphasizes the conditions in which the teaching occurs, but the key line comes at the close: "Over the plains,   snow-whirling clouds." The value of such teaching seems uncertain to Snyder and the image at the end suggests that the language acquisition of these Boiler Company employees will create a storm of confusion rather than clarity. Snyder, however, was quite wrong in his doubt about the benefits of such education, as he admits in his interview with John Rossiter and Paul Evans: "I was teaching English to Matsushita engineers and administrative people through the sixties and I had a certain amount of disbelief as to what effect that was going to have in the world. Now I can see that their grand strategy was real and that my contribution to the success of Japan in the world is back there somewhere in the sixties!"[30]

One poem near the end of this section that Snyder has chosen to include in *The Gary Snyder Reader* is "Farewell to Burning Island" (111). This poem is quite graceful in its sparse language and the successful merging of the image of the "white bird," which will likely ride the ship as part of its own routine migration across the ocean, with the implied image of the poet traveling the Pacific once again between Japan and the United States.

Part Six, "Shasta Nation," comprises thirty-three poems written during the same years that he was putting together *Regarding Wave*, *Turtle Island*, and *Axe Handles*, and two years beyond that. This section reads very much as a miscellany in which the tone and topics of the poems move about frequently with little connection between one poem and the next, although at various points clusters of related poems do work together. It opens with "First Landfall on Turtle Island" (115), which records the family's approach to California on his return from Japan. Its exclusion from *Turtle Island* probably resulted from the poem's sentimental tone. A rather sarcastic, humorous poem early in this section is "No Shoes No Shirt No Service" (125), which meditates on the common restaurant door warning Snyder found upon his return to the States. He thinks of all of the kinds of people who have lived and flourished in history who had no need of shoes and wore only what was appropriate to where they lived and how they would be denied the opportunity to eat. In a closing that echoes the end of "Logging" in *Myths & Texts*, Snyder observes that another round of volcanoes will renew the soil of the American Pacific Rim, describing such kalpa-cycle violence as "Shiva's dancing feet / (No shoes)." Another kind of humor is represented by "'The Trail Is Not a Trail'" (127), which plays with the philosophy of the *Dao De Jing* and prefigures the more successful poem in *No Nature*, "Off the Trail." Although Snyder almost never writes poems about writing poems as some poets do, "Poetry Is the Eagle of Experience" (128) describes various forms of work and activities as animals, and the process of clarifying the mind as a matter of constantly clearing a trail that repeatedly becomes overgrown. Yet in the midst of all of these necessary distractions a poem suddenly materializes before his eyes as a gift from nature. Such gifts are not owned by an individual but circulate like any other aspect of nature, as suggested by "Calcium" (129), a poem that emphasizes the diversity of the flow of minerals through the world. Like water, calcium is not consumed in the sense of being used up but is moved from one place to another, serving in one instance to nourish a pregnant doe and in another to contribute to the hardness of cement. "Poetry Is the Eagle" and "Calcium" emphasize systems rather than things and Snyder carries over this systemic emphasis in "High Quality Information" (130), where he gives it a Buddhist twist. In this poem, Snyder emphasizes the establishment of pathways for processing information, for enabling people to move forward in time and space, not armed with data but armed with neural pathways that enable a systemic integration of new data with the old. That such activity becomes automatic rather than willed is suggested by the penultimate poem of the section, "At White River Roadhouse in the Yukon" (148). Snyder finds that the bell a person wanting to buy gas uses to wake the roadhouse master reminds him of the temple bell in Japan. And once more experiences elide as Snyder establishes a parallel between "sūtras" and gasoline, both fuel for people to continue on their way.

"The Persimmons" (149-51), which was written while on a visit to China in 1983, is perhaps the most fascinating of the poems in this section since it exposes the superficiality of the exotic that too often distracts people from the profundity of the ordinary. The occasion of the poem is an excursion to the Great Wall and the Ming tombs, but along the way Snyder notices the bountiful harvest of persimmons, a fruit which predates any of the Chinese empires. As a result, the persimmon becomes a far more significant symbol than the ones he has been brought to see. While the tombs tell of kings who, even after death, consumed the fruits of the peasants' labor, the persimmons tell of a far greater historical continuity: "the people and trees that prevail." Of this poem, Scott McLean comments that "Gary finds in the circumstances of the market our essential nature. It is not defined by the heroic gestures enshrined in great walls or by the trip to the tomb; it is closest to us in the life of the people and the trees that we oftentimes pass by, bound for the wonders of civilization."[31]

"Tiny Energies," a series of short, mostly haiku-style poems, comprises the seventh section of *Left Out in the Rain*. Like most haiku, these poems gain little from stylistic or thematic explication. For instance, "For Berkeley" (158), which poses a question about the city's fruits and roots, could be read as eliciting a positive response from its residents regarding their knowledge of self and place; it could also be read as a challenge to the home of California's major research university and one of the centers of the hippie movement to prove that its intellectuals have accomplished something constructive with their talent. In contrast, the tongue-in-cheek poem " 'There are those who love to get dirty' " (176) leaves no doubt as to its intended meaning, which claims the superiority of tea drinkers as people who combine the abilities of both mind and body and are, therefore, nondualist. The final poem in "Tiny Energies," "How Zen Masters Are Like Mature Herring" (178), is quite straightforward in its remarks about Zen masters, but highly ambiguous in its final line, "These big ones feed sharks." The ambiguity is resolved, however, when one learns that Snyder has compared himself as a poet with a shark cruising at the top of a food chain in an interview conducted in Hawaii.[32] In commenting on the epigraph to this section, Scigaj notes that "in the 'Tiny Energies' section of *Left Out in the Rain*, Snyder found further confirmation of this non-dualistic interpenetration of mind and labor in the ecologist H. T. Odum's observation that tiny amounts of energy are amplified along the food chain when transferred in the right form."[33] In like manner, the messages of these tiny poems can be amplified through their reception and dissemination by readers, since, as Snyder notes, "[Odum] says that in concert such low-energy-demand, high-effect, small systems are like poems, or he says, like religion, which control values."[34]

In the last section, "Satires, Inventions, & Diversions," two items stand out. The first is "Sestina of the End of the Kalpa" (187-88), which exemplifies the outrageously inappropriate fusion of a highly formalized European poetic structure and an Eastern theme of the world's destruction and thereby succeeds in treating apocalypse carnivalistically. The second ends the volume. Snyder closes *Left Out in the Rain* with a humorous tale titled "Coyote Man, Mr. President, & the Gunfighters" (206-209), which is one of Snyder's first formal contributions to the art of American storytelling. This tale is based on a third-century B.C. Chinese story by the Daoist Chuang-tzu, but the characters are drawn from Native American and cowboy traditions and applied to contemporary national politics. Snyder calls for an end to militarism and centralized governments. In concluding his 1987 study of Snyder, Yamazato makes a general statement that seems pertinent to ending an overview of *Left Out in the Rain*: "The problem of civilization remains the central issue in the poet's thinking, and his future poetic efforts will continue to address this problem."[35]

8

Of Wildness and Wilderness in Plain Language
The Practice of the Wild

Since the publication of *Axe Handles,* Snyder has continued to address the central problem of civilization but in a more diversified way. He has written poetry, given poetry readings, written prose, and begun teaching as a permanent member of a university faculty. *The Practice of the Wild*, brought out by North Point Press in 1990, is a work qualitatively superior and more significant than any other prose volume Snyder had published up to that time. It is a sophisticated yet clear, complex yet uncomplicated, unified book about knowing how to be in this world. That kind of being requires both materially experienced and mythically figured knowledge—a concept first introduced in his undergraduate thesis and demonstrated in his first poetic sequence. *Practice* is structured along the same lines as that of *Myths & Texts*, which is to say that "Snyder's writing is rhetorically structured by the alternation of attention on 'texts,' or perceived reality, and 'myths,' or the symbolic and storied dimensions of existence."[1] In one of the early reviews of *Practice*, Ray Olson claims that Snyder's essays "constitute the finest wisdom (and also ecological) literature of our time."[2]

Until the publication of *Practice*, *Earth House Hold* had been his only prose volume treated critically in its own right and the prose most often quoted, with perhaps the exception of the essay "Four Changes" at the end of *Turtle Island*. Yet *Earth House Hold* is not a unified work but a selection of discrete pieces that work together because of the life and mind behind them; a full appreciation of that collection is to some extent dependent on the reader's knowledge of Snyder's poetry. *The Practice of the Wild* functions on a different level of organization, being thematically unified by a discussion of the interrelationships of the meanings of freedom and responsibility, wilderness and wildness, humanity and nature, mind and body, conscious and unconscious, and knowledge and action.

It seems very much the case that Snyder did not view himself as a writer of prose to any significant extent until he began turning his various talks of the late-1970s through the mid-1980s into the chapters of *Practice*, even though he had been publishing a variety of prose pieces throughout much of his career. For example, the year after the publication of *Earth House Hold* the associate editor of *Sallyport*, the Reed College student arts magazine, asked him if he had any superstitions and Snyder answered, "Yes, I don't write prose." In response to the follow-up question, "None at all?" he answered, "Not unless I feel it is absolutely indicated that I should do so."[3] This rather circuitous answer suggests that Snyder viewed prose writing as a task imposed from the outside, not so much an inspiration from the muse as a chore from society. And it is the case that many of his prose pieces were indeed written by request rather than by his own initiative, or else gleaned from his copious journals. In fact, between the publication of *The Old Ways* in 1977 and *Practice*, Snyder started two different prose projects, one on the Ainu of Japan and one on ancient China, neither of which he finished.[4] But in a 1992 interview, Snyder explained that

> I discovered about three or four years ago that I could write prose. Not that I hadn't written prose before, but I somehow had not allowed myself to take it seriously as an exciting creative venture. I stumbled onto that in the course of writing *The Practice of the Wild*. So I did have to laugh at myself on several levels. One was that I realized willy-nilly that I myself had unconsciously thought real writers or serious writers are prose writers. . . . And it has to do, I think, with the willed character of prose writing. . . . There's a deliberateness about prose. . . . There is definitely a quality of poetry that requires you let it be given to you, at least my feeling about poetry is that way. . . . And the pleasure for me was coming to the point in my life where I realized I could write prose by being that deliberate and at the same time I wouldn't necessarily lose my access to poetry, that I could do both.[5]

The Practice of the Wild has been narrowly defined as "nature writing," compared time and again with Thoreau's *Walden*, and discussed in terms of primitivism and nostalgia. But the Anglo-American tradition of nature writing has tended to be based on a sense of the author's alienation and distance from the natural world and a male desire to be reunited with something felt to be missing or lost. Thoreau had to leave Concord and go to the woods to try his two-year experiment of simple living by Walden Pond and in so doing embodied the romantic notions of human alienation from nature and nostalgic yearning to return to some Edenic ideal.

Snyder is concerned instead with people conducting practice in place. As he remarked in an interview with David Robertson conducted while Snyder was completing *The Practice of the Wild*, "I hope that the book I am now writing will be stimulating to a broad range of people and provide them with historical, ecological, and personal visions all at the same time. I would like to see the book be political in the sense of helping people shape the way they want to live and act in the world."[6]

The Practice of the Wild leaps beyond the traditional limitations of the genre of nature writing. It is environmental writing in its fullest sense and treats in detail ideas that Snyder could only present in outline in his poems.[7] As Sharon Ann Jaeger notes, "Gary Snyder's eco-essays in *The Practice of the Wild* are a superb example of re-inhabiting language. They exemplify his poetics of embodiment, an experientialist poetics, and enact the multiple modes of his cognitive rhetoric."[8] While the volume is optimistic, it is not idealistic in the sense of being utopian or naive. Robertson's comment to Snyder is pertinent here: "One of the things I like so much about your prose writing is your ability to lay out a vision of life as it ought to be, at the same time recognizing very hard-headedly that actual life is rooted in ambiguity and frustration over uncompleted goals."[9] Robertson may in part be responding to Snyder's recognition reiterated since the early-1970s, first to Ekbert Faas and then to numerous other interviewers including Robertson, that "we are entering into a really critical age. Things are bad and they are going to get worse."[10] But, as Snyder maintains throughout *The Practice of the Wild*, he also knows that they can get better.

"The Etiquette of Freedom"

The first section of *The Practice of the Wild*, "The Etiquette of Freedom," begins with the notion of a "compact" as one of the forms of proper relationships among all entities who inhabit this earth. Snyder realistically recognizes that these arrangements include predatory as well as symbiotic, mutually beneficial ones. In what humans consider the wild reaches of the world, nonhuman creatures work out their lives in relationships that are conditioned first and foremost by the various food chains of their bioregions. To date, as Snyder points out, contemporary humans are the worst example of creatures disrupting their own and other creatures' food chains. To counter this process

Snyder emphasizes the need to educate people so that they will work to cease "causing unnecessary harm" to other beings as well as to themselves.[11]

From the notion of "compact," Snyder moves to an investigation of the popular American dream of "wild and free" and describes that dream in terms of a freedom that is achieved only when people recognize the real conditions of existence in which they participate. A crucial component of those conditions is "impermanence," which Americans in particular seem to fear, given their attitudes toward aging and dying. Snyder considers the need to recognize this fundamental condition of existence so important that he made it the starting point of his editorial statement for the 1978 *CoEvolution Quarterly*, where he wrote: "Everything is impermanent anyhow, why bother to protect?" And he gave as part of his own answer to the question, "The present is an emergency case. . . . The stakes are all organic evolution. Any childish thoughts of transcending nature or slipping off into Space must wait on this work—really, of learning finally who and where we are, acknowledging the beauty, walking in beauty."[12] Snyder's perception and conception of "impermanence" are based explicitly on Buddhist doctrine. And, as Jaeger notes, Buddhism functions in *Practice*, as well as elsewhere, "as both an epistemological and an ethical matrix for experiencing self and world."[13] The recognition of impermanence has to be understood, then, in the context of "The Four Vows," which Snyder helped translate as part of *The Wooden Fish: Basic Sūtras & Gāthās of Rinzai Zen* in 1961, the first of which is "sentient beings are numberless; I take a vow to save them."[14] To realize freedom, Snyder argues, people are going to have to begin to build a civilization that can come to terms with and sustain "wildness," which is one of the forms that impermanence takes in the material world. Suspecting that his readers do not have a very good sense of such terms as "Nature, Wild, and Wilderness" (8), Snyder elaborates the derivations and definitional developments of these three words.

What people have for centuries termed the "wild" is that which has an ecosystem sufficiently flexible that humans who have not previously participated in it may enter it and survive. In contrast, contemporary cities are so inflexible and closed that wild vegetation and animals haven't much of a chance for long-term survival. It is important to remember, however, that human beings at various historical moments developed within and as functioning parts of wild ecosystems.

Snyder then relates language to body, swerving around the popular Western tendency to separate mind and body or to perceive them as in contradiction with one another. He points out that "language is a mind-body system that coevolved with our needs and nerves" (17); i.e., it is psychic and physical, since the psyche is part of the body. And poetry enters the picture as one of the ways in which language can serve the reeducation of human beings to their own wild origins to facilitate reinhabitation. As a communal aesthetic activity, poetry—whether in the oral performance or on the printed page—participates in the process of life investigating itself, which is to say nature investigating itself and, as Jaeger notes, "re-inhabitation is a living *together*, not a hermit's existence but a communal interchange."[15]

"The Place, the Region, and the Commons"

Having developed the idea of wild ecosystems and the wildness that must be reasserted along with recovering wilderness, Snyder turns his attention to conceptions of place. He emphasizes here the ways in which peoples relate to the land by means of an understanding of locale, region, and community. He begins with a position shared by Wendell Berry and numerous Native Americans: non-native Americans are a set of rootless, un-placed and dis-placed peoples, and this condition is fundamentally unhealthy; it produces dis-ease. Snyder starts with a concept of home as hearth and moves to an understanding of region based on local specifics and on one's apprehension of that region as a living, interactive place, not a national or governmental abstraction composed of dotted lines on a distorted map (one can't help but think here of those dotted lines dividing the Great Lakes into Canadian water and American water).

The "commons" is a European practice of setting aside land for communal activities, and Snyder applies this idea to the sharing of "natural areas." Various forms of commons can be found around the world, including in Japanese farming villages. In the United States, commons were a rare feature of the East but did turn up in the West, due to climate and topography, and have been developed perhaps most fully in relationship to equitable access to water within the borders of the United States, but not equitable between the U.S. and Mexico. Snyder believes that it is absolutely necessary to return to a system of commons and that this system needs to be used worldwide and should be extended to include such aspects of the biosphere as the air and the oceans. A current threat to such biospheric commons is the political concept and economic practice of trading so-called credits for airspace to build buildings taller than zoning ordinances allow or credits for carbon emissions to allow a heavier polluter to *borrow* pollution allowances from a lighter polluter across industries or across national boundaries. On the land, Snyder thinks that the greatest hope for recovering the commons lies in instituting localized bioregional governments and community practices. Fundamentally, "bioregionalism is the entry of place into the dialectic of history. Also we might say that there are 'classes' which have so far been overlooked—the animals, rivers, rocks, and grasses—now entering history" (41). Such a designation of "classes" is clearly not based on a humanist or Marxist conception of that term, but rather on a Buddhist conception of all things as being whorls in the grain of energy flows, each just as substantial and nonessential as the next. Snyder renders these claims concrete by relating the way he and others who inhabit San Juan Ridge are learning their place and their role in that locale.

"Tawny Grammar"

In this section of *The Practice of the Wild* Snyder turns his attention to manifestations of bioregional practice in terms of the cultural specifics of peoples and what the healthier cultures have in common. He draws on his experiences in Asia as well as North America to develop his points. In Alaska, Snyder finds significant parallels between the means by which the Inupiaq are attempting to raise their children and the practices of the San Juan Ridge school back home. One of the issues that Snyder discusses here is the relationship between oral transmissions and written transmissions of cultures. In a literate society, he notes, "books are our grandparents" (61), because in oral cultures it is the elders who transmit the cultural lore and values by means of stories.

Such considerations lead Snyder into meditations on nature writing, nature as a book, and an ecology of language. Snyder claims that grammars, like metaphors, are ways of interpreting reality, and that "tawny grammars" come from nature itself in its myriad manifestations. Snyder's point is not so much to argue for the organic and evolutionary character of language as to deflate the anthropocentric egotism of those who like to imagine "language as a uniquely human gift" (77). His logical maneuver here also contradicts those who argue that all of nature is a social construct since it is described and understood in human minds through the mediation of language. Snyder flips this orientation of privileging language over material phenomena by defining language itself as a material phenomenon arising from the world in which humans participate rather than arising from the human mind as a metaphysical construct.

After all, the mind exists as part of the brain and nervous system, with thoughts—including linguistic thoughts—forming by means of electrochemical cellular activity. Without the right balance of minerals within the brain necessary for synaptic activity, no individual can form words.

"Good, Wild, Sacred"

Tom Clark, writing about *The Practice of the Wild* as a whole, claims that "the essays are deployed poetically, less like steps in an argument than as spokes radiating around a single, urgent, central theme: the need for re-establishing those traditional practices of wilderness that once linked humanity in a single, harmonic chord with the animals, plants, lands and water."[16] "Good, Wild, Sacred" can he seen as being structured in the same way. Snyder begins with this triad of key concepts, centered on "wild," and works through a series of reflections on historical and present-day experience. He speaks of the contradiction within an "agrarian theology" that holds that humans render themselves more holy by "weeding out" the wild from their own nature, at the same time that their having done the same to cattle and pigs has altered those animals from "intelligent and alert in the wild into sluggish meat-making machines" (79). In the process of attempting to elevate themselves, humans have degraded nature and reduced natural intelligence. Snyder necessarily rejects any theology based on a separation of the physical and the spiritual and speaks approvingly here of Native American beliefs that connect land and spirit.

From the spiritual practices of North America's inhabitory peoples, Snyder then turns to what he has learned about spirit and place from the aboriginal people of Australia. In particular, he focuses on the ways in which their stories about themselves as people are intimately tied to the land in which they live. In that land different types of sacred places exist, some of which Snyder was privileged to visit. He was told that some of those places were defined as "teaching spots" and some as "dreaming spots." This experience prompts him to meditate on "dreamtime," which he believes "is the mode of the eternal moment of creating, of being, as contrasted with the mode of cause and effect in time" (84). Differentiating between the linear time frame that dominates Western thought and the dream time of aboriginal peoples leads Snyder to think of Buddhism, particularly the Avatamsaka Sutra, and the practices of Japan's aboriginal people, the Ainu. Snyder reflects sadly on the fact that in present-day Japan so little of the Ainu and Shinto practices in relation to the sacredness of land remain.

Toward the end of the essay, Snyder circles back to the North American present and eventually to the land in which he lives, where the essay started. He makes an extremely important point that runs counter to much of European and American thinking that has been current for centuries: "It is not nature-as-chaos which threatens us, but the State's presumption that it has created order" (92); and, further, "Nature is orderly. That which appears to be chaotic in nature is only a more complex kind of order" (93).

"Blue Mountains Constantly Walking"

The essay "Blue Mountains Constantly Walking" heavily depends for its meaning on Snyder's deep and abiding philosophical, spiritual, and aesthetic debts to Japan and Buddhism. Snyder begins the essay by talking about Dōgen, the thirteenth-century Buddhist monk, and his "Mountains and Waters Sutra," delivered in 1240. He then links Dōgen's attention to mountains to the practice of Buddhist pilgrimages and attitudes about sacred mountains, such as Mt. Hiei, which is near Kyoto where Snyder lived during most of his time in Japan.

Snyder not only provides historical information about such pilgrimages but also includes personal experience. It is useful to remember that while Snyder was in Japan he took vows with the Yamabushi monks, as he describes some of that initiation here. The Yamabushi are a sect of mountain ascetic monks, and Snyder reminds his reader that "in East Asia 'mountains' are often synonymous with wilderness" (100), particularly since they are the terrain impervious to wilderness-destroying agriculture. But mountains cannot be understood properly in a vacuum, since they enter into relationship with the rest of nature. Dōgen's sutra is, after all, about "mountains and waters," because, as Snyder observes: "mountains and rivers indeed form each other: waters are precipitated by heights, carve or deposit landforms in their flowing descent, and weight the offshore continental shelves with sediment to ultimately tilt more uplifts" (101-2). Poems in *Regarding Wave* are informed by this attitude as can be noted when Snyder remarks here that a mountain range is sometimes referred to "as a network of veins on the back of a hand" (102), an image which also appears in that volume. But that concept of the interrelationship of mountains and waters as a process lasting throughout the life of the biosphere is expressed as early as "Poem Left in Sourdough Mountain Lookout," written in the early 1950s (*Left Out in the Rain*, 42). What is most important, however, is not the ability to make associations among the different aspects of nature— mountains like veins, bodies like streams—rather, it is being able to realize that there is no nature as an entity but only *naturing*, a process of interaction and mutual transformation. Solidity consists of energy transformations in an apparent, but only apparent, period of stasis. As Snyder remarks about each human being in the essay, "Reinhabitation," "we are all composite beings . . . whose sole identifying feature is a particular form or structure changing constantly in time."[17]

"Ancient Forests of the Far West"

According to Clark, "Ancient Forests of the Far West" comprises "the crowning component of this stirring, thoughtful field report on the tenuous state of the wild in our time."[18] Interestingly enough, Snyder uses as epigraph for this essay the same lines from Exodus that he quotes in "Logging 2" of *Myths & Texts*. Thus he explicitly loops back to poetry written nearly forty years earlier. In the opening section of the essay he loops back even farther to youthful experiences growing up and working in those Far West forests. This essay provides one of the clearest pictures Snyder has presented of the events behind the poetry of the "Logging" section of *Myths & Texts* as well as early poems, such as "The Late Snow & Lumber Strike of the Summer of Fifty-four" in *Riprap*.

Snyder uses these personal memories as a way of detailing an appropriate type of logging, selective and sensitive to the bioregion and to the individual trees that are dying. From this lesson of the right way to do things, Snyder switches to the history of U.S. forest management, as well as to an analysis of the ecological specifics of the ancient western forests. Snyder notes that "the forests of the maritime Pacific Northwest are the last remaining forests of any size left in the temperate zone" worldwide (130). And he details the history of the loss of corresponding forests in the Mediterranean and East Asia before returning to the threats that the surviving forests face from the U.S. government and its various agencies. Snyder speaks lovingly and respectfully of the forests of his own region and the need and ways to protect them. This essay ends with a determined anger in which the tasks of Snyder and reader alike are delineated: "We must make the hard-boiled point that the world's trees are virtually worth more standing than they would be as lumber, because of such diverse results of deforestation as life-destroying flooding in Bangladesh and Thailand, the extinction of millions of species of animals and plants, and global warming. . . . We are all endangered yokels" (143).

"On the Path, Off the Trail"

Paths and trails have served writers as metaphors for an entire series of human activities, both spiritual and physical, for centuries. In this essay Snyder participates in this tradition by developing his own literal and metaphoric senses of these terms. He also introduces the concept of "networks" to distinguish between two aspects of an individual's life. As Snyder sees it, community is grounded in place, while work is often grounded in associations that take one beyond place into a network of people engaged in the same or related tasks. As a result "networks cut across communities with their own kind of territoriality" (144). The problem for Snyder is that in the present day people often relate only to their network and fail to establish themselves in their community as well.

Snyder turns to Asia to develop a notion related to path and trail— that of "way," which includes the idea of path but extends it to an entire perception of being, to the realms of philosophies, religions, and ideologies. Art is understood as one of the ways that people travel, which Snyder discusses in terms of the relationship between tradition and creativity. This discussion in turn brings him back to a relationship addressed at the beginning of *The Practice of the Wild*, which is that of freedom and responsibility. Manifestations of this relationship can be thought of in terms of discipline and spontaneity, as well as models and innovation. Snyder here resorts again to Buddhism and the various means by which its masters have tried to teach the relationship of the tradition, discipline, and path of Buddhist practice and individual experience—the last marked by the distinction between prescribed forms of meditation and the individual experiencing of enlightenment. Snyder concludes that "there are paths that can be followed, and there is a path that cannot—it is not a path, it is the wilderness. There is a 'going' but no goer, no destination, only the whole field" (151). He then immediately departs the realm of metaphor to talk about his own experience, which led him to study Zen in Japan, as well as to return to the United States as the place to practice what he had learned. Snyder ends with a warning about the relationships of freedom and discipline and spontaneity, tradition and innovation: "But we need paths and trails and will always be maintaining them. You must first be on the path, before you can turn and walk into the wild" (154).

"The Woman Who Married a Bear" and
"Survival and Sacrament"

In "The Woman Who Married a Bear" Snyder brings together tradition and innovation, myth and experience, with a popular Native American tale of intersexuality between humans and other animals— a story that he has worked into his poetry since the writing of "A Berry Feast." He begins with the mythical story; then, rather than explaining the tale, he begins to relate the history of bears in North America. This history too becomes a story, as Snyder retells with more realistic details rather than mythic ones the bear-human marriage myth. Like any good myth, Snyder's story educates readers about the world, specifically about the lives of bears and their relationship with their environments. Then, with his version of the story ended, Snyder relates the source of the tale and a little information about the Native American woman who told it, followed by a suggestion of the ubiquity of bear-human stories through references to Greek mythology.

The reader may keep waiting for Snyder to analyze the story, but he never does. Instead, he ends with another story, about a Native American bear dance he witnessed in 1977. What is revealed here, rather than claimed or explained, is the power that myth can carry in the present day and the ways by which it can help bridge the gap between animal and human that, as the story of the woman who married a bear suggests, once did not exist.

"Survival and Sacrament" serves as Snyder's conclusion to *The Practice of the Wild*. It begins on an ominous note by warning of the terrifying difference between death and the "end to birth"; that is, between an individual's death and the end of the coming into being of an entire species. Since their arrival in North America white human beings, as colonizers, settlers, and profligate consumers, have not only witnessed but also caused the "end to birth" of countless species at an ever-increasing rate with no conception of the suffering involved or the long-range effects on the ecosystems of this continent and the entire planetary biosphere. Snyder points out that excessive human reproduction, particularly in the past three hundred years, is a crucial dimension of this problem. In other places he has emphasized how nuclear power is a major threat to the ongoing process of birth because of its lasting effects on animal and plant genetics: "Nuclear power plants are to industrial technological society as smack to an addict. Hence difficult to block. Yet it must be borne in mind that all other insults to the earth may heal themselves in time; but the disruption of the gene pool—the treasure of all life—is irreversible. Keep that foremost in mind when making plans and strategies."[19]

Snyder opens his conclusion with a warning, but he ends it with a promise of covenant. That promise begins with the argument that a true human quest "requires embracing the other as oneself" and that a movement in the world is growing that recognizes just such a necessity (180). This necessity does not take the form of developing a modern advanced civilization, as one might expect, but of developing a wilder culture, a "culture of the wilderness" (180). This phrase encapsulates a dual recognition. One, nature is always a social construct in terms of the limits of human understanding and interaction with the rest of the world; and two, society is always a natural construct arising in relation to, and on the basis of, natural conditions of existence. Snyder closes his book with a discussion of "Grace," both as prayer and behavior, as a socially constructed natural act which recognizes that "eating is a sacrament" (184). This expression comes right out of Rinzai Zen practice, as well as numerous other spiritual traditions.[20] To approach eating with respect is to recognize human integration with the rest of the world in which people live and die, and in which people cause other beings to live and die as well, either necessarily or capriciously. By this emphasis on grace Snyder has returned to the beginning of *The Practice of the Wild*, teaching his readers about a particular form of the "etiquette of freedom," one which recognizes and gratefully affirms human responsibility.

9

Sifting and Selecting
No Nature and A Place in Space

Two years after publishing *The Practice of the Wild*, Snyder again turned to poetry and brought out *No Nature: New and Selected Poems* in 1992. He followed that project three years later with his second major volume of prose, *A Place in Space: Ethics, Aesthetics, and Watersheds*. Both of these volumes constitute selected works, with significant new material added to each. The poetry is maintained in chronological order, but in *A Place* the prose is organized achronologically according to the three topics that comprise the subtitle. Although portions of *A Place* are drawn from the prose section of *Turtle Island* and the slim 1977 book, *The Old Ways*, they have been revised for this volume and it makes sense to read those essays as chapters of a cohesive new book rather than in their originally published form. Such is not the case with *No Nature*; so with it I will speak briefly about the implications of Snyder's selection process for his previously published poems and then discuss the fifteen new poems.

For many long-time readers of Snyder's poetry, the title of *No Nature* probably took them by surprise. Fully aware of the unsettling function of his title, Snyder provided an explanation in his preface:

> Nature also means the physical universe, including the urban, industrial, and toxic. But we do not easily *know* nature, or even know ourselves. Whatever it actually is, it will not fulfil our conceptions or assumptions. It will dodge our expectations and theoretical models. There is no single set "nature" either as "the natural world" or "the nature of things." The greatest respect we can pay to nature is not to trap it, but to acknowledge that it eludes us and that our own nature is also fluid, open, and conditional.[1]

No Nature includes selections from all of Snyder's previous full-length books of poetry. Indicative of their influence on his poetic development, Snyder included a generous portion of the Cold Mountain translations as well as the majority of the *Riprap* poems, whereas in *The Back Country* section the translations of Miyazawa Kenji's poems were not included. Roughly a third of *Myths & Texts* has been omitted. *The Back Country* has been heavily scaled back, with two-thirds of the "Kālī" section being dropped. With *Regarding Wave*, it is primarily miscellaneous pieces that Snyder omitted, keeping in the three "Regarding Wave" sections those poems that depict his relationship with Masa and the community life of the Suwanose tribe. With *Turtle Island*, Snyder preserved most of the "Manzanita" section while dropping some of the more didactic and hunting-related poems of "Magpie's Song," and keeping most of the "For the Children" section while omitting all of the prose. Thirty-two poems, a significant portion, of *Axe Handles* has been left out. Not surprisingly, the majority of poems from *Left Out in the Rain* have been omitted, but Snyder has chosen to include poems that provide a historical range indicative of the development of his poetic craft. It is difficult to discern a single pattern in Snyder's selection process, but it can be noted that some of the poems for which he was criticized for sexism have been left out, as well as some of the hunting poems, for which he has been criticized in American Buddhist circles. Also, at least in the case of *The Back Country* and *Regarding Wave*, the selected versions read as more unified collections than the originals.

"No Nature": The New Poems

"How Poetry Comes To Me" opens this section with a deceptively simple-looking poem (361), which takes on complexity as the reader meditates on its implications. Snyder's description identifies "poetry" as something that comes to the poet from the external world, like a wild animal. It is an active entity rather than a static object. It does not arrive, however, with a clear-cut statement or goal, as indicated by the verb "blundered" in the first line. Having arrived, it remains "frightened," and due to this fear the poet must meet it halfway. The entity's arriving at night suggests that it is akin to dreams, something from the unconscious. At first, these images might seem to be contradictory, that poetry comes both from the outside world and from the unconscious, but only if the unconscious is viewed as the unique property of a single individual. Here, rather, the unconscious into which the poet taps is a collective one, both in the Jungian sense of the "collective unconscious" and in the sense of the unconscious expressing itself in poetry through language, which is social in origin.

The poet does not simply entrap or receive this entity and out pops a poem. Rather, the campfire could be read as the poet's rational consciousness, understanding, and information, including the knowledge of poetics. The light, then, could be understood as a metaphor for craft as well as consciousness. The poem in this kind of reading takes shape in a liminal zone through the interaction between the unconscious and the conscious, and in the interaction between the external world's stimuli and the poet's word craft for shaping experience into an aesthetic artifact. The poem is both inspired and wrought. The role of craft here is that of focusing the experience down to a necessary set of images, as suggested by the way that the poem moves from an opening eight-syllable line to a concluding four-syllable line.

The following poem, "On Climbing the Sierra Matterhorn Again After Thirty-One Years" (362), in contrast, is both simple in appearance and content, being basically a modified haiku. It expresses the value and power of cycles and repetition in human experience. Curiously enough, however, while the first two lines are quite explicit about their content, the final line leaves unstated what the primary object of Snyder's "love" might be.

"Kyšiwoqqóbɨ" returns to two subjects that recur throughout Snyder's poetry (363), the relationship between knowledge and naming and the possibility of reinhabitation. Here Snyder is reflecting on the origin of the particular smell of a tree called "Jeffrey Pine," but known to Piutes as "Kyšiwoqqóbɨ." In asking what "Piute children" would have said about smelling this tree, Snyder is not concerned with the particular words used in one language or another but with the difference in viewpoint expressed by such words. He thinks of the smell of "pineapple," which would have been unknown to the Piutes, while they may have thought of the smell of plants that have become extinct since European colonization of the Americas. By thinking that he hears the Piute name "From the dust, from the breeze," Snyder is feeling his way toward a sense of knowing this place intimately and having a historical conception of human-nonhuman relationships here. The reference to "Piute children" links up with the signature line, informing readers that the poem is based on a July 1982 trip with his son Kai on the eastern side of the mountains near Mammoth in southern California. There is thus both a reference to the historical inhabitants of the area and the generational connection of the handing down of knowledge between them and Snyder and between Snyder and his son. At the same time, impermanence and liminality appear at poem's end. The "voice" that may be speaking the Piute word is like the "it" that comes blundering toward him in "How Poetry Comes To Me," while "the dust" and "the breeze" remind him of the transience of human presence in this and any other place.

The generational and reinhabitory emphases of the previous poem are continued in the following one, "The Sweat" (364-65). Describing a sweat lodge in Alaska, Snyder reflects on the aging of the women in the group and then on his own aging. The key point here is the acceptance of the aging process and a certain kind of satisfaction at reflecting on all the older people assembled in this community. In regard to this point as it is made in *Practice*, Jaeger provides a comment relevant to the appreciation of "Kyšiwoqqóbɨ" and "The Sweat": "Thus Snyder covers the two aspects of his re-inhabitation model—people (or living beings) grounded in place, and in particular, a place where others have lived before and where new generations will live after the deaths of the current inhabitants."[2]

The next poem of the "No Nature" section continues these emphases but with a different twist. In "Building" (366-67), Snyder takes a position about the relationship of local history to national history and the relative importance of each. He traces the history of the building of his home, Kitkitdizze, as well as the San Juan Ridge schoolhouse and the Ring of Bone Zendo. The activities that comprise local history are set against the backdrop of the official history that begins the poem with "The Vietnam War" and ends it with the war in "the Persian Gulf." In contrast to such destruction is the home-building, community-building activities of Snyder's family and neighbors. The penultimate stanza sets the claim that "our buildings are solid, to live, to teach, to sit" against government corruption, but also contends that both the national history and the local history are part of larger cycles of human natural history. In the brief final stanza, the cycles of the moon are the backdrop for the closing line: "Sharp tools, good design." The kind of building that concerns Snyder here is both larger than politics and highly political, in as much as these specific buildings contribute to the construction of an alternative way of life that rejects the government's "Lies and Crimes" and attempts to fit into the natural cycles. Snyder seems to suggest in his final two stanzas that not all cycles must continue indefinitely but that those human cycles of activity in line with the greater natural cycles may prevail over the cycles of destruction that have dominated so much of human history.

Many of the new poems in *No Nature* are quite playful and humorous. "Building" is an exception in terms of its high seriousness. Stylistically it is also the most prosaic of the poems with its strong narrative structure and long lines, yet quite successful nevertheless. But as if to protect himself from being too serious and, perhaps, too self-righteous, Snyder follows "Building" with "Surrounded By Wild

Turkeys" (368). Basically, he compares himself and other human beings with a group of turkeys passing through his property, with the obvious connotation that goes with referring to a person as a "turkey." But under this humor, some serious points are made. One, these turkeys are not indigenous to the region, but decades after their introduction have managed to survive and thrive through adaptation to their locale. Two, the backdrop for this mini-migration is a forest fire; conflagrations displace people. If read immediately after "Building," the reader unavoidably connects this fire with those from the wars mentioned in the previous poem. Three, Snyder remarks that one of the things that turkeys and humans have in common is that our offspring "Look just like us." Again, with the narrative of the building of a schoolhouse in the previous poem fresh in a reader's mind, one cannot help thinking of the rather pointed implication of this comparison. If our children are going to be just like us, how should we be behaving; what kind of building should we consider to be important? What methods should we employ in adapting to our locale and in learning to survive?

"Off the Trail" (369-70), which follows "Surrounded," along with "Ripples on the Surface," is one of the two most accomplished poems among these fifteen. "Off the Trail" opens with the line, "We are free to find our own way," and later alludes to the *Dao De Jing* axiom that "the trail's not the way." Jaeger provides an extended analysis of this poem in light of remarks in *The Practice of the Wild* and the "cognitive metaphor" that life is a journey. She notes that "the title of the poem is invested with special meaning for Snyder within his spiritual outlook: ' "Off the trail" is another name for the Way,' he writes, and 'sauntering off the trail is the practice of the wild.' " Jaeger goes on to point out that the poem is addressed to a narratee, Snyder's wife Carole Koda, to whom the poem is dedicated, and as a result readers/ listeners overhear the poem. Such a device is typical of many Romantic poems and seems particularly appropriate for a poem that is, finally, a love poem above anything else. As Jaeger notes, "the poem emphasizes that both partners are aligned in the same direction. . . . No end of the landscape of rocks and trees is in view, implying that there will be no end to this partnership, a quality embedded in the American culture model of marriage."[3]

Some other aspects of the poem worth noting are Snyder's emphasis on specific detail on the one hand, through which he demonstrates that different species establish trails running in different directions appropriate to each one's needs; and his recognition that the place does not determine the quality of the relationship, on the other hand. Just as "no place is more than another," so too Gary and Carole must find their own way through their life environment to make their relationship work. The final aspect of the poem deserving comment is the playful way in which Snyder weaves a highly spiritual language throughout the poem in both direct and subtle ways. The directness comes with the invocation of the *Dao De Jing* and the directive it provides on how to read the use of the word "way," as well as "trails" and "paths." The subtlety comes through the use of such phrases and words as "Been here before," as in reincarnation, "practice," as in spiritual discipline, and "bedrock," as the foundation of faith and experience that lets them temporarily part knowing they will rejoin each other later.

"Word Basket Woman" returns to the issue of multigenerational inhabitation (371-72), as Snyder attends to his European heritage as represented by one of his great grandmothers whose grave he visits in Kansas. While paying tribute to her, he reflects on the fact that she was a poet who wrote of the horrors of war, and contrasts her compassion with Robinson Jeffers's cold aloofness. While Snyder would in most venues ascribe his ability to recognize the preciousness of both plants and animals to his Buddhist beliefs, here he admits that there must have been something in the European heritage of his own family that helped bring him to the kind of life he practices in the Sierra Nevada, a place geologically far removed from the plains of Kansas.

The next poem, "At Tower Peak" (373-74), is reminiscent of the early poems of *Riprap*. Snyder contrasts the rejuvenating experience of mountain climbing with the increasingly urbanized world where "Every tan rolling meadow will turn into housing." But he does not end with the illusion of the individual being able to separate himself from the rest of humanity through ascetic retreat to some pure, wild, place—and in this instance, this poem can be read in relation to his criticism of Jeffers in "Word Basket Woman." As he observes near the end of the poem, "It's just one world," and the contradictions must be worked through and from within. He will reinforce this one world image in the final poem of the volume, "Ripples on the Surface." But before doing so, he will include five poems of uneven quality and distinctly different tones.

"Right in the Trail" is the only truly humorous one of the five (375-76), and perhaps the most successful as a result of its tone. In it, the poet is studying a large pile of bear excrement. Not surprisingly, the story of "The Woman Who Married a Bear" is alluded to in the first stanza. And while that woman gained some specific lessons to bring back to her people, the poet seems perplexed as to how to interpret this nonlinguistic sign. While he imbues it with cosmic significance, in reality at most he can only discern what the bear has been eating of late, "(mostly still manzanita)." Jaeger notes of this line that "the parentheses around the 'manzanita' are an example of Snyder's playful poetic craftsmanship, as they constitute an outer enclosure neatly corresponding to the outer crust enhulling the information within the scat."[4] The poem concludes with two stanzas of direct address to the bear. They function to demonstrate proper etiquette toward other species and to admit the presence of the bear into the sense of local community. This poem embodies Snyder's remarks in the preface that "the greatest respect we can pay to nature is not to trap it, but to acknowledge that it eludes us."

"Travelling to the Capital" is quite different in tone and seems to suffer from the closing lines Snyder appends to it (377). Working through establishing various contradictions, such as a waiter who must use pliers to take the caps off of bottles of Perrier, the poem's key contradiction is the blooming of the "sakura," Japanese cherry trees, in the midst of Washington, D.C. Perhaps because of the highly ephemeral quality of such blossoms and their long literary history in Japan as a symbol for loss and sadness, Snyder paints a bleak picture of the present that unfortunately reads like a cliché. His closing statement is too didactic without sufficient preparation throughout the poem for the polemic to be emotively affective for most readers.

The next poem, "Thoughts on Looking at a Samuel Palmer Etching at the Tate," critiques pastoral tradition leaving out the fate of the domestic animals so lovingly represented in its artwork (378). Some of the lines in this poem sound rather affected in their style, such as "They stamp and steam in chilly morn," as if Snyder is imitating pastoral style even as he critiques the romanticism of the pastoral. This poem reprises a topic that Snyder has addressed more effectively in *Turtle Island* poems. Likewise, "Kisiabaton" (379) reiterates the theme of "Kyšiwoqqóbɨ" but not as effectively, perhaps because the knowledge of the local tribal name for the tree is not linked with any specific inhabitory practice and the point of this event occurring in Taiwan is not developed. "For Lew Welch in a Snowfall" is a more effective poem than the preceding two (380). The tone of melancholy works well insofar as Snyder regrets the reduction of the life of a close friend to "one more archive," but the closing stanza with its mild notion that life goes on fails to take advantage of the scene that has been established.

Fortunately, Snyder saved one of the best poems of this group to serve as the conclusion to the volume as a whole. "Ripples on the Surface" will no doubt be one of Snyder's lasting poems and one likely to be frequently selected for anthologies. It opens with a quotation distinguishing different kinds of ripples on the water, which refers to a way of reading nature.[6] In mid-poem he remarks: "Nature not a book, but a *performance*." He concludes by deconstructing the dichotomy of house and wild, of human and nonhuman, announcing: "No nature / Both together, one big empty house." The final line echoes the Buddhist image of the phenomenal world that we perceive as nonessential. Or, in the words of *The Diamond Sutra*, a Buddhist text very important in Snyder's Zen training, "As to any Truth-declaring system, Truth is undeclarable; so 'an enunciation of Truth' is just the name given to it."[5]

Yong-ki Kang has developed an extended reading of this poem that sheds light not only on "Ripples on the Surface" but also on more general aspects of Snyder's poetics. In "The Politics of Deconstruction in Snyder's 'Ripples on the Surface,'" Kang notes that "while the western mind stresses *ri* (the universal) over *ji* (the particular), Zen thought does not accept the hierarchical dichotomy of *ri/ji*. Snyder's poetic efforts to describe his individual experiences or observations, which stem from his own direct contact with nature, well-imply his intention to resist the *ri*-oriented westerner's mindset." As part of this resistance in the opening stanza of "Ripples,"[6] according to Kang, Snyder contradicts the idea that definitions determine reality: "the water may perform innumerable faces so as to dodge our homocentric definition of it. 'Salmon passing,' 'breezes,' or 'a humpback whale' register their own meaning on the surface of the water."[7] The resistance is then continued in the fourth stanza through what Kang perceives as "a significant deconstruction of language" through which "the nature/culture dichotomy is effaced."[8] Further, contends Kang, Snyder's "linguistic deconstruction of 'wild' and 'house' also represents the theme of ecological interconnectedness," which is necessarily both "deconstructive and reconstructive at the same time" because "Snyder does not deny human stewardship in the task of preserving wilderness. Because Snyder's view of nature allows a ground for self-deconstruction, his environmentalism ultimately takes a dialogical position between nature and humanity, between primitivism and techno-scientism—the ongoing dialogue toward the ecologically sustainable transformation of self and culture."[9]

Indeed, Snyder's alternation in the fourth stanza between "the little house in the wild" and "the wild in the house" leads right back to the humorous, yet deeply significant sensibility of the title of *Earth House Hold*, through the absent term *oikos*, the ancient Greek root for both *house* and *ecology*. This house is necessarily "empty" in both senses that Kang discusses: one, it is empty in the sense of the Buddhist concept of *sunyata*, which can be understood in this context as void of fixed universal essence; two, it is empty in that none of the words used to define this ecology/house fix it into an object for observation. Rather, humans are always participants in a process, in what I referred to earlier as *naturing*.

Essays Old, New, and Renewed

Unlike the arrangement of *No Nature*, which allows for a separate discussion of just the new poems, the arrangement of *A Place in Space* requires a consideration of the old, the new, and the renewed—in the sense of revised—essays in relationship to each other as well as to the development of Snyder's thought over the forty years of writing that these essays represent. The pieces collected in *A Place* are of three basic types: one, like the chapters of *The Practice of the Wild*, many of these began as oral presentations that were revised to varying degrees for publication; two, pieces composed as written essays; and three, reviews of, and introductions to, the work of others. Although the majority of them were delivered or written prior to the publication of *Practice*, Snyder makes it evident in his introductory "Note" that he anticipates that many readers will come to these pieces for the first time in *A Place* and likely after having read *Practice*. As a result, he remarks that this volume "can be considered a further exploration of what 'the practice of the wild' would be."

Upon its publication, *A Place in Space* received generally favorable reviews. For example, Kenneth Olliff emphasizes "a casual and intimate style that is reminiscent of Aldo Leopold" and goes on to say that "seeking a 'planetary and ecological cosmopolitanism,' *A Place in Space* proclaims human and nonhuman alike inseparable and worthy of celebration." Stuart Cowan in another review emphasizes that "these pieces call us to the difficult art of living well in place— which requires a certain porousness to both wild nature and our own complex histories." And Donna Seaman remarks that "Snyder analyzes our troubled relationship with the earth from a fertile triumvirate of perspectives: that of a Buddhist, an environmentalist, and a poet. . . . This bracingly pragmatic and unerringly spiritual volume reaffirms Snyder's prominent place in American literature and discourse." In a review essay, the well-known environmental ethicist J. Baird Callicott walks through the volume commenting on its contents in an autobiographical mode. He emphasizes that "Snyder is an integrationist, not a segregationist. The trick is to (re)inhabit the land well, not to back off and just leave it alone." And of the book itself, he remarks that it "is a very carefully assembled literary ecosystem. . . . it is a great book."[11]

I. Ethics

The first part of *A Place in Space* is labeled "Ethics" and consists of ten essays of varying length and sophistication. Just as in his "Note" where he places Buddhism first, he places "Ethics" first in order of attention. The first three essays are the weakest in the entire volume, but, as Callicott suggests, Snyder has likely included them because they reveal Snyder's own intellectual development and provide a context for his growth as a poet and activist. The narrative poem "Smokey the Bear Sutra" continues this history of intellectual development, showing how Buddhism and poetry can function as integral parts of activism, but it also divides the first three essays from the later more substantial ones.[12] This poem is amazingly humorous, particularly in Snyder's appropriation of Smokey the Bear, "a terribly American cultural icon," as a Buddhist deity, one of the manifestations of Fudōmyō-ō,[13] and in the closing lines, "Drown their butts / Crush their butts," which do not refer to cigarettes but to the promoters of consumer capitalism (27). As a "sutra," this poem is by definition written for the purpose of moral instruction, and as is common to this Buddhist genre contains various mythical and legendary figures. Snyder, however, takes it beyond the traditional figures expected to be found in a sutra by introducing locally appropriate figures. As Jaeger aptly notes,

> In the sutras, anecdotes often involve the Buddha, bodhisattvas, and bhikkus, while by analogy with the sutra form, Native American tribal tales deploy figures such as Bear and Coyote and Raven to make their points about divine, human, and other living beings, so that the bear as a Native American totem and savior-figure, perhaps the most powerful animal in the Western wilderness, is part of the subtext here.[14]

In a note appended to the poem, Snyder explains the mythical allusions and the circumstances of its creation and dissemination. Written to be distributed at the Sierra Club Wilderness Conference held in San Francisco in February of 1969, Snyder declared that it could be reproduced for free and, as a result, it has been widely distributed throughout the world in the past thirty-plus years.

The first substantial essay in *A Place* is "Four Changes, with a Postscript," which was originally published and widely distributed in 1969, then slightly revised for inclusion in *Turtle Island*.[15] For *A Place*, Snyder added "Postscript (1995)." Snyder observes that, although this essay is very much a part of its historical milieu—the anti-war, black liberation, and hippie movements of the late-1960s—"the apprehension we felt in 1969 has not abated." Snyder cries out against the destruction of the ways of life of "the few remaining traditional people with place-based sustainable economies," and concludes that "naive and utopian as some of it sounds now, I still stand by the basics of 'Four Changes' " (46).

Just what are these basics, then? The four changes that comprise his focus consist of population, pollution, consumption, and transformation. In each section, he outlines "The Condition" under the categories of position, situation, and goal, followed by "Action," which is broken down into "social/political," "the community," and "our own heads." Under "Population," he points out that human beings are a part of the fabric of life that has expanded beyond sustainability. Under "Pollution," Snyder defines the term, identifies human production of wastes as excessive and calls for a cleaner environment. In the "Our own Heads" section of "Pollution," he quotes Thoreau and calls for understanding a "balanced cycle." The "Consumption" section continues in the same vein and Snyder criticizes the U.S. Forest Service and ends with a concern about the "complication of possessions." With "Transformation" Snyder changes emphasis. "Everyone, " he claims, "is the result of four forces: the conditions of this known universe (matter/energy forms and ceaseless change), the biology of his or her species, individual genetic heritage, and the culture one is born into." Evolution is then defined as finding spaces and gaps within these conditions to "experience inner freedom and illumination" (41). Civilization, according to Snyder, has become the very enemy of the people who have created it, and only through a change of consciousness based on direct, material experience is there a hope of turning things around for the species and the planet. "Four Changes" was written as a manifesto, which explains its declarative and hortatory style, not at all like the colloquial, personal style of much of *Practice* and the "Watershed" essays later in the volume.

The next essay of the "Ethics" section is "The Yogin and the Philosopher," which was originally delivered at the 1974 conference, "The Rights of the Non-Human." Of particular interest here is Snyder's delineation of what has been termed the Great Subculture.

Snyder relates the Eastern concept of the yogin with the Native American and indigenous cultural concept of the shaman, once more seeking a syncretic blend translatable into one of the roles of the modern poet. Snyder concludes that "one of the few modes of speech that gives us access to that other yogic or shamanistic view (in which all is one and all is many, and the many are all precious) is poetry or song" (51). As Snyder has said elsewhere, he views here the roles of the yogin, the shaman, and the poet as being identical when it comes to the task of speaking for the nonhuman to humans.

In "Energy Is Eternal Delight," the poet's task is fundamentally defined as defending the "diversity and richness of the gene pool" (52). One of the things that poetry can accomplish in this regard would be to help people seek "nonmaterial, nondestructive paths of growth" in opposition to continuously expanding human consumption (53). Although Snyder takes his title from the visionary poet William Blake, he takes his philosophy here primarily from Buddhism. Not only does he depict his own Zen training, but also makes the explicit claim that "Buddhists teach respect for all life and for wild systems. A human being's life is totally dependent on an interpenetrating network of wild systems" (54). While the language here might be understood in terms of ecology and cybernetics, the ontology is a Buddhist one in which Snyder is alluding both to the image of Indra's jeweled net and to the Buddhist concept of dependent co-origination, *pratītya-samutpāda*.

Snyder concludes the "Ethics" section with three substantial essays, all based on talks given in 1990 and 1992. Not only do these three essays continue to intertwine Buddhism and ecology, but they also integrate the local and the planetary in very specific ways. The first of these is "Earth Day and the War Against the Imagination," originally delivered in 1990, and, as Snyder notes, twenty years after the first Earth Day and his initial Earth Day speech. In 1970 he spoke to the students at Colorado State University in Greeley. In 1990 he is speaking mainly to local people living in the South Yuba River region of northern California. Snyder defines the first Earth Day as a turning point for the rise of a new environmental movement and the shifting of energies within the American counterculture. Snyder then provides a capsule summary of some key global environmental issues, including deforestation, overpopulation, and the inequitable distribution of wealth in the world before working his way toward more regional and local environmental issues. As with the transition between *Turtle Island* and *Axe Handles*, one sees here part of a transition in Snyder's prose to a more balanced way of delivering a warning.

Rather than a message that makes people feel that the environmental crisis demands and all-or-nothing response, "Earth Day," and many of his other more recent chapters in *A Place*, make people feel that change is possible and that there are many ways and levels on which people can contribute to such change. His writing in the 1980s and 1990s reflects a recognition that ways have to be found to enable the largest number of people possible to contribute to environmentally beneficial change from whatever starting point each can assume. While Snyder stands squarely behind his sense of the intensity of the crisis, as his "Postscript (1995)" to "Four Changes" indicates, his sense of how to motivate people to participate in responding to the crisis has altered.

While "Earth Day" could be labeled as hortatory, "Nets of Beads, Webs of Cells" and "A Village Council of All Beings" could be labeled as demonstrative. The former reflects Snyder's participation in a debate about the interpretation of the first precept of Buddhism, "cause no unnecessary harm," which is often interpreted as a prohibition against eating other animals. As Snyder works his way through the issues of raising domesticated animals, hunting, or eating accidentally killed animals, he concludes that "the very distinction 'vegetarian/ nonvegetarian' is too simple" (67), because it fails to take into account bioregional particularities and the inequities of the global economic system. Finally, Snyder concludes that rather than laying down universal strictures, members of the Buddhist community "must each find our own personal way to practice this precept, within quite a latitude of possibilities" (72); he then goes on to remind his audience that "to save the life of a single parrot or monkey is truly admirable. But unless the forest is saved, they will all die" (73). This demonstrates a strategy by which Snyder attempts to mediate the conflicts between local particularities and universalizing systems, which includes religions that are not place-based but claim to be true for everyone.

In the prefatory note to "A Village Council of All Beings," Snyder explains that this talk was delivered in northern India within the general topic of "ecology and spirituality" and that it gave Snyder a chance to "enlarge on my own thoughts about how ecological insights and bioregional organizing might help a Buddhist society under siege from the witless expansionism of the industrial world" (74). Snyder begins with defining ecology and then critiquing the notion of scientific objectivity emphasizing that human beings are completely within nature. He then depicts an ecosystem as a "mandala," a kind of spiritually powerful design, and then returns to the theme of his previous essay by pointing out that all of life is involved in eating other beings as part of the ongoing energy transfers of the universe. According to David Robertson, "mandalas are concentric diagrams (mandala means 'circular' in Sanskrit) that depict the interrelationships between fundamental Buddhist concepts and states of mind. They are used as aids in study and in meditation and can be drawn, printed, or woven. In design and in use they are analogous to the sand paintings of various native North Americans."[16]

Having established the ecosystem as a place for Buddhist practice and spiritual realization, Snyder then defines eating in terms of "*puja*, a ceremony of offering and sharing" (77), which in turn should arouse feelings of compassion, the key emotion in Buddhism demonstrated by all bodhisattvas. Snyder then interweaves these points by referring to a previous speaker at the conference that he identifies as "a remarkable lay Buddhist philosopher" (74): "As Tashi Rapges said, the spontaneous awakening of compassion for others instantly starts one on the path of ecological ethics, as well as on the path towards enlightenment. They are not two" (78). In like manner, as Robertson points out, the "three" described spaces of the mandala are not actually three but one: "The space created by mandala for dharma practice can be none other than the spatial order of the true universe, which is in turn the spatial order of the real universe."[17]

Having established his fundamental interconnections of ecology and spirituality by means of Buddhism, Snyder is quite careful not to make his subject a sectarian issue. Instead, he points out that "the awakening of the Mind of Compassion" is not created by or experienced by the followers of any one religion, but has been experienced and can be experienced by anyone, and needs to be in this time of ecological crisis. He concludes the talk by taking the bioregional concept of a "Council of All Beings," which he attributes to John Seed and Joanna Macy and extends it to the idea of a "*Village Council of All Beings*" in relation to the basic social unit of the region in which the conference took place (79).[18]

II. Aesthetics

The first seven of the eleven chapters of this section consist of one short essay on Chinese poetry based on various talks Snyder has given and six forewords to a diverse group of books written or edited by other people. While these forewords are all tied to their initial circumstances of composition, they are often revealing about Snyder's own poetics and his own poetical training. In particular, the influence of classical Chinese poetry and the importance of the oral tradition are emphasized. In "Amazing Grace," Snyder distinguishes the oral tradition as a form for remembering rather than memorizing, and explains the relationship of that distinction to the difference between "direct experience" and "hearsay" (94). The sensibility about the world that is embodied in the oral songs of the Ainu represents for him both a precise knowledge of the human place in the natural world and a type of intergenerational teaching that must not be lost: "We now see the Ainu not as a fading remnant, but as elders and teachers whose playful sense of their own bioregion points a way to see and live on our planet as a whole" (98). In these remarks one sees that Snyder's conception of aesthetics is clearly not an exclusively structural one, but also an ethical and thematic one.

In "A Single Breath," Snyder links meditation and poetry. It is interesting to note, however, that he is not suggesting meditation as a device for thinking up poems or receiving poetic inspiration; rather, he is emphasizing the similarity of the two as complementary disciplined activities. He develops this complementarity through a discussion of the role of poetry in formal Ch'an/Zen training halls. For a gathering of poets who meditate, Snyder wrote: "Meditation is the problematic art of deliberately staying open as the myriad things experience themselves. Another one of the ways that phenomena 'experience themselves' is in poetry. Poetry steers between nonverbal states of mind and the intricacies of our gift of language" (113). Snyder then launches into a lively consideration of the idea of "*Beyond wild*" (114), specifically as it relates to meditation and getting to known one's own mind: "You find that there's no one in charge, and are reminded that no thought lasts for long. . . . A poem, like a life, is a brief presentation, a uniqueness in the oneness, a complete expression, and a gift" (115).

"The Politics of Ethnopoetics" is the longest essay in the "Aesthetics" section and has been revised for publication in *A Place*. It was originally delivered at an ethnopoetics conference in Milwaukee in 1975 and addresses an issue very much under debate in anthropological and poetic circles since that time. Snyder opens this essay by taking a clear-cut position on what politics means to him: "This politics is fundamentally concerned with the question of what occidental and industrial technological civilization is doing to the earth" (15). In explaining his understanding of ethnopoetics, Snyder defines the people whose poetics would be studied as those who practice an ecosystem culture rather than a biosphere culture, the latter being defined as the culture of centralized states that can wreck one ecosystem and "keep moving on" to exploit others (131). What has probably attracted the most attention to this essay in the past, however, is his promotion of the Gaia hypothesis popularized by James Lovelock, Sidney Epton, Lyn Margulis, and others. For *A Place*, though, he has deleted that portion of the original essay.

What may now be more prominent and controversial in this chapter is his claim that "all poetry is 'our' poetry. Diné poetry, people poetry, Maydy poetry, human being poetry" because "everyone on earth is a native of this planet" (141). It is important to realize here that Snyder is not attempting to efface ethnic identity or to erase ethnic differences, but rather to call on people to pay attention to each other's art for the lessons it can teach us all about how to live together on this one planet with the rest of the entities that comprise our local ecosystems. For Snyder, poetry is not property but a form of knowledge by design intended to be made public and to be handed down from one generation to the next. And, as his Earth Day speech indicated, those who would live in a particular place have an obligation to learn the lessons of those who have preceded them and those who live alongside of them.

In the 1977 version of this essay, Snyder concluded that the study of ethnopoetics would only make sense if it assisted contemporary peoples in reinhabiting the planet along the lines of the old ways. But in *A Place*, he has altered his conclusion in two ways. He emphasizes that "the study of ethnopoetics provides would-be poets and scholars with hundreds of models . . . that enrich our sense of human accomplishment without stealing anything from anybody" (147). He then significantly adds that such "would-be poets and scholars" will have incurred a debt for which they need to make some compensation: "The way to express gratitude and respect for these teachings of poetry, music, and song is to join in the work of helping your nearest endangered subsistence society in its struggle against the rape of land and culture" (147).

"The Incredible Survival of Coyote" is also reprinted from *The Old Ways*. Snyder emphasizes once again his indebtedness to Native American cultures for his own beliefs and practices. As he notes, "there is something to be learned from the Native American people about where we all are. It can't be learned from anybody else" (156). This essay also helps to explain the strong presence of Coyote throughout so much of his poetry. Snyder explains that "Coyote was interesting to me and my colleagues because he spoke to us of place, and became almost like a guardian, a protector spirit. The other feeling—our fascination with the trickster—has to come out of something inside us" (159). But how is it that a Native American trickster figure can come out of something inside of nonnative peoples? Snyder's answer is direct, even if contested: "When the Coyote figure comes into modern American poetry, it is not just for a sense of place. It is also an evocation of the worldwide myth, tale, and motif storehouse" (160). Such an answer turns back to his argument about all poetry being "people poetry" and his Jungian-based belief that all human beings participate in a collective unconscious with localized manifestations.

Snyder concludes the "Aesthetics" section with two relatively recent chapters, "Unnatural Writing" and "Language Goes Two Ways." For many readers interested in Snyder's work, the first of these two will be of particular interest because Snyder spells out his own definition of contemporary "nature writing." First, he rehearses the history of the nineteenth-century style of nature writing as well as natural history writing, and notes the denigration of it by the literary establishment—a situation that is only now being challenged and altered. He then argues that if an expanded definition is employed then it will be recognized that nature writing is an ancient human activity, one that was perhaps never so devalued as it has been in the modern period. In order to criticize this devaluation, Snyder returns to his view on language presented in *The Practice of the Wild* and also critiques deconstruction. For a "New Nature Poetics," Snyder wants his readers to think about "wild writing," with the idea that the natural world should instruct writers about their craft. In his conclusion, he provides nine points by which to define the "New Nature Poetics," which it is important to note cuts across genres and is not limited to a sense of nature writing as "nonfiction prose," which is a mainstay of most definitions of that term.

"Language Goes Two Ways" continues his concern with "wild writing" and language as a wild system. Snyder makes a case for "natural language," arguing that *"truly excellent writing"* is practiced by those who have gone through training in "Good Usage and Good Writing, and then loop back to the enjoyment and unencumbered playfulness of Natural Language" (177). Snyder upends common conceptions of language by emphasizing that language is "basically biological," that people have manifold interactions with the world "including human communication, both linguistic and nonlinguistic," that the orderliness of language is a reflection of order in the world, that humans need to let the world instruct them as fully as possible, and that "good writing is 'wild' language" (178-79). In what may come as a surprise to his readers, Snyder then demonstrates his main points by quoting the English Puritan poet John Milton and remarking that "discipline and freedom are not opposed to each other" (180).

III. Watersheds

Of the three sections of *A Place in Space*, "Watersheds" contains the highest percentage of material written in the 1990s, and, as a result, displays most prominently the development of Snyder's prose style from his writing in the early-1960s. As the section title suggests, it turns away from an emphasis on literature toward an emphasis on inhabitation based on the kinds of values and practices enunciated in the first two sections allied with a very explicit bioregional agenda.

"Reinhabitation" is the oldest of these eight chapters. Taken from *The Old Ways*, it recapitulates points made in "The Yogin and the Philosopher," with special emphasis on defining the term "inhabitation" and pointing toward the kinds of practices that need to be implemented to achieve reinhabitation, with some autobiography included along the way. Snyder emphasizes that "there are many people on the planet who are not 'inhabitants," and as a result "intellectuals haven't the least notion of what kind of sophisticated, attentive, creative intelligence it takes to 'grow food.' " The emphasis on food growing becomes immediately clear as Snyder points out the historically bioregional character of human life up until the relatively recent past (184). Snyder is quick to provide a response to the almost immediate complaint that being bioregionally based, locally attuned inhabitants means being parochial. As he notes about various indigenous peoples, "inhabitation does not mean 'not traveling.' "

Interestingly enough, Snyder sees the need to provide a Buddhist critique of the contemporary concept of the self, with its attendant beliefs in personal autonomy and the ideology of individualism, as part of persuading people of the benefits of reinhabitation: "we are all composite beings, not only physically but intellectually, whose sole individual identifying feature is a particular form or structure changing constantly in time. . . . Part of you is out there waiting to come into you, and another part of you is behind you, and the 'just this' of the ever-present moment holds all the transitory little selves in its mirror. . . . knowing who we are and where we are intimately linked" (189). As Jaeger notes, "re-inhabitation is a living *together* in place. . . . Individuals derive their significance from their place and from their interrelations to other living beings, both people, animals, and plants."[19]

To make it clear that his conception of reinhabitation is not simply a hippie-style, new-age imitation of hunter-gatherer lifestyles, Snyder ends "Reinhabitation" with a section titled "Summing Up." In it he refers to Wendell Berry's "The Unsettling of America," an essay that provided the title for a highly popular critique of American nomadism published by the Sierra Club in 1977. Snyder comments, "I saw old farmers in Kentucky last spring who belong in another century. They are inhabitants" who are under attack by the civilization that is also producing the people whỏ are trying to become reinhabitants: "Reinhabitory refers to the tiny number of persons who come out of the industrial societies . . . and then start to turn back to the land, back to place" (190).

"Reinhabitation" is followed by four smaller chapters with a variety of emphases. "The Porous World" combines two vignettes written for a local watershed newsletter. The other three chapters are based on presentations made at academic events. "The Forest in the Library" was presented at a dedication of a wing of the main library at the University of California, Davis, while "Exhortations for Baby Tigers" was a commencement address at Snyder's alma mater, Reed College. "Walt Whitman's Old 'New World' " was originally delivered at a conference on Walt Whitman in Madrid, Spain. Of these, only "The Porous World" is being reprinted in *The Gary Snyder Reader*.

"The Porous World" consists of two parts, "Crawling" and "Living in the Open." In these, Snyder emphasizes the value of a reinhabitory lifestyle that involves intimate, daily contact with a person's environment. In the first part, Snyder describes the exploration of a forested area near his home. There is so much understory growth that "it's not easy to walk upright through the late-twentieth-century midelevation Sierra forests" (192). As a result, the hiking party must abjure their hominid pride and get down on all fours from time to time to make any headway. Snyder's point is that only through a joyful exercise in humility can human beings either regain or maintain the proximity to nature that is necessary for us to understand and appreciate the biological diversity that is everyday and everywhere experiencing decimation. In the second part, Snyder writes about trying to live a porous life so that all of the creatures in the local ecosystem have a space in which to survive and thrive, which includes sharing the space that humans have carved out for themselves. Snyder's focus here is on how ex-urbanites are altering the marginal environments between the wild and the domesticated: "As people increasingly come to inhabit the edges and inholdings of forest lands, they have to think carefully about how they will alter this new-old habitat" (197). This second part is as practical and serious as the first part is playful and joyous while both are clearly written for a local audience, although with obvious implications for any potential reader.

"The Forest in the Library" speaks of the value of academic knowledge and its interrelationship with the wild land that the very library physically displaces. Eloquently written, Snyder emphasizes the library as a storehouse of information and wisdom, a type of "gathered nutrients" to be endlessly recycled "where the artists and writers go, to be cheerfully nibbled and passed about" (202, 203). With "Exhortations for Baby Tigers," a 1991 commencement address, Snyder begins by reminding the Reed College students of their location in place and time, bioregionally, historically, and politically. Snyder warns the students not to accept the glitter of the end-of-the-millennium American culture, warning them that "we need planetary diversity in nations as much as we need human diversity in society or biological diversity in the forest" (207). Befitting his title, Snyder speaks of the need to have courage and generosity to accomplish social change and to accept the idea that "it is the *world* that gives meaning to each of us" (210). Snyder closes with a variety of proverbs and quotations, with the one that I find most eloquent coming from Robinson Jeffers: " 'corruption / never has been compulsory' " (212).

Finally, "Walt Whitman's Old 'New World' " may have surprised his initial audience. Snyder has been influenced by Whitman and praised his poetry, but here he criticizes a specific Whitman text, "Democratic Vistas," because "we miss the presence of people of color, of Native Americans, of wilderness, or even the plain landscape" (215). For Snyder, Whitman in his desire to celebrate a post-war United States in the late-1860s glossed over some of the tragedies occurring to the native species, human and nonhuman alike. But if Whitman were alive in the 1990s, Snyder believes that "he might well give his heart to the new native and bioregional movement with as much foolish optimism as he gave to his own uniquely enlightened version of the nineteenth-century fantasy of progress" (218). Here Snyder explicitly calls for a rejection of any faith in the nation states of the previous two centuries and instead supports "the emergence of the natural nations of the future," which he believes will be bioregionally based (217).

"Coming into the Watershed," delivered and originally published in 1992, has already been reprinted numerous times and become the older Snyder's equivalent to "Four Changes." It has been widely recognized as a bioregionalist manifesto. It begins with a narrative about a trip Snyder and his son Gen took from Kitkitdizze down to the ocean north of Arcata, California, to Trinidad Head. Snyder notes the subtle yet significant changes in the landscape and observes that "these are the markers of the natural nations of our planet, and they establish real territories with real differences to which our economies and our clothing must adapt" (220). Snyder then meditates on the concept of "California," and concludes that it consists of at least six distinct regions. Snyder cries out against the fact that for most "Americans" "the land we all live on is simply taken for granted—and proper relation to it is not considered a part of 'citizenship' " (223).

Snyder calls for the breaking up of the United States "into seven or eight natural nations" (227). The basis for such "natural" divisions would be the "bioregion," which Snyder attempts to define in some detail based on the concept of a "watershed." And it becomes quite clear that Snyder's emphasis is not on "nation" but on "natural," and that he foresees the eventual end of "nationalism" as an ideology: "Bioregional concerns go beyond those of any ephemeral (and often brutal and dangerous) politically designated space" (232). And while this manifesto is in many ways quite utopian, Snyder also warns that any sense of community commitment arising from such a bioregional vision "cannot be ethnic or racist. . . . anyone of any race, language, religion, or origin is welcome, as long as they live well on the land" (234).

The conundrum of such a proposal, of course, would be the working out of disputes over the interpretation of what it means to "live well on the land," since many Americans think they are already doing just that even as they destroy its ecological viability with blinding rapidity. This essay also returns to the kind of self-assured tone that has appeared in earlier Snyder manifestos and which various reviewers and readers have criticized. Yet, it is precisely the tone one ought to expect in a manifesto; as for the utopian character of this bioregional document, it is clearly meant as a visionary statement on the basis of which more practical and pragmatic actions can be taken. As Snyder recognized quite clearly in a 1990 interview in which he was asked about the "actual possibilities of the bioregional movement,"

> The actual possibility in the real world at the moment is as visionary social theatre. We are doing not street theatre, but mountain, river, and field theatre. We present a larger vision than most people have been willing to permit themselves. Our project is theatrical and imaginative at the moment, but ultimately very pragmatic as it moves down the line. And, as arts always are, just a little bit ahead of its time.[20]

"The Rediscovery of Turtle Island" elaborates on and demonstrates some of the ideas expressed in "Coming into the Watershed." Snyder critiques various forms of instrumental reason and the tendencies of postmodern theorists to support such ways of thinking. He charges that "these positions still fail to come to grips with the question of how to deal with the pain and distress of real beings, plants and animals, as real as suffering humanity; and how to preserve natural variety" (239). Snyder reminds his audience that he is not talking about going back in some romantic way to an idealist image of the world as garden, but that there are ways of relating to the world that can be distinguished as destructive and restorative. "We are still laying the groundwork for a 'culture of nature,' " he believes, that will be based on "a noninstrumentalist view that extends intrinsic value to the nonhuman natural world" (240, 241). Snyder then turns to autobiography, as he has done in most of the chapters in this section of *A Place*, to elaborate on his conceptions of Turtle Island and bioregional inhabitation. He closes the essay with a Buddhist-based statement that "we are all indigenous to this planet" (250), suggesting that the fundamental problem is human awareness and consciousness, which must be clarified to address the problem of human behavior.

Snyder ends the "Watersheds" section and all of *A Place in Space* with "Kitkitdizze: A Node in the Net," a very local chapter on his own home. The biography of home begins with the focus on the individual, then widens to community and family. The way that Kitkitdizze is developed is discussed in parallel with the way that the community began to come together around bioregional/ watershed issues, particularly in relation to public lands management. That work led to various types of mapping of the region that contribute to the establishment of the Yuba Watershed Institute. The node in the net is the relationship of the singularity to the universality, or the local to the regional: "Lessons learned in the landscape apply to our own lands, too. So this is what my family and I are borrowing from the watershed work as our own Three-Hundred-Year Kitkitdizze Plan" (261). The responsibility for such long-range planning is necessitated, Snyder argues here, by the recognition that "my home base, Kitkitdizze, is but one tiny node in an evolving net of bioregional homesteads and camps" (262). This net can be understood quite fruitfully as a mandala, in which Snyder is referring both to the physical world-space of various homesteads and community-based organizations and to sacred space. Each of these homesteads and camps reflects back upon the others and each is participating in the practice of realization and mutually reinforcing one another. As

Robertson contends, "we can then consider a bioregion as a unit of space where, by locating ourselves there, we place ourselves in a physical, mental, and spiritual relationship with the whole. At the moment that relationship is felt, not just grasped with the intellect, the moment it is realized, not merely postulated, bioregional will become sacred space. Bioregion will be mandala in all of its meanings."[21]

Just as a mandala is meant to be used as an aid in study, *A Place in Space* is also meant as an aid for the study and practice of bioregional reinhabitation. Such reinhabitation needs to be, Snyder both argues and demonstrates, ethical and aesthetic, morally appropriate and beautiful, as is the volume itself. Snyder's tone changes throughout this volume, reflecting both his own artistic development and the varied purposes for which the chapters were composed. What many readers will find refreshing is the increasing infusion of personal experience alongside of highly informed explanations of diverse concepts of Buddhism, ecology, and bioregional living. *A Place* clearly has an internal cohesion in which many concepts and images are reiterated, refined, and clarified through examples and illustrations. Although much can be gained from reading the volume selectively for specific themes, the pattern of the whole deserves a reading from cover to cover.

10

The Calligraphy of Water on Rock
Mountains and Rivers Without End

Shortly after completing *Myths & Texts*, Snyder began work on another long poetic sequence, *Mountains and Rivers Without End*. It took quite a bit longer than the first sequence to complete: forty years instead of three years. Over those decades he published nearly two dozen individual pieces designated as parts of *Mountains and Rivers*. In 1965, he published *Six Sections from Mountains & Rivers Without End* and in 1970 published *Six Sections from Mountains and Rivers Without End Plus One*. Most of the criticism published up until 1996 was based on these limited samples and necessarily had more to say about individual sections than about the poem as a whole. Some of this criticism may no longer be particularly useful, given that the final sequence contains thirty-nine sections, some not previously published, others significantly revised, and some poems identified as part of the sequence-in-progress omitted from the final version, such as "Hymn to the Goddess San Francisco in Paradise," "Down," and "Greasy Boy."

Clearly, Snyder did not have a full understanding of the poem's overall design and structure when he began the sequence, nor did he ever claim such knowledge. As interviews and his own commentary at the end of the sequence, "The Making of *Mountains and Rivers Without End*," indicate, his conception of the poem changed over the years. The single most significant change came from his reading of Dōgen in translation in the late-1970s, particularly the "Mountains and Waters Sutra." His sense of the structural significance of Chinese scroll paintings also appears to have evolved during the composition process. What does seem to have developed early and remained a constant throughout was the importance of Japanese Nō drama as one of the organizing devices for the sequence.[1] As late as 1989, Snyder responded to a question about *Mountains and Rivers* with these words: "It is not easy to say where it stands. . . . I don't know what shape it will take until I lay it all out again."[2] A key element to the determination of that shape came with the writing of the final section, "Finding the Space in the Heart."[3] Once he had written it, he was then able to fill in the gaps, complete revisions of individual poems, and make the final decisions about what to include and exclude from the completed work.

Like *Myths & Texts*, *Mountains and Rivers* is a mythopoetic work, interweaving textual and mythical elements and substituting one for the other. As a result, some of the sections are as highly allusive and elliptical as ones in that first sequence. But there are other sections that are much more narrative and others more referentially descriptive, so that some of them are among the most accessible pieces of Snyder's poetry. Since Snyder has provided titles for all of the sections of the sequence, I will refer to them here as "poems," while retaining the term "sequence" for the poetry as a whole. The book also contains the prose explanation that I mentioned earlier, authorial notes on some of the poems, and a publication record.

The structure of the sequence has two fundamental bases. The first demonstrates a spatial arrangement that contains a temporal element, the Chinese scroll painting. Its spatial character as a type of painting is obvious; its temporal character is not immediately so, but has two main aspects. One, being a scroll it has to be viewed by means of the viewer unrolling it and viewing the scenery as if from a moving boat, and Snyder employs such moving-boat imagery in the first poem. Two, the scroll housed in the Cleveland Art Museum that Snyder depicts in the opening poem is typical of the genre in that at the end of the painting there are attached colophons written over several centuries, reminding viewers that this object has influenced people throughout time. Thus, a spatial form becomes temporal.

The second base demonstrates a temporal form with a spatial element: the classical Japanese Nō play, in particular the *Yamamba* by Seami. Nō has a tripartite structure, *jo-ha-kyū*, with the middle section often extended, so that *Mountains and Rivers* has a *jo-ha-ha-kyū* structure, as Eric Todd Smith notes.[4] It is useful to note their meaning in the literary form from which they originated, *renga*, a type of Japanese linked poetry. As Earl Miner explains, the one-hundred stanza linked poetry of *renga* used four sheets of paper: "The first front was considered a stately introduction (*jo*), and the fourth back a fast close (*kyū*). All the rest was the development or breakage section (*ha*), with fluctuation, agitation."[5] According to Bob Steuding, this Nō influence means that the sequence will be "basically constructed around the journey motif"; in the *Yamamba*, he continues, " 'hills,' meaning mountains, represent life; and one's travels in these hills, in terms of the Buddhist 'Wheel of Life,' are the endless round of reincarnation."[6] But even interpretation of the title is complicated by the fact that in Chinese the characters for "mountains" and "rivers" when placed together form the ideogram for "landscape." And "mountains and rivers" is also the name of the genre of Chinese landscape painting to which the scroll belongs.

Finally, it becomes important to distinguish the meaning of "journeying." In Nō, which is Buddhist influenced, and Buddhism itself, the journey is not the same as the Western quest. As Steuding indicates, it follows the "wheel" of life, reflecting a certain circularity. In Nō plays such as *Takasago*—alluded to in *Myths & Texts*—the traveler is not the protagonist but more an internal audience for " 'The Doer' (or the principal actor; *shite* in Japanese)," according to Katsunori Yamazato, "[who] is the spirit of one of the pine trees who in the shape of an old man engages in a conversation with a travelling priest." A Nō play, then, often revolves around "The Doer" telling his or her story and thereby gaining release as a ghost from this world, with the play ending quickly with a celebratory song or dance. In *Myths & Texts*, Snyder has the line "The Doer stamps his foot," with Yamazato commenting that such action is a "characteristic movement of the Doer."[7] And near the end of the opening poem of *Mountains and Rivers*, "Endless Streams and Mountains," Snyder has the line "stamp the foot, walk with it, clap! turn,"[8] which sounds like stage directions for a Nō performance. But here Snyder is describing himself viewing and ritualistically responding to the scroll painting in the Cleveland Art Museum, which raises the question of whether throughout the sequence Snyder will be the traveler or the spirit who must tell his story to gain release, or both. Both Anthony Hunt and Smith observe that the lines following the one I have quoted above suggest that the story to be told will not be Snyder's personal story but a story of the land-in-process, the travelers upon it, and the spirits within it.[9]

With the foregoing in mind about the structure of the sequence and the history of its germination and development, it seems to me inappropriate to label it an "epic" as several reviewers and critics have done. Clearly, the end was not foreseen from the beginning, nor does the action begin *in media res*, both of which are typical features of Western epic poems. Further, with Homer, Virgil, Dante, and Milton, all considered epic poets, their subject matter reflected a belief system held either by the dominant culture or a significant cultural minority, and the action takes place in a mythical past or theological locale. Whatever the setting, the action of the epic poem takes place in a location absolutely separated from the world of the contemporaneous audience and involves heroes of a stature no longer considered attainable by that same audience. None of these criteria applies to *Mountains and Rivers*.

While ancient epics sung the deeds of a period of nation-building or civilization-founding, they were not culture-building acts so much as culture-consolidating ones. They were not providing a vision for a new state but the positive perspective to take on the contemporaneous one through a revisionary depiction of the state's origins in an imagined or legendary golden age. Later epics served a similar purpose for religions. Snyder's poetic sequence, however, is visionary rather than revisionary in comparison. It casts doubt on the efficacy of a nation-state as an institution for the future. It also repeatedly refuses to maintain the epic distance, either spatially or temporally, that Mikhail Bakhtin rightly sees as the fundamental distinction between the epic and the novel.[10] *Mountains and Rivers*, however, must also be distinguished from Western definitions of the novel. The last lines of the final poem that loop back to link up with the opening poem serve to frame the sequence, not in terms of narrative structure or plot, but in terms of *spatiotemporality*. They provide an opening and a closure, just as any scroll painting must eventually run out of canvas, but they do not posit a beginning or an end to the processes depicted. The closing, with words depicting the ink brush lifting off the page, emphasizes that the writing of a poem occurs within the limited time frame of a compositional process contained within the span of a single human life embraced within the arc of an indefinitely unfurling universe: "The space goes on" (152).

The non-epic structure and its successful realization in *Mountains and Rivers Without End* arises from Snyder's Buddhist belief in mutual co-arising, or interbeing, on the one hand, and his deep bioregional commitment to reinhabitation, on the other. These beliefs enable him to overcome the modernist infatuation with spatiality posed in opposition to temporality in the high modernists' headlong flight from a universe perceived as contingent rather than fixed. They also enable him to overcome the even more specious postmodernist obsession with temporality as an overcoming of spatiality, as in the "post-" prefix fetish of so many of its intellectuals.

I prefer to think of this sequence as not only a great *non-epic*, but also an *un-American* one. As Snyder has demonstrated and voiced over the years, his allegiance is not held by the United States as a political entity. Snyder does not give his loyalty to a government laid over a territory, but rather to the "soil" upon which a way of living is developed. Further, he commits himself to a bioregional, reinhabitory culture-in-the-making. As an engaged artist as well as an environmental activist, Snyder contributes to this culture-in-the-making through his writing. Myth-making along these lines works as both cultural critique and cultural creation. *Mountains and Rivers Without End*, then, is produced in the service of a culture-building process, which will lead to political and social formations fundamentally different from the United States and what is called *American* culture today. As Snyder remarked in 1965, "We won't be white men a thousand years from now. We won't be white men fifty years from now. Our whole culture is going someplace else. The work of poetry is to capture those areas of the consciousness which belong to the American continent, the non-white world."[11] In regard to the designation "white men," Snyder clarifies his use of "White man" in "The Hump-backed Flute Player," by saying that it "is not a racial designation, but a name for a certain set of mind. When we all become born-again natives of Turtle Island, then the 'white man' will be gone" (161).

There is another reason for suggesting that this sequence is un-American: it draws on a territory far more extensive than the United States and does so in an effort to break away from an American frame of mind. Indeed, it is virtually globally inclusive. At the same time that it contains macroscopic references to tectonic plates and fault blocks that vastly exceed any illusion of geopolitical determinations, the sequence also contains microscopic references to places and species largely unaffected by the shifting fortunes of political borders, such as the Great Basin sagebrush and its various cousins in Japan, Europe, and China. There is also the global spatiality of the passage through various cities and cultures and the temporal territory of the sequence to consider. The latter swings from the barely imaginable two-million-year global water cycle to the highly immediate moment of "Now in the nineties desert night" (151). In between there are the temporal continuities of various cultures, ecosystems, and plant and animal species. Finally, there is the coalescence of spatiality and temporality in a spatiotemporality found particularly in the dream poems, such as "Journeys," and the mythic poems, such as "The Blue Sky." Such spatiotemporality is both utterly archaic and utterly postmodern in the awareness of the mutability of these two linear constructs—at least as they are typically envisioned in contemporary American thinking— for depicting processes as if they were either locations or events.

Such spatiotemporality is certainly at play in the second to the last poem of the sequence, "The Mountain Spirit," in which the geological temporality of some "three hundred million years" (145) is punctuated by the timeless queries of the mountain spirit, even as the spatiality is specifically designated as that of the Great Basin, which in turn is a landed space created by a vanished sea. At the same time, the spatiotemporality of the literary tradition of just this section extends from the Nō theater of Japan through a Hindu story of Krishna, Buddhist stories from India and China, to nineteenth-century Wovoka's Ghost Dance religion (see Snyder's notes to this poem on p. 162). The place, the time, and the culture that can integrate and philosophically and spiritually appreciate all of that will certainly not be recognized as *American* according to any definition of that term in use today.

From an aesthetic direction, Hunt also relates an important way of reading the sequence. In a detailed study of the landscape scroll tradition and the specific scroll at the Cleveland Art Museum, Hunt reports that one of the historians who has studied the scroll claims that its structure has a musical quality and that it can actually be scored. Hunt takes this argument and applies it to Snyder's sequence, tying it in with Snyder's discussion of how to sing a mountain range in one of his interviews. Hunt concludes that

> The sung rhythms of the Sierra may be heard just as surely as the periodicity of the ridges and gorges of the Cleveland scroll; the sections of *Mountains and Rivers Without End* also lead toward an observable rhythm. . . . However one chooses to measure the beat, it is clear that a cadence does exist and that it exists on several levels. . . . Any way one looks at it or hears it, rhythm is a "way in" to the poem.[12]

Reinforcing this point about the rhythm of the sequence, Snyder responded to an interviewer's question about having it finished by saying, "Now I have further work with it though—I'm learning how to read it aloud."[13]

The two epigraphs for the book, one from Milarepa and one from Dōgen require a few words. "The notion of Emptiness engenders Compassion," says Milarepa, while Dōgen paradoxically addresses how a "painted rice cake" can "satisfy hunger" (ix). Smith explains this epigraph by remarking that "in the Mahayana sense, emptiness, or *shunyata*, does not mean simply 'nothingness'. . . . Rather, emptiness means that everything in the universe is empty of individuality; everything is connected to everything else. When Milarepa says that emptiness 'engenders Compassion,' he means that if we understand that all things are related we will act compassionately in the world."[14] Leonard Scigaj, in turn, interprets the Dōgen epigraph by building on the work of Kazuaki Tanahashi, asserting,

The key is to recognize, as Tanahashi does in his seventh note, that "the enlightenment of various buddhas cannot be separated from verbal expressions of enlightenment." The labor of artistic creation through words is just another of the many ways that one can realize enlightenment. It is inseparable from everyday practice. "Painted hunger" is the creative effort to achieve in the practice of writing the state of emptiness, the śūnyatā of hunger, through which one achieves enlightenment.[15]

The special experience of artistic practice is fundamentally no different from the quotidian experience of daily-life practice. Each can contribute to an understanding of emptiness and from that understanding arises compassion, which requires a person to engage the world rather than deny or transcend it. *Mountains and Rivers*, then, is both a representation of an engagement with the world over several decades and an act of engagement as such.

Part I

The sequence is divided into four parts, containing nine, ten, ten, and ten poems respectively. "Endless Streams and Mountains" begins Part I of the sequence. Snyder provides the Chinese phrase for this title, *"Ch'i Shan Wu Chin,"* which connects this poem with the genre of painting that the scroll represents. The first line of the poem refers not to the painting, however, but to the viewer who must clear his or her mind in order to enter the space created by the painting. This announcement of the preparatory activity of the viewer also serves as the preparatory activity of the poet who is about to describe a visual art form by means of words. As will be demonstrated near poem's end with lines about the "brush" and "the moist black line" (9), writing and painting should not be understood as opposing media, since both are visual. In particular, Snyder invokes the imagery of calligraphy to link the two here and, later in the sequence in "Night Song of the Los Angeles Basin," to link it with signs that can be read in the phenomenal world, which includes nature and culture together. The significance of calligraphy as a form of writing developed in connection with the Chinese characters of both written Chinese and written Japanese should not be underestimated, as Snyder himself emphasizes its importance in "The Making of *Mountains and Rivers Without End*." The calligraphy he learned as an undergraduate at Reed led him later at Berkeley to "a class in sumi—East Asian brush painting. . . . Though I lacked talent, my practice with soot-black ink and brush tuned my eye for looking more closely at paintings" (153).

That attention to paintings led him to recognize in East Asian art the Buddhist sense of "a chaotic universe where everything is in place" (153), a point made quite explicitly in "Bubbs Creek Haircut." It also led him to a book that referred "to a hand scroll (*shou-chuan*) called *Mountains and Rivers Without End*" (153). Snyder further points out that he resolved to undertake the writing of this sequence as a result of a conversation with the Japanese artist Saburo Hasegawa, in the course of which Hasegawa "spoke of East Asian landscape painting as a meditative exercise" (154). Through linking painting and writing via calligraphy, Snyder links the viewing of the scroll, the writing of the sequence, and the reading of the sequence as meditative exercises.

Like the scroll painting itself, its description in the poem is intensely active and yet presented with the same emotional tranquility and feeling of unhurried timelessness that such paintings evoke. Although not highly allusive to material outside the sequence, "Endless Streams and Mountains" has its own type of complexity in terms of a series of phrases and words that allude to other parts of the sequence and that are highly symbolic philosophically. For instance, in the first stanza water permeates the scene not only in the streams and rivers but also in the air itself and forms a "web." That web-like quality can be seen both in the way that a word like "river" or "stream" describes not the separate molecules of water in a given place but their motion as a cohesive unit, and in the way that water molecules are linked in the two-million-year biospheric water cycle. In the second stanza, the "path" is described as actively moving through the landscape. It, therefore, is not an object but becomes an activity linking the trail it forms with the people who follow it. At the same time, its activeness invokes the symbolic meaning of the word in terms of the *Dao De Jing* and the concept of the "Way" in Buddhism. Similarly, the "stairsteps" of the fourth stanza are also depicted as moving across the land, just as the land itself is depicted as geologically active. Here the three men on land are depicted in a relationship with one another that parallels the prior depiction in the stanza of the relationship of "Big ranges," "little outcrops," "rocky uplifts" and other mountainous elements.

As the description of the painting draws to a close, Snyder emphasizes its boats and boatmen. One of them is "lost in thought," while "The watching boat has floated off the page" (6). A highly ambiguous remark invoking the spatiotemporal relationship of painting as a scroll, it also returns to the issue of perspective and the position of the viewer. Here the "boat" is both an object and an activity, especially since it does not have a fixed location. The viewer/reader is also an object and an activity without a fixed location. Everything is in motion without a fixed point of rest and yet everything is, at any given moment, in a particular place.

But the end of the painting is not the end of the scroll, which is not the end of the poem. Rather, the scroll continues and "tells a further tale" (7). This tale consists of the colophons in which various owners and viewers of the painting comment on the painting's meaning and beauty, beginning in 1205. Its history is traced until its arrival in Cleveland.

With that history presented, the poem issues an imperative: "Step back and gaze again at the land." This line contains a multiplicity of meanings. The addressee could be the poet-viewer of the scroll being instructed to change his perspective while viewing the painting. The addressee could be the reader of the poem, who is told to change his or her perspective on the foregoing description. The addressee could be the poet, the viewer, and the reader, all of whom are being told to shift their perspective from the artistic rendering of landscape to the phenomenal landscape itself. The poem emphasizes the first meaning through a return to the imagery depicting the landscape within the scroll. That, however, does not negate the other meanings that can be inferred, because the viewing of the painting is not a static moment, but an ongoing activity linking the aesthetic representation and the phenomenal representation of the world, both of which always contain perspective through the physiological particularities of human sight. Such perspective can be altered through a vision that involves all of the senses and all of the mind.

There is an additional element that must be noted about the final section of this poem and that is its ritualistic features. The line, "stamp the foot, walk with it, clap! turn" (8), connects the activity of the viewer with the features of the typical introductory character in Nō, who is responsible for guiding the audience through the drama. The poet, who is identified as an "I," who is implicitly Gary Snyder, a few lines later has established himself as a character in the drama rather than as its author. Through this device, Snyder is able to vary his presence, as Hunt notes, throughout the poem. Sometimes he is the authorial commentator, at other times a narrator repeating dialogue, at other times a character from whose point of view a poem in the sequence is related, and at other times a character in the action commented on from the nonidentical viewpoint of a narrator. Thus, as Snyder has commented in various places, a human being does not have a single, unified self, but many selves, and those selves are not even autonomous but are co-originating with the rest of the world.[16] And so, various Snyders can appear in the poem whereby the experiencer need not be identical to the mythographer.

"Endless Streams and Mountains" closes with a set of lines in italics, which will be repeated later in the two poems "The Mountain Spirit" and "Finding the Space in the Heart":

> Walking on walking,
>   under foot   earth turns.
>
> Streams and mountains never stay the same. (9)

In his "Mountains and Waters Sutra," Dōgen speaks of mountains and waters walking, a concept Snyder discusses at some length in "Blue Mountains Constantly Walking" in *The Practice of the Wild*. Here, then, we can interpret the first phrase as referring to human beings walking on the land that is itself always in motion. The second line reminds readers that the earth is constantly turning even when we are standing still, so that we are, in fact, never standing still. The representations of reality in common language tend to resist this sense of continuous motion through space, as in the phrase, "the sun rises," which it does not. Rather the earth rotates us toward and away from the sun, which everyone knows but conveniently forgets in the ongoing effort to imagine the possibility of stasis. But *"walking"* is not merely motion here; journeys are not merely travel; rather, as the final line indicates, *"walking"* is a process of continuous change—the meaning of the verb *naturing* if such a verb could exist in American English—and, in spiritual terms, the opportunity for ongoing transformation. *"Walking on walking,"* then, may be read back into the opening line of the poem, "Clearing the mind." As other poems in the sequence will clarify, walking can be one form of meditation, one type of ritual—as in "circumambulation"—one part of the spiritual path toward enlightenment.

It is not surprising with this conclusion to "Endless Streams and Mountains" to find the word "walking" in the opening line of the next poem, "Old Bones" (10), one of the poems in the last group to be written for the sequence. A ritual poem, "Old Bones" pays homage to the spirits of the animals and people who have preceded contemporary humankind; it also reflects the Nō structure of the sequence. The poem also emphasizes a mountainous terrain, which will be a major scene of confrontation in "The Mountain Spirit," one of the closing poems of the sequence.

"Night Highway Ninety-Nine" was written in Japan in 1961 and originally published in 1962. It has undergone some revision since its appearance in *Six Plus One*. According to a letter to Philip Whalen, Snyder views it at his *"sashiuta*, travelling song," an opening component of the traditional Nō play.[17] This tradition of the "traveling song" clarifies the connection between hitchhiking and certain kinds of Buddhist practice. A close-to-home example for Snyder of such practice is the monk named in the Portland section, Sokei-an Sasaki. He was a Japanese Zen master who wandered the Pacific Northwest in the early-1900s and who was instrumental in the establishment of the First Zen Institute of America.[18] Even though "Night Highway" is structured according to the sequence of the towns the poet passes through, it actually weaves together experiences from several different years out of chronological order. And when Snyder names "the Goodwill" in the third part of the poem, it becomes evident that all of these exchanges bear the imprint of "Bubbs Creek Haircut," which was published in the poetry magazine *Origin* the year before "Night Highway" appeared, although it is placed a little later in this volume. Similarly, allusions to Buddhism, such as the story of buttermilk in Portland, and other religious practices are interlaced throughout the sections. In particular, the notion of breaking through the illusion of permanence and the appearance of the solidity of things is emphasized, as when the narrator remarks in part five: "The road that's followed goes forever; / In half a minute crossed and left behind" (21). These lines refer back to the prose epigraph by Lew Welch. They also link up with Snyder's poem in *No Nature*, "Off the Trail" (369-70).

In "Night Highway" these lines about "The road that's followed" are initially read in relation to the Welch epigraph and the Beat/ dharma-bum rejection of mainstream American culture, but they can also be read in relation to the dangers of religious dogma and the empty, mechanical practice of rituals—one of Snyder's initial complaints about Buddhism in Japan in the mid-1950s, as noted by Katsunori Yamazato and Timothy Gray.[19] This concern becomes evident in the conclusion that the idea of the highway itself, of the fixity of "99" as a road that can be infinitely followed, is an illusion of permanence. Upon reaching San Francisco, the narrator of the poem realizes that his adventures are of significance only to himself. As a traveling song, it signals the positive character of "walking" and the potential insights that might be derived as a consequence, but the ending suggests a recognition that practice in realization does not depend on traveling, or on staying put, but on "clearing the mind" of the illusion that one's way is *the* way.

"Three Worlds, Three Realms, Six Roads" (25-30), which has not previously been collected, was first published in *Poetry* in 1966 as six separate poems, although Snyder already considered them a single part of *Mountains and Rivers*. Snyder explained to Katherine McNeil that at that time he was interested in "a kind of oblique looking. Each one of those poems is entirely about a place; it doesn't say anything about the individual except by implication, what an individual can do there; and it's by the arrangement of the choices that some picture of a personality and a character emerges."[20] This kind of impersonality connects well with the lack of a self-described narrator in "Endless Streams and Mountains" and a kind of positing of anonymity of the traveler, whose *true self* is not something autonomously or uniquely given at birth, whether genetically or through the provision of a soul; rather, the traveler becomes someone through the experience of practice. As with the choices made in each of the parts of the poem, the person is composed of a series of accidentals, if you will—a mixture of genetic inheritance, circumstances of an early childhood environment, the fortunes and misfortunes of adult circumstance, and so on. The person must then make of them what he or she can. What one can do in Seattle is not the same as what one can do in Portland, or aboard ship, or in Kyoto, nor would two different people do exactly the same things in each place. No place is presented here as intrinsically superior but only different, so that the speaker can get lost in San Francisco just as well as he can get lost in the mountains outside of Kyoto. But the final three lines suggest a spiritual lesson to be learned in all of these circumstances: "Throwing away the things you'll never need / Stripping down / Going home" (30).

The two longer poems, "Night Highway" and "Three Worlds," are followed by the very short, eight-line poem "Jackrabbit" (31), originally published in 1988. This poem complements "Old Bones," as these two short poems frame the longer ones. "Old Bones" pays homage to ancient ghosts and "Jackrabbit" pays homage to animal spirit guides, with both of them utilizing the supernatural aspects common to Nō. While "Three Worlds" might be defined as a what-you-know poem, "Jackrabbit" is a what-you-don't-know poem. Here, the speaker is once more on the road and directly addresses a jackrabbit he spies on the roadside with humility, reverence, and awe. He credits the animal with having greater knowledge of himself—and by implication the human realm—than he has of the rabbit and the natural world. What the speaker signals, however, by his tone and politeness is his openness to being educated by whatever guides the world will provide.

"Jackrabbit" is followed by two poems that were part of the original *Six Sections* volume. "The Elwha River" is a dream-vision prose poem, the only one totally blocked out in paragraphs rather than stanzas. It has been significantly revised from its original version, with the entire second section, written six years after the first, having been deleted. In addition, Snyder has efficaciously changed the words of the "teacher" in the poem. The complex interconnections of dreams, memories, and memories-within-dreams in this poem suggest that both dreams and recollections are prone to error in relation to the natural world. But at the same time both may also be accurate in establishing a balanced human relationship with that natural world, regardless of the *facts*. As with the interrelationship of "myths" and "texts" in Snyder's first sequence, this poem establishes that readers should treat as equally informative the mythic and realistic events portrayed throughout the sequence.

In "Bubbs Creek Haircut" (33-38), Snyder begins with a first-person autobiographical narrator preparing for a journey. What is interesting to note about the placement of this poem is that it suggests that all nine poems of the first part of *Mountains and Rivers* may comprise a preparation for departure in the Nō tradition. Snyder's speaker gets a haircut before entering the mountains, and it turns out that the barber has been where this speaker intends to go. In the second stanza, reality unravels a bit in the Goodwill store. Discarded items are described as having lives of their own and the proprietor is referred to as "The Master of the limbo drag-legged," invoking the mythic image of a limping god to be found in the Western tradition. Snyder establishes a mood of expectancy, indicating that for the speaker in the poem this journey represents a crucial quest, an ascetic experience that is supposed to produce spiritual results.

The next few stanzas begin an actual journey and initiate a process of interweaving memories, presenting events in a collapsing of time and space. Attachments are being dropped away in the same way that the speaker sheds his hair; the implication that the haircut was a preparatory ritual is reinforced here, its being akin to the shaving of Buddhist acolytes' heads in imitation of the Guatama Buddha. And that story suggests something to the reader about the barber, since it was not a man but the Hindu god Vissakamma who shaved the Buddha.[21] Quickly Snyder brings readers to a vastly different land from the one he has left, a land of mountains and waters, rocks and ice. He warns readers that they have reached a world of spirits in which the laws of the city no longer apply and in which visions may be experienced. The lake and its flowing waters in the mountains depicted in this stanza symbolize the concept of the universal womb, network of energy, through which all material entities pass.

But in order to reach this lake, the speaker has had to involve himself in a series of human and economic exchanges, embodiments of the abstract concept of "goodwill." The experiences with his friends "Locke" [McCorkle] and "A.G."[Allen Ginsberg] are divided by the memory of a failed haircut. The reality of segregation related in this haircut story indicates that goodwill is not yet universal. His final exchange involves being drafted to carry messages between trail-crew camps.

The observation of the "deva world" mountain lake—i.e., a place filled with good spirits—leads the narrator into a strange meditation, first referring to the Goodwill proprietor as "King of Hell" and then moving into a celebration of the dance of Parvati, who is both the consort of the Hindu god Shiva and an earth goddess figure.[22]

Hunt views the entrance of Parvati as a moment of revelation in which Snyder realizes that his path to enlightenment will go not by the route of being a world-renouncing mountain ascetic—perhaps in the likeness of Han-shan—but by the route of Tantra and immersion in the physicality of the world.[23] This route requires him to recognize the total interpenetration of all of nature. Thus at the end of his ecstatic meditation, he is able to see the equivalence of objects in the Goodwill basement and the wild nature around him in the mountains: "a room of empty sun of peaks and ridges / a universe of junk, all left alone" (36). The final phrase here indicates acceptance of a viewpoint that recognizes that all is interconnected and simultaneously unique, and yet not conforming to any humanly conceived organizing principle—"a chaotic universe where everything is in place" (153).

The next section returns to everyday memories that reiterate the theme of goodwill. But all this remembering ends with a revealing parenthesis: "(on Whitney hair on end / hail stinging bare legs in the blast of wind / but yodel off the summit echoes clean)" (37-38). One not only can have visions in the mountains but also can experience the purification that comes from the recognition of a deep spiritual lesson.

The poem then moves to a conclusion revealing that the haircut which began the poem also happened long ago, that "all this" recounted in the poem "comes after," including the memory of the haircut in which the poet recognizes its deeper significance. And that significance is contained in the return to "the double mirror waver" of the barbershop's mirrors. Snyder informed Ekbert Faas, when explaining "Bubbs Creek Haircut," that "multiple reflections in multiple mirrors, that's what the universe is like."[24] These mirrors are not Snyder's own trope but one that arises from a well-known story about the Chinese master Fa-Tsang trying to explain the Hua-Yen Buddhist doctrine of interpenetration to the Empress Wu Tse-Tien. In that story he designs a totally mirrored room to display infinite reflections of the Buddha-figure set in its middle.[25] In like manner, Snyder has designed a totally mirrored poem in which the mirrors that begin and end the poem reflect, through the medium of the poet's memories, the interpenetration of events across space and time.

In *Six Sections Plus One*, Snyder provides the date for the poem's composition as "20.IV.60." It was written, then, not when the poet was immersed in the Sierras but when he was immersed in *sanzen*, formal Buddhist meditation, in Kyoto. What is perhaps most interesting is that it records Snyder's poetic depiction of a moment of sudden enlightenment about a crucial Buddhist teaching a few months before he had just such an experience in his own life, June 11 of that year. He wrote to Yamazato: "I was shelving books in the stacks of the Ryosen-an library, and while pushing a book into its place suddenly and totally saw myself together with all other entities of the universe, each totally 'in place' and beautifully so."[26] "Bubbs Creek Haircut," based upon the poet's own experiences in the American West and, apparently, premonitions of his experiences in Japan, opens up to the reader a new way of perceiving the world that breaks through physical appearances and rationalist constructs, suggesting a set of relationships by which that world works that are different from the ones dominant in American culture. At the same time, the discrepancy between Snyder's depiction of a *kensho*, a sudden moment of spiritual recognition, as happening in the mountains and its actual occurrence in a library, heightens his point made earlier with "Night Highway" that practice in realization can occur anywhere and that, as remarked in "Off the Trail," "no place is more than another" (*No Nature*, 369).[27]

Snyder follows the oldest poem of the sequence with one of the newest, "Boat of a Million years." A brief, lyrical poem set in the Red Sea, it takes the reader from one realm of Snyder's formative experiences, the mountains, to another, the ocean. The poem's conclusion reiterates a previously established point: human beings are not in control of their own destiny; and while the world may be ruled by chance or by cosmic design it certainly is not ruled by human design. Snyder makes this point by undercutting a claim made by the Catholic philosopher Teilhard de Chardin. While the ship on which he works may be plotting its own course, just as humans have done in the Red Sea since at least the days of the ancient Egyptians, such plotting has little to do with where humans end up or how the world works out its own direction, for "We are led by dolphins toward morning" (39).

The final poem of the first part of *Mountains and Rivers*, "The Blue Sky" (40-44), is probably the most difficult and highly allusive of these first nine. In speaking with McNeil, Snyder provided a helpful comment: "That poem is based on the sutra of the Buddha of healing, Bhaishajyaguru, otherwise known as Yakushi. . . . It's the jump from the healing impulse in Buddhism to a North American shamanistic healing that I'm really trying to get across."[28] It is precisely this mixture of Buddhism and Shamanism that is key for appreciating "The Blue Sky." As Beongchen Yu explains it, in this poem Snyder combines both Hsuan Tsang and Koko'pilau (a.k.a. Kokop'ele, Kokopele) "in the figure of 'Old Man Medicine Buddha,' the archetypal healer, and thereby justifies his personal convictions about the poet's function as a shaman."[29] Several critics have initiated explications of this poem.[30] One, Julia Martin, makes an extremely helpful observation: "The eye is shifted from one fragment to the next, and yet the poem is about making 'whole'? Yes! The poem must foreground this process, because to conceive of 'wholeness' outside the continual play of difference and interdependence, to desire the attainment of a transcendent Absolute . . . is, according to the teaching of sunyata [emptiness], to remain bound by that desire."[31]

"The Blue Sky" ends Part I with paradoxical images. One, "The Blue Sky / is the land" and, two, that land is "where the eagle that flies out of sight // flies." When Snyder gets to his description of the Great Basin at the end of the sequence, he exclaims that "the ground is the sky / the sky is the ground / no place between" (151). As Martin observes of "The Blue Sky," "the blueness of the sky . . . is after all the color not, in the ordinary sense, of 'something' but of vast spaciousness. In Native American tradition, the eagle that flies so high that it is out of sight is a symbol of healing. Here it becomes an image of all things which, gone beyond into blueness, are devoid of essence." And, further, "yet the eagle continues to fly: form is emptiness, but emptiness is also form. The other side of sunyata is tathata, thusness, suchness, which means that the eagle is real, sufficient as it is. The awareness of this is freedom from desire."[32] Healing produces a freedom from desires for illusory achievements and material things, such that the traveler of the sequence—having cleared the mind, greeted the various spirits, opened himself to both exterior phenomena and interior phenomena (as in dreams), included encounters with both mountains and waters as potentially spiritually transformative—

is now prepared for his journey through the rest of *Mountains and Rivers*.

Part II

Part II begins with "The Market" (47-51), which is designed to look like "Night Highway," with the names of cities in the right-hand margin to identify the sections of the poems. It records a series of Snyder's reflections made during an experience in India, which includes earlier experiences from the U.S., the boat trip from Japan to India, and a side trip to Nepal. It reflects another act of traveling, appropriately opening the *ha* section of the sequence, which consists of both Parts II and III. In contrast to "Bubbs Creek Haircut," it expresses doubt about the pervasiveness of "goodwill" in the world and the degree to which commodity fetishism obscures human recognition of the interdependence and co-creativity of the universe. As Snyder indicated to Faas, the reader can only go so far with this poem because it raises a question that Snyder will have to answer later in the sequence: "When you break your customary set of equivalences, then where do you go?"[33] The river Ganges mentioned at the end of the poem and the cities identified in the margin define the poem's settings as being urban centers in mountain and river locations. But Snyder seems more concerned with the way that economics erodes human community and the way that commercial exchange seems to flow unobstructed and unabated through even the most traditional cultures.

The demonic elements of "The Market" prepare the way through tone and imagery for "Journeys" (52-56), which works a bit like "The Elwha River" in that it utilizes the interpenetration of dream imagery and historical memory. It takes the reader through several worlds both to break down normal channels of rational thought and to tap into the unconscious through archetypes and myths. The first part is another dream sequence in which a bird becomes a woman who then leads the first-person narrator through a subterranean journey. Her gift of a slice of apple awakens him, an obvious parody of the Adam and Eve myth. The second and third parts, with no apparent indication of being dreams, depict the narrator and others as traveling in a strange land. As primitive hunters they reach a plateau where they flee the sun in awe of its power while shooting arrows at it.

The next two parts seem to be individual recollections of real events, but their relationship to the primitive hunter story remains unclear. The sixth part heightens whatever confusion the reader may have because it is a journey into the mountains that ends "now I have come to the LOWLANDS" (54). The last three parts of the poem are crucial to unraveling its mysteries and the elliptical relationships among its preceding parts. The seventh part returns to the dream format, depicting a scatological urban nightmare. The eighth part, in contrast, takes place in the quotidian world, portraying a bus ride. But by now the distinction between dream narratives and this travel narrative has blurred—all are journeys, with the physical and the psychic interpenetrating. In the final section, the narrator is traveling again with a friend. It begins: "We were following a long river into the mountains" (55). The spiritual components presented in "Bubbs Creek Haircut" are also here: water as energy, mountains as form, and friendship as human interaction. The last section starts out like the preceding travel narrative, but then:

> Ko grabbed me and pulled me over the cliff—
> both of us falling. I hit and I was dead. I saw
> my body for a while, then it was gone.
> Ko was there too. We were at the bottom of the gorge.
> We started drifting up the canyon, "This is the
> way to the back country." (55-56)

As in "Bubbs Creek Haircut," a moment of *kensho* is depicted here. The narrator has shed his ego and with it his sense of body as separate from the rest of the world. Smith in *Reading* reveals that "Ko-san" was a nickname for Snyder's teacher at Daitoku-ji. Given Snyder's interests in etymology, he may also use "Ko" for his companion's name since it is the Indo-European root for "together"; and given "The Blue Sky," it may also be an abbreviation of Kokop'ele. Snyder may very well also be rehearsing a little myth of the Mahā Prajña Pāramitā Hrdaya Sūtra (or Heart Sutra), which espouses the doctrine that form equals emptiness.[34] What is a canyon but an empty form, defined by the space between cliffs? What is emptiness but the experience of relationship? The answer to these questions provides the possibility for a great sense of liberation. As Robert Aitken helpfully remarks, *"At the very cliff-edge of birth and death, you find the Great Freedom. . . .* The biggest joke in the universe is that there is nothing to depend upon. When you see that joke, then you are free to get up when the alarm clock goes off."[35]

Two of the very significant and late additions to *Mountains and Rivers* are the two urban-based poems devoted to Los Angeles and New York. The first of these, "Night Song of the Los Angeles Basin," appears in the second part and the other in the third part. The poems are quite distinct in emphasis, yet both attempt to present positive lessons about these two grand megalopolises on opposite shores. "Night Song" (62-64) opens with "Owl" but close at hand is the "calligraphy of cars," which leads to a stanza recognizing that the freeway system is the defining characteristic of this city. As this meditation gains momentum, mythic images begin to appear. But the speaker quickly turns away from the internal-combustion-engine-based trails to those of the animals who are survivors, such as the vole and the mouse, pocket gopher and marmot. These are the creatures that catch Snyder's attention in contradistinction to the "drivers" who remain anonymous and indistinguishable in their automobiles. All of these animals, of course, need water to survive, and thus one of the key elements of the sequence enters the poem as a ghost. For those unfamiliar with Los Angeles, Snyder's remark that the L.A. river "never was there" may be confusing. He refers here to the fact that the entire "river" has been paved to become a concrete channel, much of which is bone dry except for a thin band of water running down its center.

As he does in the New York poem, in "Night Song" Snyder depicts the wealthy of the city as a particular kind of animal. Here they are koi fish fighting over crumbs in the way that such fish do in dirty, overstocked ponds usually for tourist display. The poem closes reinvoking the "Owl" as someone who will outlast the koi. But before this final stanza, Snyder sets off a line by itself, "will long be remembered," which refers to the freeways as if they already are something existing in the past. The city here is represented as highly transient and built upon the unsteady pilings of speculative capital at the eventual mercy of the water cycle. Snyder alludes extremely obliquely in this poem to the history of water plans in southern California, which have been essential for its urban sprawl. (In *The Fudo Trilogy*, Snyder published "The California Water Plan," a poem that many readers thought would be part of *Mountains and Rivers*.) Water is continuously drained off from distant places to keep Los Angeles from returning to the conditions of its parched past. In this poem Snyder seems to view Los Angeles as a chimera, an illusion that traps people in the kind of longing that the Buddha saw as breeding dissatisfaction and perpetual longing. This condition, called *duhkha*, is brought about by the *skandhas* of human thought, through which "we are propelled into discursive thought, projection, and an unfulfilling cycle of mind-states referred to as the Six Realms."[36] The animals that populate the poem, however, provide an alternative vision of what is *really* there.

"The Flowing" (68-72), originally published in 1974 and only slightly revised, links together descriptions of a series of rivers in different parts of the world to depict a sense of all rivers as a single form of the virtually endless flowing of the water cycle. The opening section, "Headwaters," describes the spring that constitutes the beginning of the Kamo River near Kyoto. Snyder singles out this river because its origin is enshrined with a statue of Fudō-myō-ō, which he here images in the role of a world transformer: "Lord of the Headwaters, making / Rocks of water, / Water out of rocks." This mythic imagery is also quite literal in that the spring that initiates the Kamo emerges from a cliff.

The second section, "Riverbed," links the Kamo with the Yakima River in Washington State and the Columbia River system. Here Snyder's attention focuses on human and animal activity in the form of salmon migrating upstream and Native peoples catching them, reminding the reader of the water-as-life image that is obliquely introduced in "Night Song of the Los Angeles Basin." The "Falls" section takes readers to Yosemite where Snyder describes the life of the stream that creates the falls all the way back to its headwaters originating in snowmelt "rocked between granite ribs." The water here may be seen as a metaphor for the activities of a countercultural wanderer who works his or her way through the contemporary cultural landscapes and "then soars off ledges." The "water cycle" explicitly invoked in this section emphasizes the inexorable inevitability of process and change. Snyder then brings the mountains more forcefully into the poem through attention to geological activity, which parallels, although more slowly, the activity of the water. The final section, "Rivermouth," becomes a song of praise, with both the river's mouth and the poet's mouth part of a singular interaction. Even as the water rushes into the poet's open mouth, his praise rushes out. The poem ends in a sexually ecstatic moment, one in which Snyder identifies the speaker as explicitly a maker of poems to reinforce both the ritualistic character of the poem itself as a song of praise and the speaker's assuming the responsibility of responding to nature's inspiration.

Following "The Flowing," "The Black-tailed Hare" (73-74) reiterates the relationship of mountains and waters to each other, but also brings in the role of plant life in helping to generate the headwaters of the streams and rivers that bring water down from the unlivable heights of mountains to the lower altitudes of human inhabitation. This poem, originally titled "The Rabbit" when first published in 1968, complements "Jackrabbit" and "The Blue Sky." It also contains language reminiscent of John Muir's descriptions of California mountains, particularly their glaciers and snow banners. The hare in this poem is an animal spirit-guide teaching the narrator about the sources of potable water. His point that "the / mountains and juniper / do it for us" functions on several levels. One, all life on the planet is interconnected, enabling each other to come into being. Two, human and other animal life are dependent on the same sources for nutrients and so what one species does to the water supply affects other species. Three, the "juniper" have a particular role to play because forests are a factor in the amounts of precipitation that fall in various locations. The junipers are also a factor in the gradual erosion of the mountains by water and by the actions of the trees themselves.

The last poem of the second section of *Mountains and Rivers* is "The Hump-backed Flute Player" (79-82), one of the major poems of the sequence. That the Heart sutra, which Julia Martin discusses in relation to "The Blue Sky," is important to *Mountains and Rivers* is made explicit in "The Hump-backed Flute Player." In this poem, Snyder identifies two crucial figures for his mythopoesis: Hsuan Tsang, the Chinese wandering Buddhist who brought the Heart sutra and others from India to China in the seventh century A.D.; and, Kokop'ele, the Hopi kachina humpbacked flute player who carried seeds and warmed the air with his flute in the spring. These two also serve through their similarities to link Buddhism and Shamanism, a connection Smith emphasizes in *Reading Gary Snyder's* Mountains and Rivers Without End.

Hunt, in his pre-completed sequence reading of this poem, emphasizes the swirling, arcing shape of the Kokop'ele petroglyph that adorns the first page of the poem in *Mountains and Rivers* and has been used by Snyder in the past. He concludes that the key image for this poem is one of emptiness, suggested by a variety of associations and even, I would add, by the spatial arrangement of the fourth line of the poem: "his hump   a pack." Hunt goes on to argue that "it is possible to see the entire poem as Snyder's informal version of a formal Vajrayana ritual known as 'meditating on a deity.'"[37] In line with this argument, Hunt develops a significant discussion about the rhythm and sound of this particular poem, similar to his discussion of the musical qualities of "Endless Streams and Mountains." In addition, Hunt notes that the poem emphasizes vision, as both seeing and envisioning, in part through such characters as Kokop'ele, Hsuan Tsang, and Wovoka. And the poem links these visionaries with the traveler through the sequence in terms of their packs—or in Wovoka's case his hat—and the pack carried by the hitchhiking narrator of "Night Highway."[38] Kokop'ele and Wovoka enable Snyder to link the philosophical and spiritual issues of Buddhism with the Great Basin, the former a Hopi figure and the latter a Piute visionary. At the end of the poem Snyder also introduces "Bristlecone Pine" and "Pinyon Pine" as characters who represent the oldest and the youngest of trees in the mountains edging the Great Basin. Such trees echo the use of tree-spirit characters in Nō and also may represent a metaphor for the Indian tribes, who are the oldest human inhabitants, and Snyder and other "born-again" native Americans, who are the youngest.

Beyond these figures, Snyder also introduces Tārā, who, he remarks in "The Making of *Mountains and Rivers Without End*," is a central figure in the entire sequence. Early in his thinking about the composition of the sequence while in Kyoto, he claims that "I came to see the yogic implications of 'mountains' and 'rivers' as the play between the tough spirit of willed self-discipline and the generous and loving spirit of concern for all beings: a dyad presented in Buddhist iconography as the wisdom-sword-wielding Manjushri, embodying transcendent insight, and his partner, Tārā, the embodiment of compassion, holding a lotus or a vase" (155). Tārā, then, might be understood to balance out the "Mountain Spirit," with both of them the focus of poems in the final part of the sequence. And yet, Snyder concludes his remarks about the making of the sequence by noting that he thinks of it "as a sort of sūtra—an extended poetic, philosophic, and mythic narrative of the female Buddha Tārā" (158). Indeed, Snyder ends the sequence emphasizing compassion, suggesting that wisdom cannot be such without activation through compassion, while compassion—as in his own life—can provide the starting point for gaining wisdom.

Part III

This section of the sequence opens with "The Circumambulation of Mt. Tamalpais" (85-89), which actually records a ritualistic, meditative walk that Snyder and his cohorts, Philip Whalen and Allen Ginsberg, made in 1965. Tamalpais was well-known to Snyder by then, as David Robertson relates in *Real Matter*.[39] As recorded in the poem, these three are engaging in a particular kind of ritual known as *pradakshina*, "the religious rite of circling clockwise a sacred object."[40] Snyder had learned about such rituals while in Japan, especially as a result of his contact with the mountain-dwelling Yamabushi Buddhist. Robertson, as a result of an interview with Whalen and Snyder together, concludes that they "wanted to make an opening for Buddhism in American culture."[41] Certainly they were a part of a significant increase in Buddhist practice in the United States that occurred in the 1960s and has continued to develop since then, but such interest would have expanded with or without this particular ritual. What their circumambulation did accomplish, however, was to enshrine Mt. Tamalpais as a ritualistic site not only for Buddhists but also for others who wanted to make a gesture of their commitment to wild nature in America. Robertson points out that circumambulations of the mountain became common after the popularization of their walk and remain so today.[42] As far as the sequence is concerned, it would seem that "Circumambulation" functions in the second part of the body of the sequence in much the same way that "Flowing" does in the first part. Each is a ritualistic celebration of one of the main elements of the poem, mountains and waters, and places the narrator in each case in the position of the traveler who is seeking spiritual purification. The difference between the two, however, is significant in that in "Circumambulation" the traveler is explicitly assuming responsibility for the ongoing protection and veneration of the land.

"The Circumambulation of Mt. Tamalpais" is followed by "The Canyon Wren" (90-91), a poem that records what there is to lose when wild nature is not revered and protected. It was originally published in *Axe Handles* (see its discussion in relation to that volume in chapter 7). The poem not only depicts the river's rapids as an aspect of wild nature that has been lost to human engineering, but also depicts the wren's song as nature's own ritual and celebration. When "The Canyon Wren" closes with the lines, "These songs that are here and gone, / here and gone / to purify our ears," the reader can think not only of that particular song and that particular river, and not only of this particular poem and this particular sequence, but also the doctrine of emptiness and the concept of impermanence that permeates the sequence. And yet, what is impermanent here? If the closing stanza is read back into the stanza that quotes Dōgen's remark, "mountains flow / water is the palace of the dragon / it does not flow away," then readers might conclude that it is the dam, which submerges the rapids, that will prove to be far more impermanent than the river itself. Readers might also conclude that while one particular set of rapids may disappear—after all geological and hydrological activity themselves will cause such disappearances even without human intervention—there is no possibility of an end to rapids in the world, either literally or metaphorically. Such is not an argument against environmental activism or defense of wild nature, but a recognition that not all defensive actions will be successful and that which is lost can be recorded to educate oneself and to educate others about the entire spinning world.

In "Arctic Midnight Twilight Cool North Breeze With Low Clouds Green Mountain Slopes, White Mountain Sheep" (92-95), Snyder opens the poem by defining it as a "song," which can be interpreted as a poem of praise. Given that it immediately follows "The Canyon Wren," readers will likely recall the closing lines of that poem emphasizing that songs of nature can "purify our ears." As the canyon wren lives in its place, so too do the Dall sheep who are the subject of the poem. These hardy arctic animals live in a land of mountains and waters, while the altitude of their abode makes it also seem that they live poised "half in the sky" and half on the earth. As a result, within this poem they become liminal creatures, not only of the phenomenal world of sky and ground, but also of the natural and the spiritual realms.

Snyder moves through the poem switching between these realms, combining description of the behavior of the sheep as physical beings and meditations on the metaphysical implications of their lives and their deaths as "Vajra sheep"—i.e., sheep associated with Vajrayana, or Diamond Vehicle, Buddhism. These sheep become spiritual teachers because the precariousness and hardiness of their lives teach the meditating poet about both "impermanence" and "shapeshifting," which is to say both the transitory qualities of material existence and the potential for individual spiritual transformation. Later in the poem, the speaker relates his following the sheep in their practice in the world through using one of their trails as a path for the ascent of "Midnight Mountain." And as he follows this trail he undergoes a transformation:

> At rest in a sheep bed
> at the cliff-edge of life and death
> over endless mountains
> and streams like strips of the sky. (95)

The traveler becomes one with the world through entering into the dreamtime of the sheep by lying down in their "hidden / sheltered beds." And later, with the "Sheep gone," the speaker will "arise to descend   to unbuild it again." This line links "Arctic Midnight Twilight" with "An Offering for Tārā," which will come later in this section. It does so by obliquely foreshadowing the reference there to Milarepa's spiritual training through building and rebuilding stone houses. Once again, the traveler/poet/reader is called on to clear the mind and look to other animals for guidance through this world, as will also be recommended in "Haida Gwai North Coast, Naikoon Beach, Hiellen River Raven Croaks" (103-104). Here his guide is the mountain sheep and there it will be the birds of the sky and the salmon off the coast.

"Walking the New York Bedrock Alive in the Sea of Information" (97-102) radically shifts location but maintains the same kind of view, made possible in part because the poet composed them relatively close together. In a poetry reading in New York, he commented on "Walking the New York Bedrock" by saying that he had just come out of the Brooks Range in Alaska, the setting for "Arctic Midnight Twilight," and was able for a few days to walk around New York City employing the same perspective as he had in the mountains. Snyder explains about the opening of this poem that it records his waking up from a nap taken during those days on a ledge in Central Park. At age eighteen, when he was preparing to ship out during the summer from New York, he had to wait for several weeks to get his seamen's papers and during that time he had to camp out in Central Park, where he found a safe and solitary ledge.[43] It is from this ledge that the poem begins, which is to say that it commences at a site of wild nature within the metropolis.

From there Snyder views Manhattan and the people in it through a variety of organic metaphors. He also looks at the buildings, the subways, the streets, and the people in all of them in terms of energy and information flows—all in process rather than as static entities—which allows him to use both mountains and waters imagery. The poem is rife with humorous commentary about the economics driving nearly all of the activity, but at the same time serious remarks are made about how the power of capital enables the buying of the world's art and the maintenance of class hierarchies. But even such hierarchies are imaged in metaphors of the natural world, such as a peregrine swooping on a pigeon. John Whalen-Bridge makes a useful point when he remarks that "the gap between the rich and the poor, between the bottom-feeders on the street and the species in the high-rise condominiums is not *accepted* in this poem, but the gap is understandable." And he goes on to argue that the satire of the poem results in the city losing "its 'epic distance,' and [it] is cut down to size, to a habitable size. . . . The practice of the wild can occur" anywhere.[44] While in the earlier poem about Los Angeles, Snyder looked to the wild animals and ghost waters of that place for his organic imagery, here he renders all that he sees in organic imagery based on the concept of energy flows rather than static entities.

As in the first two sections of *Mountains and Rivers*, Snyder has some very short poems in the third section. One of these is "New Moon Tongue" (105), which in highly abbreviated form recapitulates numerous images found throughout the sequence and in particular in this third section. The spirituality of "Blue" is invoked, while the "enduring time" or timelessness of "a million years" is also called up.[45] Here both are introduced in the service of an appreciation for the extended presentation of eating and food chains that represent the impermanence of life and the ecological regeneration of all material phenomena. Also, as with the "emptiness of intelligence" in "Arctic Midnight Twilight," the instinct of wild animals is identified as an alternative to ego-bound human consciousness. The cycles of nature are represented here both in terms of the new moon, which in its darkness links instinct and the human unconscious, and the sniffing and licking of the "lips and / reaching tongue" of the deer. As long as humans are alive they remain, with other animals, in the cycle of eating and being eaten, being born and dying, which can be understood in relation to the practice of *puja* introduced in the next poem. Such a reality can be greeted with dismay and despair or with celebration and respectful appreciation, which is the tone of this poem.

"An Offering for Tārā" (106-113), which is divided into three numbered parts, is set in the Himalayas, where the town and the fields themselves are built upon the erosion of mountains. What is particularly impressive for Snyder about this high altitude home is the way that the mountains provide water through the melting of glaciers for a region that receives virtually no rainfall. Snyder also links this locale with the one in "Arctic Twilight" through reference to wild sheep. House=home=*Oikos*=ecology is indicated by gravel being made into walls and Milarepa building stone houses as a form of ritual purification and practice, as well as the growing of food through the interaction of erosion to create soil and glaciers melting to create flowing water.

Having established the village as home in Part I, the traveler enters an individual home in Part II and encounters a shrine to Tārā. Here Tārā as a bodhisattva is depicted as making a commitment to having the body of a woman as a form of compassion in order to help other sentient beings. In this section, the reader is introduced to "blue sheep," who are the color of healing introduced in "The Blue Sky" and may be linked to the Vajra sheep of "Arctic Midnight Twilight." They live amidst continuous geological transformations and within enduring time marking out naturally defined cycles of activity.

Part III of the poem opens with the Indus River. The first section, then, presents land and mountains, the second section a household and Tārā within those mountains, and the third section waters connecting the Indus River in the Himalayan mountains with the Yuba River in the California mountains—and implicitly Snyder's home with the homes of Ladakh. Tārā appears here again as part of the sharing represented by the harvesting of grain, which is made possible by the interbeing of mountains and waters. And through this association with the harvest and the compassion and generosity it implies, she is then linked with love, family, and community, all of which encompass the animals, the people, and the land. Interestingly enough, Snyder intrudes a parenthetical about nation-states and their wars defining them as something clearly quite alien to community and compassion. To this parenthetical Snyder contrasts two italicized lines: *"space of joy / in the heart of the moment."* The chant at the end of the poem, which speaks in defense of the white hawk of the region, is clearly a prayer not only for the continuation of the bird but also for the future of the village, which is like the hawk perched "On the lofty rock."

As with the mention of the Yuba River of California in the previous poem set in the Himalayas, the brief poem, "The Bear Mother" (113), makes mythic connections across the continents. The Bear Mother is also an earth goddess figure here, like Tārā. There is also a sharing of food, the fruit provided by the mountains and waters. It is followed by "Macaques in the Sky" (114), which closes out Part III and appears to be set in Taiwan. It is another animal goddess poem, like the previous one, but here the image of the goddess is invoked by the actual behavior of a group of Rhesus monkeys. The mother who takes her child on an airborne ride through the trees is recognized as doing so in the same way that the Earth is hurtling through space as part of the spiral-armed spinning galaxy. Given the emphasis on the many manifestations of Tārā presented in this section of the sequence, it is likely that the monkey mother is a disguised version of Tārā. With the line, *"as we hang on beneath with all we have,"* standing on its own, readers can easily infer that the monkey mother is not only *"mother of the heavens,"* as the poem claims, but also the earth itself, which is constantly turning underfoot.

Part IV

The epigraph to the opening poem of Part IV of the sequence, "Old Woodrat's Stinky House" (119-21), sets up links with "Macaques in the Sky." Although invoking mythic figures he has used as early as *Myths & Texts*, "Coyote and Earthmaker," Snyder actually emphasizes geological history. In so doing he initiates one of his equivalence listings, as in "The Market." The enduring time of wild nature is contrasted through this listing with the brevity of human lives and cultures. And yet "a breath is a breath"; that is to say, it is both ephemeral/transitory as his listing has demonstrated, and it is the seed syllable of all life, the eternal present in which all actions occur.

Snyder concerns himself in mid-poem with bioregions and their ecologies, focusing on Yellowstone and the Great Basin, so that the traveler can be understood to be coming out of the mountains to engage the wood rats who exist right alongside humans. Or are humans just like wood rats, fouling their own nest through "ten thousand years"? The answer to this question is suggested by Coyote's admonition at poem's end to "learn your place."

The second poem of Part IV, "Raven's Beak River At the End" (122-24), involves a return to Alaska. Two key connections to note here are the rhythm of the poem as it traces the river back from its emptying into the ocean to its headwaters; like "The Flowing," then, "Raven's Beak" is a song. But the second connection suggests that it is a healing song rather than a celebration song, on a par with "The Blue Sky." Toward the latter part of the poem, the "Mind in the mountains" becomes one with the environment, so that it becomes like/is the river, as well as being the animals that depend on the river for their existence. Human beings are living at the end of an ice age like the other animals, yet we are "Off alone." This concluding line can be read as both a literal and a metaphoric statement, both positive and negative. We have separated ourselves from the rest of our animal kin who are living in this interglacial temporal niche. But like the eagle at the end of "The Blue Sky" our flying off can become an act of healing in two distinct senses. One, obviously, would be the changing of our ways; the other would be to retreat from our continued invasive behavior of every wild place.

"Earrings Dangling and Miles of Desert" (125-27) takes the reader into the Great Basin and focuses on an appreciation of plants, whereas previous poems emphasized animals. The poem interweaves images of the phenomenal world and the noumenal world of the mythic realm with plants providing linkages between continents. The appreciation for the plant world at end of the poem is based on this sense of the relatedness between emptiness and life. The appreciation for the plant, Artemisia, in this poem sets the tone for the placement of two love poems, "Cross-Legg'd" and "Afloat" (128-29, 130-32), immediately after it. They link the romantic relationship of Gary and Carole with images from other poems. "Afloat" also takes the reader back to the opening poem of the sequence as the section moves toward closure. The boat here becomes in a sense the human body, even as it is a kayak, which lets Snyder present an image of the merging of two individuals into one combined identity as a couple: two souls in one kayak body. "The tiny skin boat" becomes both the kayak and the human form.

"The Dance" (133-36) is an important poem in relation to the Nō structure of the sequence and in preparing the way for the appearance of the "Mountain Spirit" and the resolution of the sequence. The poem tells various versions of the role of Ame-no-uzume in bringing the Goddess of the Sun out of the cave in which she was hiding through engaging in outrageously humorous behavior. It is worth noting that in both the Jean Herbert and Allan Grapard translations of the Japanese that Snyder quotes, Ame-no-uzume is said to have "stamped" her feet, an act that can be associated with the ritualized action of The Doer at the opening of a Nō drama. This action suggests to me that the poet is establishing a comparison between her action of calling forth the goddess and the poet's own experience of encountering a goddess in "The Mountain Spirit" later in the section. Smith makes the point that "the poem invokes the shamanic dance of Noh, with its ability to '[call] forth the spirit realms' (*MR* 155) of mountains and waters, in order to stretch the reader's perspective of what exactly constitutes 'The Dance.' The poem ultimately suggests that all of existence is engaged in a dance."[46]

This humorous and playful poem is followed by a ritualistic poem about purification, "We Wash Our Bowls in This Water" (137-39). At Shinto shrines throughout Japan, which are often found alongside or even within Buddhist temple compounds, there will be a *temizu-ya*, a roofed structure over a stone basin with flowing water and bamboo ladles so that visitors can purify themselves before approaching the religious site. This poem functions in the same way, enabling a purification of the poet and the reader. The use of the word "bowls" here also suggests a connection with Snyder's Zen monastery training where the eating of meals is treated as a sacred activity, and Snyder remarks in the notes section: "This poem incorporates a Zen training-hall meal verse" (162), the likes of which he had helped to translate years earlier in compiling *The Wooden Fish*. This Northwestern/Alaska poem begins with an epigraph about the water cycle and then relates a raft guide's explaining the various hydrological phenomena of a white water river. In mid-poem Snyder makes an offering to the water spirits, which will counterbalance the spiritual experience in the mountains that will be related next, so that mountains and waters are maintained in poetic balance. In this poem, as with "The Canyon Wren" and "The Hump-backed Flute Player"—as discussed respectively by Scigaj and Hunt—the vehicle of sound as a way to enlightenment is posited. The poem ends emphasizing each individual's own responsibility to help other sentient beings to enlightenment through compassion and action.

According to Smith, "The Mountain Spirit" (140-47) is the key poem for the entire sequence. In it, Snyder in the California mountains on the western edge of the Great Basin encounters the "Mountain Spirit" who challenges his beliefs and questions the value of his poetic sequence, which he is then obligated to recite to her. In his recitation he works through the geological relationship of mountains and waters, of minerals and genetic life, as embodied by the history of the Great Basin. Figures from other poems are invoked and in the end the poet has freed himself and the "Mountain Spirit" through a playful, celebratory embracing of the impermanence posited by Milarepa's doctrine of emptiness. Here, the poet becomes simultaneously the spirit telling the story that grants release and the traveler who gains enlightenment through hearing the story told. If readers perceive of the gods and goddesses, the bodhisattvas and the travelers, human beings and their egos, all as illusory forms without a stable essence or independence but interconnected elements of the swirls of energy that comprise the phenomenal universe both inside and outside the human body, then, of course, the Mountain Spirit and the poet/ traveler here are one and the same, and the former is immanent in the latter. Also, the geological history of the Great Basin is part of the evolutionary history of human beings.

"Earth Verse" (148) is a simple, elegant poem about the continuous awe-inspiring character of the planet with its manifold phenomena. It serves as both an envoy to "The Mountain Spirit" and a prologue to "Finding the Space in the Heart." The real question for the reader, although unstated in the poem, is how human beings will respond to the phenomena unfolding before their eyes, ears, nose, mouth, and skin. It establishes an appropriate tone for the reader's entering the final poem of the sequence, "Finding the Space in the Heart" (149-52), which is a highly personal poem, from start to finish, unlike the opening poem of the sequence. It depicts the passing of the years of an individual life and the ongoing visits by the poet to the Great Basin, seeing it differently each time, gaining shocks of recognition from the various experiences.

On page 151, Snyder has arranged two indented stanzas that invoke the language of the Heart sutra, so that the Great Basin indisputably becomes a mandala for that particular sutra, and that sutra's foundational teaching of impermanence becomes the bedrock, as Smith observes in *Reading*, for the philosophy of the poem; but I think Smith emphasizes the foundation over the building there. Impermanence is the starting point for the recognition of interconnectedness, mutual co-arising, or interbeing, as it has variously been translated. The extension, which is Snyder's responsibility and his answer to the question, *"who can?"* at the end of "We Wash Our Bowls," is the expression and practice of compassion. To emphasize or demonstrate only the recognition of impermanence would fail to grasp the opening epigraph of the sequence, "The notion of Emptiness engenders Compassion" (ix). Snyder's sequence demonstrates precisely such engendering, not only within an individual life but also, through "Finding the Space in the Heart," within generational continuity and human social change.

I accentuate this point because nowhere does Snyder portray himself as Manjushri needing completion by Tārā (wisdom by compassion), but rather suggests by "The Mountain Spirit" that the human individual needs/has both within him or herself, i.e., both masculine and feminine attributes. It is pertinent here that in his foreword to Robert Aitken's *Taking the Path of Zen*, Snyder emphasizes compassion in explaining Aitken's influence on his own life: "Those letters [from Bob Aitken] helped me to understand that my stubborn and cloudy bohemian radicalism needed considerable work if it were to approach anything like real compassion."[47]

At the end of *Mountains and Rivers Without End*, "the space goes on" as human beings work out their destiny with the rest of the planet, but the poem ends just as any single life will end and will always be—whether painting, poem, or person—a fragment of the larger endless process of reality, and simultaneously a microcosmic whole. The space goes on because the reader must respond to the sequence, just as viewers of the landscape scroll responded with their own signatures, comments, and poems. Just as Snyder's sequence, then, becomes an extension of the scroll painting, so too the reader's actions can become an extension of Snyder's poetry.

Conclusion
As Mountains and Waters Remain, the Poet Continues Walking

While the publication of *Mountains and Rivers Without End* may very well represent the pinnacle of Snyder's poetic career, it in no way represent its culmination. Nor should his career as a writer be limited to the genre of poetry. His work since 1996 indicates that he continues to write both poetry and prose, that he continues to work with the mountains and waters trope, and that he will persist in environmental activism into his seventies. In these remaining pages, then, I will summarize his ongoing work, with special attention to some previously uncollected essays and poems appearing in *The Gary Snyder Reader*.

The Gary Snyder Reader:
Prose, Poetry, and Translations, 1952-1998

As to be expected, the vast bulk of this large volume consists of previously published material mainly collected from his full-length books. It even includes nearly a third of the *Mountains and Rivers* sequence. Looking at the table of contents, a reader sees that Snyder has made a very deliberate effort to represent himself here as a multi-genre writer who is a poet, an essayist, and a translator, who has been "weaving the Buddhist Teachings quietly into my books."[1] He has also included sets of letters to Philip Whalen and Will Petersen, most of which have previously appeared in print, and two previously published interviews. In regard to translations, not only has Snyder included a selection of "Cold Mountain Poems" and five of the Miyazawa Kenji translations, but also two translation chapbooks that originally appeared in limited and relatively unknown editions, *Sixteen T'ang Poems* and *Long Bitter Song*. Four selections from his copious journals appear here treating Japan, Australia, Ladakh, and Botswana and Zimbabwe. Other prose consists of three chapters from *The Great Clod* project, which he discontinued in the eighties, and four additional essays on miscellaneous topics, all of which have been previously published but not previously collected. Finally, Snyder has also included three previously uncollected poems, all written since the completion of *Mountains and Rivers*.

The Great Clod Essays

From the available fragments, it becomes clear that Snyder had envisioned *The Great Clod* as a sweeping historical study of the relationship of nature and culture in East Asia. " 'Wild' in China," for example, is concerned with the perception of the "wild" in Chinese thought as reflected in its literature dating at least as far back as the fourth century A.D. Snyder notes that in the *Classic of Songs*, nature is described in detail and is clearly proximate and directly experienced by the writers. But by the time of the Six Dynasties there is already a stepping-back from such proximity and a tendency toward panoramic landscapes. As a result, Snyder is interested in the poets who stand out in their attention to specificity, such as T'ao Yuan-ming and Hsieh Ling-yün. Why? It seems to me that they epitomize precisely the kind of engaged artistry that Snyder is concerned with promoting and maintaining in the contemporary postmodern world, which also tends toward surface panoramas and generalized landscapes rather than the loving attention to detail that comes from daily immersion in the natural world. True to the quote from his Bukkyo Dendo Kyokai acceptance speech in the previous paragraph, Snyder weaves Buddhism into this essay, tying spiritual and philosophical beliefs into attitudes toward nature. He concludes that the Buddhist spiritual doctrine that all sentient beings were capable of achieving enlightenment mixed well with Chinese natural philosophy. As this essay moves into a meditation on trying to define the nature poetry of China, one can see Snyder meditating also on the cosmic and poetic implications of his own mountains and rivers project, particularly in terms of emptiness and silence, but also wilderness and inhabitation.

"Walls Within Walls" shifts focus. Historically taking up where the previous essay left off, this one is concerned with Chinese urbanization and the destruction of wilderness. Snyder is particularly concerned here with the gradual loss of writers' direct and accurate knowledge of the nature they were ostensibly depicting. This condition he views as directly connected with the destruction and extinction of various species. Again, the relationship between ancient China and contemporary America is easily recognized. The other essay from this project, "The Brush," displays similar concerns. The three together show a high level of unity, although each has a slightly different focus.

Miscellaneous Essays

The four miscellaneous essays, not surprisingly, are not nearly as interconnected as those from the *Great Clod* project. And it is this very variety that makes them as equally interesting. "Walking the Great Ridge Omine, on the Womb-Diamond Trial" was originally published in the *Kyoto Journal* in 1993, about a decade after the *Great Clod* essays appeared mainly in *Co-evolution Quarterly*. It is useful here to recall David Robertson's remarks about mandalas and Snyder's own experience with the Yamabushi, or mountain-way monks. This essay explains a number of interconnected phenomena in Snyder's autobiography. One, shortly after arriving in Japan he made contact not only with the local mountains near Kyoto, where he would be living, but also encountered a mountain deity who would become of paramount importance in his poetry, Fudō-Myō-ō. Two, this experience with the mountains enabled him to relate the landscape of Japan, much more highly inhabited than any he had heretofore encountered, with the mountains of the Pacific Northwest, which had been such a formative influence on his life up until the time he left for Japan. Three, the introduction to the Yamabushi tradition enabled him to make contact with a living ritual practice that had certain similarities with the envisaged life-style of his poetic alter ego, Han-shan, at a time when that poet's landscape was unavailable to Snyder for exploration. Four, as Snyder notes, the Yamabushi provided a contemporaneous and experiential link with the traveling monks found in many Nō dramas, providing a more personal connection with that dramatic art form than otherwise might have been possible for him. Much of this essay is given over to the record of a 1968 circumambulation of the Omine Ridge, a sacred and perhaps originating site for Yamabushi practice, which in some ways links through Snyder's own spiritual practice the newest established Buddhist mandala site of Mt. Tamalpais in the United States with one of the oldest in Japan (see chapter 10 on "The Circumambulation of Mt. Tamalpais").

"Walking Downtown Naha" takes readers from mountains and wilderness to the nearly sea level city of Naha, Okinawa. Naha is the largest city on this small island and is the capital of Okinawa prefecture. As Snyder's report of a walk taken in the 1980s indicates, much of the city was destroyed in the Battle of Okinawa late in World War II, but there are some old parts of the city still standing. And in these twisting, tiny back streets, many of them covered arcade-style, Snyder finds not only a certain wildness, but also wild nature surviving amidst the multi-centuried layers of local culture and commerce. In many respects, "Walking Downtown Naha" is the prose equivalent of "Walking the New York Bedrock," one of the poems in *Mountains and Rivers Without End*. In both cases, Snyder works hard to think through the ecosystemic implications of urban environments.

The other two miscellaneous essays collected in the *Reader* are oriented toward intellectual issues, particularly concepts and arguments emanating from academia. "Is Nature Real?" is a response to various academic attacks on the concept of "wilderness" that Snyder sees as playing into the hands of corporations and others who would destroy whatever vestiges of undeveloped nature can still be found that have economic value. Fundamentally, Snyder is making the case that while the academic intellectuals that he targets here consider themselves highly sophisticated, they are actually quite naive when it comes to the stakes involved in the interpretation of their ideas as governmental and commercial policies. "Entering the Fiftieth Millennium" is quite different in tone, but is even more academically oriented, which only makes sense since it was originally delivered at the annual meeting of the Modern Language Association, the largest professional organization of university and college professors in North America. While "Is Nature Real?" focuses on the practical results of the positions that intellectuals take in relation to nature and the need therefore to be more responsible in terms of their impact on immediate public policy, this essay emphasizes the opposite end of the intellectual spectrum. Here Snyder basically argues that the intellectuals he is addressing have too narrow a perspective on culture. He makes two specific points: one, multiculturalism has to be understood diachronically as well as synchronically; two, contemporary behavior has to be viewed in terms of how it will be evaluated by our descendants. These points are interrelated. Only by thinking deeply about how we should understand the actions of human beings who lived ten thousand years before us can we begin to think about how our actions will be understood by people who live ten thousand years after us (an argument relevant to reading the new poem, "This present moment"). Snyder is also trying to break people loose from the typical American short-term, immediate gratification mindset that both produces millennialist anxiety and is exacerbated by a dating system that makes it seem as if human history is only two thousand years old.

None of these eight essays will be studied or taught in terms of their literary qualities, even though they are well written and stylistically sophisticated and diverse. So why include them in the *Reader*? Snyder has become a public individual, who is increasingly viewed not only as a poet or a writer but also as a major ecological thinker of the contemporary period. These essays contribute to that more filled-out image of Snyder as a public intellectual who is working unstintingly to reshape American and world cultures toward more sustainable practices and more compassionate spiritual and philosophical beliefs. They also demonstrate his ability to speak to a variety of audiences. Unlike much of the writing that appears in *Earth House Hold*, the prose collected since that time indicates an author attempting to express his ideas to a range of audiences through a variety of mechanisms.

New Poems

While Snyder is gaining increasing recognition as a public intellectual, he nevertheless remains primarily a poet in most of his readers' eyes. And for that audience he has included three new poems in the *Reader*. Like the essays collected here, these poems are surprisingly varied in tone, style, and content.

"Icy Mountains Constantly Walking" is dedicated to the Irish poet Seamus Heaney and records a trip that Snyder took to Ireland for some poetry readings. Slow and meditative in tone and rhythm, "Icy Mountains" reflects on the long, slow sweep of history, both cultural and natural, and the minuteness of any individual voice within that sweep. There are two distinctly significant aspects of this poem worth noting. The first is its demonstration that Snyder is going to continue to work with the mountains and rivers trope. While the sequence *Mountains and Rivers Without End* reached a closure, mountains and waters are indeed endless and their philosophical paradigm remains continuously relevant. In the first of the three stanzas, Snyder sets up a flattened out mountains-and-waters contrast by means of fields and swamps, while in the third he appeals to the landscape of Greenland for a mountains-and-ice contrast. The second aspect is his turning this trope toward Europe rather than toward the Pacific Rim. Here Snyder recognizes the centuries of interaction of nature and culture in Irish history with the kind of attention normally reserved for China or Japan.

In contrast to the serious tone of "Icy Mountains," "Summer of Ninety-seven" is written in a playful rhythm and style replete with couplets and other rhyme schemes. Some of the lines are so brazenly banal as to evoke wincing laughter. Yet the humor overlays an understated pain. In this poem Snyder describes the remodeling of his Kitkitdizze home in 1997, which included the building of an addition. Its main purpose is to facilitate the convalescence of Snyder's wife, Carole Koda. This purpose is revealed only obliquely in the poem through reference to her leaving and the work crew grieving at her departure midway through the poem, and then in the penultimate stanza describing her return home. As the reader becomes aware of this purpose through the course of the poem, the forced rhymes and the mundane couplets becomes poignantly understandable. A deep, unstated love and heartfelt sorrow flow beneath the laughter.

"This present moment" is a four-line, ten-word untitled poem that is over almost before it begins. It seems to say almost nothing at first reading, but gradually becomes richer as a reader meditates upon its implications. Snyder plays here with a Zen sense of temporality and an archaic sense of enduring time. I think it is best understood by bringing together a sense of political expediency with a sense of timeless ritual. This moment, any moment, instantaneously ceases to exist, yet the action taken by human beings in that moment invariably has indefinite repercussions. From the perspective of political expediency there is the need to reverse the American tendency to live for the moment in such a way that no responsibility is assumed for this planet in the future when it will be inhabited by our descendants. The need for such a change can be understood by realizing the problems that have been bequeathed to the present generation by the actions of former ones. From the perspective of timeless ritual, there is always only this moment, and to live fully within it requires that a person behave as if there is nothing else more important in the world than doing what is most noble, most compassionate, or most pure at this very second. The evaluation of the degree of success in such living will only be gauged by those who live long after us. Part of their present moment will be a judgment on our own. Thus, the readers of the poem are, in effect, called on to realize that both perspectives are one and the same.

Snyder's writing and his social practice exist in both "this present moment" and in "enduring time." While each shows tremendous diversity in style and technique, the fundamentals have changed relatively little since he first began publishing poetry and first got into trouble with the government nearly fifty years ago. In his writing, prose has come to play a more prominent role in the 1980s and 1990s than it did before that time. Yet it is unlikely that any prose work he has published, or will publish, could overshadow *Mountains and Rivers Without End*. Politically, his teenage pacifist, anarcho-syndicalism has evolved into a vision of bioregional social organization. From this vantage point he was able in the winter of 1998 to provide a highly nuanced critique of the debate within the Sierra Club about taking a position against immigration to California.[2] Philosophically and spiritually he has become more explicitly Buddhist in his writing and practice, continuously clarifying a syncretism that he believes will accord with his bioregional politics; at the same time, he can display the most persuasive features of American pragmatism in his rhetoric.

After studying Snyder's writing and his life for nearly twenty years, what I find most impressive is not any particular poem, essay, or pithy statement, but rather his ability to maintain a richly developed sense of humor and an ever evolving elegant balancing of seemingly contradictory concepts. His poetry reflects the complementary relationship of Buddhism and bioregionalism in that he remains focused both on inward states of awareness—self-realization—and human practice in the world—(re)inhabitation—which can be understood as the mutually reinforcing cultivation of wisdom and expression of compassion. Certainly his remarks in the late-1960s indicate that he, like so many other Americans at that time, believed that revolution and social transformation would be the work of a single generation. Thirty years later, he has to address the question of how much has changed, and has any of it changed for the better. In addressing that question in the interview with Eliot Weinberger, which is reprinted in the *Reader*, he encapsulated the best qualities of his thinking and writing, which combine practicality and stubbornness with optimism and compassion:

> I feel that the condition of our social and ecological life is so serious that we'd better have a sense of humor. That it's too serious just to be angry and despairing. Also, frankly, the environmental movement in the last twenty years has never done well when it threw out excessive doom scenarios. Doom scenarios, even though they might be true, are not politically or psychologically effective. The first step, I think, and that's why it's in my poetry, is to make us love the world rather than to make us fear for the end of the world. Make us love the world, which means the nonhuman as well as the human, and then begin to take better care of it."[3]

Snyder's poetry, indeed, has the potential to open the "space in the heart" of each reader to love the world enough to let it, and themselves, live.

Notes

Chapter One: "Membership *in a Real World"*

1. Gary Snyder quoted in the interview, "Gary Snyder," conducted by Nicholas O'Connell and collected in *At the Field's End* (Seattle: Madrona Publishers, 1987), 308.
2. Gary Snyder, *The Practice of the Wild* (San Francisco: North Point Press, 1990), 118; see also Snyder's interview with Bill Moyers in *The Language of Life: A Festival of Poets*, ed. James Haba (New York: Doubleday. 1995), 367.
3. O'Connell, 308-309. The figures here for the years Harold Snyder was out of work are based on Snyder's emendation of his remarks to O'Connell. See also Snyder, *The Practice of The Wild*, 116-17, for a brief description of this "tiny dairy farm."
4. Carol Baker, "1414 SE Lambert Street," in *Gary Snyder: Dimensions of a Life*, ed. Jon Halper (San Francisco: Sierra Club Books, 1991), 24.
5. John P. O'Grady, "Living Landscape: An Interview with Gary Snyder," *Western American Literature* 33.3 (Fall 1998), 279.
6. Snyder quoted by David Kherdian, "Gary Snyder," in *Six Poets of the San Francisco Renaissance: Portraits and Checklists* (Fresno, Calif.: Giliga Press, 1967), 47.
7. O'Connell, 309.
8. Jerry Crandall, "Mountaineers Are Always Free," Halper, 5; see also, J. Michael Mahar, "Scenes from the Sidelines," Halper, 8-9.
9. See Crandall, 3-7.
10. O'Connell, 312. In a late-1997 interview conducted by John P. O'Grady, Snyder reiterated the importance of these teenage climbing experiences (O'Grady, 276).
11. Crandall, 6. In talking with O'Grady, Snyder mentions that he also published an article in the Lincoln High School newspaper at about the same time as the *Mazama* article (O'Grady, 277).
12. Snyder quoted by Dan McLeod, "Gary Snyder," in *The Beats: Literary Bohemians in Postwar America, Part 2, Dictionary of Literary Biography*, vol. 16, ed. Ann Charters (Detroit: Gale, 1983), 495. See also Crandall, 6.
13. David H. French, "Gary Snyder and Reed College," in Halper, 21. Snyder identifies his work as being that of a "timber scaler" in *The Practice of the Wild*, 120.
14. Such research runs through a variety of subjects from his undergraduate thesis on Native American myth, *He Who Hunted Birds in His Father's Village: The Dimensions of a Haida Myth* (Bolinas, Calif.: Grey Fox Press, 1979); to some of the chapters in his two prose books, *The Practice of the Wild* and *A Place in Space* (Washington, D.C.: Counterpoint, 1995); through such essays as "Ink and Charcoal," *The CoEvolution Quarterly* (Winter 1981), 48-50—on environmental attitudes in ancient China; and "Beyond Cathay: The Hill Tribes of China," in *Mountain People*, ed. Michael Tobias (Norman: University of Oklahoma Press, 1986), 150-52.

15. In fact, Snyder took strong exception in 1973 to an interviewer who said, "now that you're not doing physical labor." He retorted that "I not only built my own house, I do everything else around it continually. I'm farming all the time." See Gary Snyder, *The Real Work: Interviews & Talks, 1964-1979*, ed. Scott McLean (New York: New Directions, 1980), 48.

16. See Mahar, 12-13, and Baker, 25.

17. O'Grady, 283.

18. Snyder, *The Real Work*, 64.

19. French, 22.

20. On Welch and the influence of Williams and Stein, see Lew Welch, *How I Read Gertrude Stein*, ed. Eric Paul Shaffer (San Francisco: Grey Fox Press, 1996).

21. See O'Grady, 280; also Charles Egan, "Poetic Insights: An Interview with Gary Snyder," *Poets & Writers Magazine* (May/June 1995), 73. Christopher Beach treats the influence of Pound on Snyder in "Pound's Words in the Their Pockets: Denise Levertov and Gary Snyder" in *ABC of Influence: Ezra Pound and the Remaking of the American Poetic Tradition* (Berkeley: University of California Press, 1992), 190-216. Egan also points out that Kenneth Rexroth became a major influence on Snyder after he moved to the San Francisco Bay Area; likewise, Timothy Gray, in "New Lyric Worlds: Gary Snyder's Pacific Rim Communitas, 1930-1970" (Diss. University of California at Santa Barbara, 1998), 37, emphasizes the importance of Rexroth. For various discussions of poetic influence, see Snyder, *The Real Work*, and Ekbert Faas, *Towards a New American Poetics: Essays & Interviews* (Santa Barbara: Black Sparrow Press, 1979).

22. Gray, 60.

23. See Dell Hymes's account of Snyder at Indiana University in his essay, "A Coyote Who Can Sing," Halper, 392-404.

24. Snyder quoted by Kherdian, 49.

25. For details on this experience, see David Robertson, "Gary Snyder Riprapping in Yosemite, 1955," *American Poetry* 2.1 (1984), 52-59.

26. Gary Snyder, "The Making of *Mountains and Rivers Without End*," in Snyder, *Mountains and Rivers Without End* (Washington, D.C.: Counterpoint, 1996), 154; see also, Snyder, *The Real Work*, 95.

27. Barry Chowka, "The *East West* Interview," in Snyder, *The Real Work*, 94; see also, McLeod, 189; O'Connell, 313-14; and Snyder, "The Making," 153.

28. O'Grady, 280-83.

29. Snyder, *The Practice of the Wild*, 120.

30. Copies of pertinent documents and letters can be found in the Gary Snyder Archives, Department of Special Collections, University of California Library, Davis.

31. Edward Halsey Foster, *Understanding The Beats* (Columbia: University of South Carolina Press, 1992), 1-2.

32. See Chapter One, "Hipsters, Beats, and the True Frontier," in Foster; and Chapter Two, "'The Darkness Surrounds Us: Participation and Reflection Among the Beat Writers," in Michael Davidson, *The San Francisco Renaissance: Poetics and Community at Mid-Century* (1989; New York: Cambridge University Press, 1991).

33. On this period of Snyder's life, see Burton Watson, "Kyoto in the Fifties"; Philip Yampolsky, "Kyoto, Zen, Snyder"; and Hisao Kanaseki,

"An Easy Rider at Yase," in Halper, 53-59, 60-69, and 70-75. Snyder, however, did not work for Mrs. Sasaki the entire time he was in Japan, but quit the institute in the summer of 1961.

34. Letter to Will Petersen, 17 September 1956, published in *Io* no. 14 (Summer 1972), 80. Snyder also discusses the matter of seriousness many years later in the interview with Paul Rossiter and John Evans appearing in *Printed Matter* (Tokyo), 16.3 (Summer 1992), reprinted in "Gary Snyder: An International Perspective" special issue, guest ed. Patrick D. Murphy, *Studies in the Humanities* 26.1-2 (1999), 10-17. His distinction in the letter to Petersen between the spontaneity of poetry and the discipline of Zen seems to be based on a long-held belief about the fundamental nature of poetic inspiration and practice.

35. Gary Snyder, "On Rinzai Masters and Western Students in Japan," *Wind Bell* 8.1-2 (Fall 1969), 24.

36. See Snyder's letter to Lew Welch, 14 September 1957, published in *I Remain: The Letters of Lew Welch & The Correspondence of His Friends*, 2 vols., ed. Donald Allen (Bolinas, Calif.: Grey Fox Press, 1980), v. 1, 112-14.

37. See Kyger's account of their relationship in Joanne Kyger, *The Japan and India Journals 1960-1964* (Bolinas, Calif.: Tombouctou Books, 1981), especially her opening remark that Ruth Fuller Sasaki rushed them into marriage, vii. See also Yampolsky, 66, and Kanaseki, 73.

38. See Katsunori Yamazato, "Seeking a Fulcrum: Gary Snyder and Japan (1956-1975)" (Diss. University of California at Davis, 1987), 89-90.

39. A photo of such a demonstration is available in Halper, 188.

40. McLeod, 487-88.

41. Gary Snyder, "Dear Poets Commune" letter, *Anthology of Underground Poetry* #7 (1970), n.p. The *Anthology* was published by a group called the Dear Poets Commune and Snyder's letter to them is dated "22.XII.40070,"—December 22, 1970.

42. Burr Snider, "The Sage of the Sierra," *Image: San Francisco Examiner* 17 Sept. 1989, 10; see also Yamazato, "Seeking a Fulcrum," 114-17, 128-29.

43. O'Connell, 318. Snyder's winning the Pulitzer did not occur without controversy. In particular, some Native Americans were incensed that the award went to a volume of poetry by a white author that made extensive use of Native American cultural materials rather than to one of the collections published by a Native American writer in the same year. See Gray, 302-305, for a summary; for the Native American criticisms, see Leslie Marmon Silko, "An Old-Time Indian Attack Conducted in Two Parts," *Yardbird Reader* 5 (1976), 77-85; and Geary Hobson, "The Rise of the White Shaman as a New Version of Cultural Imperialism," in *The Remembered Earth: An Anthology of Contemporary Native American Literature*, ed. Geary Hobson (1979, Albuquerque: University of New Mexico Press, 1981), 100-108. It is pertinent to remark here that letters written by Silko to Snyder from the early-1970s through 1977, collected in the Gary Snyder Archives at UC Davis, include no criticism by Silko of Snyder's work. In her *Yardbird Reader* essay, it is important to note, she does not actually condemn any of his work but warns him about avoiding possible wrong directions in his treatment of Native American cultural materials. Also in the UC Davis archives are letters to Snyder from Vine Deloria, Jr., from May of 1975 through August of 1983. Throughout Deloria expresses a very positive attitude

toward Snyder and his work, congratulating him in a 7 May 1975 letter on receiving the Pulitzer.

These letters and the attitudes of other Native American writers toward Snyder, such as N. Scott Momaday, Simon Ortiz, and Nora Dauenhauer, suggest that Snyder has been lumped in with other white writers in the attack on "white shamanism" without careful attention to his actual practices and that, rather than conspiring in the silencing of Native American voices, he has actually contributed to the artistic development of some of the writers and encouraged the dissemination and reading of their works. For example, Wendy Rose negatively mentions Snyder in the opening of her essay, "The Great Pretenders: Further Reflections on Whiteshamanism" in *The State of Native America: Genocide, Colonization, and Resistance*, edited by M. Annette Jaimes (Boston: South End Press, 1992), 403-21, but doesn't actually discuss the specifics of his writing. Further, Snyder would meet the criteria she establishes on p. 418 for appropriate artistic use of Native American source materials.

44. Michael Helm, "A Conversation with Gary Snyder," *California Living Magazine, Sunday San Francisco Examiner & Chronicle* 20 November 1983, 17.

45. Snider, 16.

46. O'Grady, 287.

47. Some of the later essays of *A Place in Space* began as articles for the newsletter of the Yuba Watershed Institute, which has headquarters in Nevada City. See, for instance, "The Porous World" in *A Place*, the first half of which originally appeared in *Tree Rings: The Forum of the Yuba Watershed Institute* 2.3 (Summer 1992), 3.

48. Gary Snyder, "Entering the Fiftieth Millennium," *Profession 1997*, 35-40.

49. Egan, 75.

50. Luke Briet and Pat Grizzell, "The Recovery of the Commons: Interview with Gary Snyder and Steve Sanfield," *Poet News* (May 1984), 10.

51. O'Connell, 320.

52. Uri Hertz, "An Interview with Gary Snyder," *Third Rail* 7 (1985-86), 52.

53. Gary Snyder, *Earth House Hold: Technical Notes & Queries to Fellow Dharma Revolutionaries* (New York: New Directions, 1969), 8 and 19.

54. Bruce Cook, *The Beat Generation* (New York: Scribner's, 1971), 33; Michael Castro, *Interpreting the Indian: Twentieth-Century Poets and the American Indian* (Albuquerque: University of New Mexico Press, 1984); O'Grady, 280-83; Gray, 346; see also Gary Snyder, "The Politics of Ethnopoetics," *A Place in Space*, 126-47.

55. Quoted in Yamazato, "Seeking a Fulcrum," 129, from Gary Snyder, "A Brief Account of the Ring of Bone Zendo, I," *Ring of Bone Zendo Newsletter*, 15 October 1986, 8-9.

56. Gary Snyder, "Earth Day Speech," 22 April 1970, Colorado State College. Unpublished. Photocopy in the Gary Snyder Archives, Department of Special Collections, University of California Library, Davis; quoted by permission of Gary Snyder.

57. Gary Snyder, "Earth Day and the War Against the Imagination," speech "for Earth Day April 22, 1990, at Bridgeport on the South Yuba River in Nevada County / Nisenan Country / Western Slopes / Northern Sierra / Shasta Bioregion / Continent of Turtle Island." Unpublished. Quoted by permission of Gary Snyder.

58. I use "at one time" here because of the fact that Snyder refers specifically to the Gaia hypothesis in the version of "The Politics of Ethnopoetics" published in Gary Snyder, *The Old Ways* (San Francisco: City Lights Books, 1977), 39, but deletes that paragraph in the version of the essay published in *A Place in Space*.

59. Gary Snyder, "Little Songs for Gaia," *Axe Handles* (San Francisco: North Point Press, 1983), 47-58.

60. Julia Martin and Snyder discussed some of the problems of his using gendered images of the earth, particularly as a goddess, because of the negative uses of the identification of women and nature in Western and other societies. See Julia Martin, "Coyote-Mind: An Interview with Gary Snyder," *Triquarterly* 79 (Autumn 1990), 148-72; see also Patrick D. Murphy, "Sex-Typing the Planet: Gaia Imagery and the Problem of Subverting Patriarchy," *Environmental Ethics* 10 (1988), 155-68, rptd. in Murphy, *Literature, Nature, and Other: Ecofeminist Critiques* (Albany: State University of New York Press, 1995), 59-69. Gray's discussion of *Regarding Wave* in the fourth chapter of his dissertation is also relevant to this matter.

61. Snyder quoted in Bob Steuding, *Gary Snyder* (Boston: Twayne, 1976), 35.

62. Lee Bartlett, "Interview: Gary Snyder," *California Quarterly* No. 9 (1975), 47.

63. Woody Rehanek, "The Shaman Songs of Gary Snyder," *Okanogan Natural News* No. 19 (Summer 1984), 2-13; Gray, 313-27. Gray, by the way, uses the postmodernist theory of Gilles Deleuze and Felix Guattari in *A Thousand Plateaus I* in discussing "song's efficacy in cognitive mappings."

64. See Jody Norton, "The Importance of Nothing: Absence and Its Origins in the Poetry of Gary Snyder," *Contemporary Literature* 28 (1987), 44-47, rpt. in *Critical Essays on Gary Snyder*, ed. Patrick D. Murphy (Boston: G. K. Hall, 1990), 166-88; Yao-fu Lin, " 'The Mountains Are Your Mind': Orientalism in the Poetry of Gary Snyder," *Tamkang Review* 6-7 (1975-1976), 366-67; Wai-Lim Yip, "Classical Chinese and Modern Anglo-American Poetry: Convergence of Language and Poetry," *Comparative Literature Studies* 11 (1974), 21-47; and Ling Chung, "Whose Mountain Is This?—Gary Snyder's Translation of Han Shan," *Renditions* 7 (Spring 1977), 93-102.

65. Laszlo Géfin, *Ideogram: History of a Poetic Method* (Austin: University of Texas Press, 1982), 130. The section of this book treating Snyder is reprinted as "[Ellipsis and Riprap: Gary Snyder]" in Murphy, *Critical Essays*, 122-31.

Chapter Two: From Myth Criticism to Mythopoesis

1. Gary Snyder, *Myths & Texts* (1960; rpt. New York: New Directions, 1978). Further references to this work are cited in the text.

2. Snyder, *He Who Hunted Birds*, x. Further references to this work are cited in the text. In this chapter I treat *He Who Hunted Birds* as a reference text that informs readers about Snyder's poetry. I do that because it is a work of academic anthropological analysis distinct from the other full-length literary prose that Snyder has produced.

3. Tim Dean, *Gary Snyder and the American Unconscious: Inhabiting the Ground* (New York: St. Martin's, 1991), 84-89.

4. On this point, see Snyder's own remarks in Katherine McNeil, *Gary Snyder: A Bibliography* (New York: Phoenix Bookshop, 1983), 8-9.

5. See, for example, Robert Kern, "Clearing the Ground: Gary Snyder and the Modernist Imperative," *Criticism* 19 (Spring 1988), 158-77; Yamazato, "Seeking a Fulcrum," 41.

6. Gray, 76.

7. Gray, 77.

8. William J. Jungels, "The Use of Native-American Mythologies in the Poetry of Gary Snyder," (Diss. SUNY at Buffalo, 1973), 214. Further references to this work are cited in the text.

9. Robert Graves, *The White Goddess* (1949; amended and enlarged, New York: Farrar, Straus & Giroux, 1966), 50.

10. Howard McCord, *Some Notes on Gary Snyder's* Myths & Texts (Berkeley: Sand Dollar, 1971), n.p. McCord's book is unpaginated.

11. Tom Lynch, email correspondence, 15 December 1994 and 25 January 1999.

12. Gray, 77-78.

13. Snyder, *The Practice of the Wild*, 120, 126.

14. Gray, 81.

15. McCord.

16. Gray, 82.

17. See Gray, 82-83.

18. Gray, 83, 85.

19. Gray, 88. My entire discussion of "Logging 12" is deeply indebted to Gray's treatment of it in his dissertation (83-88); I skipped over this section of the sequence in my original treatment of *Myths & Texts*.

20. As Heinrich Zimmer explains it in *Myths and Symbols in Indian Art and Civilization* (1946; rpt. Princeton: Princeton University Press, 1972), 13-19, a "kalpa" is a single day of the Hindu god Brahma, which lasts for "4,320,000,00 years of human reckoning," while the entire "kalpa cycle" lasts "311,040,000,000,000 human years." In relation to the circularity of Native American beliefs contrasted to the "square" of industrial civilization and the linear teleology of Christianity, it is useful to bear in mind that, as Zimmer notes, "the progress and decline of every kalpa is marked by the mythological events that recur similarly, again and again, in magnificent, slowly and relentlessly rotating cycles." Circularity and cyclicity, then, function as the bridge to support a syncretic mixture of Hindu and Native American cosmology.

21. Gray, 89. By focusing exclusively on human relationships, Maura Gage, in "Identity, Masculinity, and Femininity in the Poetry of Gary Snyder" (Diss. University of South Florida, 1997), p, 387, misreads this section, claiming that Snyder places blame on the woman in the personal relationship, but the relationship is only a minor aspect of this conclusion to "Logging," which is concerned with the possibility of regeneration rather than placing blame.

22. Gray, 92.

23. Dean, 123.

24. See Gray, 99, who in turn cites Bert Almon, *Gary Snyder* (Western Writers Series 37. Boise: Boise State University, 1979), 19.

25. See Gray, 100-101, which pointed out the Garden of Eden comparison to me, for a somewhat different and more developed discussion of "Hunting 12."

26. Sherman Paul, *In Search of the Primitive: Rereading David Antin, Jerome Rothenberg, and Gary Snyder* (Baton Rouge: Louisiana State University Press, 1986), 241.
27. Gray, 106; see pp. 104-106 for his different reading of "Burning 2."
28. For a comparative discussion of Lawrence and Snyder, see Leo Hamalian, "Beyond the Paleface: D. H. Lawrence and Gary Snyder," *Talisman* #7 (Fall 1991), 50-55.
29. Paul, *In Search*, 242.
30. Robert Aitken, *Taking the Path of Zen* (San Francisco: North Point Press, 1982), 140.
31. Gray, 109.
32. Snyder quoted by McCord.
33. Aitken, *Taking the Path*,139.
34. Paul, *In Search*. 247.
35. In the mid-1980s, Snyder commented in correspondence that the second half of "Burning" and its use of Coyote is based on language from Smohalla's late-nineteenth-century messianic "Dreaming" religion, which treated Coyote as a future "Messiah." This remark about Coyote as a messiah figure also pertains to his appearance in "Hunting 16" and "Burning 11."
36. See Gray, 77.
37. See Lok Chua Cheng and N. Sasaki, "Zen and the Title of Gary Snyder's 'Marin-an,' " *Notes on Contemporary Literature* 8.3 (1978), 2-3; Yamazato, "Seeking a Fulcrum," 71.
38. See Leonard M. Scigaj, "Contemporary Ecological and Environmental Poetry," *ISLE: Interdisciplinary Studies in Literature and Environment* 3.2 (Fall 1996), 1-25.

Chapter Three: Working Rhythms

1. Gary Snyder, *Riprap and Cold Mountain Poems* (San Francisco: North Point Press, 1990). All page references given in the text are to this edition. Snyder relates the publication history of this volume in his afterword.
2. Crunk (James Wright), "The Work of Gary Snyder," *The Sixties* 6 (Spring 1962); rpt. in James Wright, *Collected Prose*, ed. Anne Wright (Ann Arbor: University of Michigan Press, 1983), 108; Paul, *In Search of the Primitive*, 214. In fact, Snyder claims that even *No Nature: New and Selected Poems* (New York: Pantheon, 1992) "has its own coherence" (O'Grady, 288).
3. For those interested in analyses of the Han-shan poems, see the following: Lee Bartlett, "Gary Snyder's Han-Shan," *Sagetrieb* 2 (1983), 105-10; Ling Chung, "Whose Mountain Is This?—Gary Snyder's Translation of Han Shan," *Renditions* 7 (Spring 1977), 93-102; Paul Kahn, *Han Shan in English* (Buffalo: White Pine Press, 1989); Jacob Leed, "Gary Snyder, Han Shan, and Jack Kerouac," *Journal of Modern Literature* 11 (1984), 185-93; Yao-fu Lin, "'The Mountains Are Your Mind': Orientalism in the Poetry of Gary Snyder," *Tamkang Review* 6-7 (1975-1976), 357-91.
4. Donald M. Allen, ed., *The New American Poetry* (New York: Grove Press, 1960), 420-21.
5. Snyder quoted in Gray, 131.
6. It is interesting to note that when Snyder assembled *No Nature* he dropped six poems from *Riprap*. It appears that different criteria guided

his selection process. For instance, he deleted two poems about women that had been criticized over the years as sexist, but which reflect his riprap poetics. Several of the other poems deleted, however, are those that are stylistically most removed from that poetics and in a couple of cases seem more poetically derivative, as in "A Stone Garden" and "T-2 Tanker Blues."

7. Yamazato, "Seeking a Fulcrum," 32.

8. On the concept of "point of attention," see Earl Miner, *Comparative Poetics* (Princeton: Princeton University Press, 1990) 181-212.

9. Gray, 134.

10. Paul, *In Search of the Primitive*, 215.

11. Susan Griffin, *Woman and Nature: The Roaring Inside Her* (New York: Harper & Row, 1978).

12. Steuding, 141.

13. See Paul, *In Search of the Primitive*, 219.

14. Charlene Spretnak, "Dinnertime," in Halper, 361.

15. While, as I have remarked, the poems are highly autobiographical, they are not purely so. While some critics have used "For a Far-out Friend" to accuse Snyder of celebrating his having actually beaten up a woman, Snyder is at pains to point out that the first line of the poem is a "fiction," not the description of an actual event.

16. Robinson Jeffers, *The Double Axe and Other Poems* (1948; New York: Liveright, 1977).

17. See Dean, 169, for a very different reading of these lines.

18. Gray, 142.

19. Thomas J. Leach, Jr., "Gary Snyder: Poet as Mythographer" (Diss. University of North Carolina at Chapel Hill, 1974), 8.

20. Gray, 152.

21. Emphasizing biography, Gray remarks that "the cedar walls of the berry-pickers cabin remind [Snyder] of his father's failed attempt at farming. . . . He does not want to repeat his father's mistakes," 154.

22. It is possible that additional poems exist in the pages of Snyder's voluminous unpublished Japan journals, but whether or not they become available to the public will depend on Snyder's editing decisions regarding the publication of those journals.

23. Paul, *In Search of the Primitive*, 220. Gray, 158-59, reads farther into the poem's images his own feminist critique of Snyder's sexism, particularly its Orientalist manifestations, than seems warranted. I don't find his imagined scenario of why there are "Men asleep in their underwear" persuasive.

24. Steuding, 50.

25. Snyder letter to Will Petersen, quoted in Sanehide Kodama, *American Poetry and Japanese Culture* (Hamden, Conn.: Archon Books, 1984), 179.

26. Kodama, 180.

27. Paul, *In Search of the Primitive*, 223. Paul slides over the fact that the culture doing such giving is a male dominated one and that, while Snyder may be reaching for a matrifocal vision here, he ends up aligning woman and nature on one side and man and culture on the other side.

28. Kodama, 182-83, 237n64.

29. Jeffers, xxi-xxii.

30. Leach, 35; cf. Charles Molesworth, *Gary Snyder's Vision: Poetry and the Real Work* (Columbia: University of Missouri Press, 1983), 20.

31. Gray, 163, 165.

Chapter Four: Passing and Returning

1. In London, *A Range of Poems* was published in 1966 by Fulcrum Press, but it is mainly a collected volume more than a new project in that Snyder did not select and organize the contents of this book in the way that he did for *No Nature: New and Selected Poems*. It contains the contents of *Riprap and Cold Mountains Poems*, *Myths & Texts*, Snyder's translations of a set of Miyazawa Kenji's poems, and a little over half of the poems that would appear in the final version of *The Back Country*. See McNeil, 24-28.

2. Gary Snyder, *Passage Through India* (San Francisco: Grey Fox Press, 1983), ix. Hereafter cited in the text as *Passage*.

3. *Caterpillar* was a small press literary magazine edited by Clayton Eshleman, whom Snyder mentions on the opening page of *Passage*.

4. Gray, 279n67.

5. Snyder, *Mountains and Rivers*, 154.

6. Faas, 138, 139.

7. McNeil, 35.

8. Steuding, 122.

9. For college professors who would want to teach *Myths & Texts* and yet find its complexity daunting, I would suggest *warming up* with "A Berry Feast," since it has a similar structure and also engages many of the same issues.

10. Gary Snyder, *The Back Country* (New York: New Directions, 1968, 1971), 3. Subsequent page references are given in the text.

11. Norton, 180.

12. Charles Altieri, "Gary Snyder's Lyric Poetry: Dialectic as Ecology," *Far Point* 4 (1970); rpt. in Murphy, *Critical Essays*, 54.

13. Altieri, "Gary Snyder's Lyric Poetry," 53.

14. Michael Castro, "Gary Snyder: The Lessons of *Turtle Island*," in *Interpreting the Indian: Twentieth-Century Poets and the American Indian* (Albuquerque: University of New Mexico Press, 1984); rpt. in Murphy, *Critical Essays*, 133.

15. Norton, 177-79; Norton builds on Altieri's discussion in "Gary Snyder's Lyric Poetry," pp. 54-55.

16. Snyder, *Mountains and Rivers Without End*, 73-74. This poem and "Home from Sierra" were omitted from *No Nature*.

17. *The Diamond Sutra and the Sutra of Hui Neng*, trans. A.F. Price and Wong Mou-Lam (Berkeley: Shambala, 1969), 60.

18. Snyder, "North Beach," originally published in *The Old Ways* and reprinted in *A Place in Space: Ethics, Aesthetics, and Watersheds* (Washington, D.C.: Counterpoint, 1995), 3; see Gray, 230.

19. Gray, 230.

20. See, for instance, "Working on the '58 Willys Pickup" and "Removing the Plate of the Pump on the Hydraulic System of the Backhoe," Snyder, *Axe Handles*, 39-40, 93.

21. Molesworth, 53-54.

22. Sherman Paul, "From Lookout to Ashram: The Way of Gary Snyder," *Iowa Review* 1.3 and 1.4 (1970), abridged rpt. in Murphy, *Critical Essays*, 74.

23. Gray, 234.

24. Mahar, 13; Halper, 432-33.

25. Robert Kern, "Recipes, Catalogues, Open Form Poetics: Gary Snyder's Archetypal Voice," *Contemporary Literature* 18 (1977), 190.

26. Paul, *In Search of the Primitive*, 253.

27. Snyder, *He Who Hunted Birds*, xi.

28. Gray, 237.

29. Yamazato, "Seeking a Fulcrum," 76.

30. Yamazato, "Seeking a Fulcrum," 128-132.

31. Gray comments on these poems that "they are much more honest in their appraisal of human relationships and more frustrated in their attempts to turn personal loss into poetic capital. Such honesty and frustration would increase even more significantly in "Kālī," 248.

32. Yamazato, "Seeking a Fulcrum," 75, 80.

33. Snyder, *The Real Work*, 7.

34. Katsunori Yamazato, personal correspondence 15 February 1999. Yamazato cites the poem about "Alisoun" in *Medieval English Lyrics: A Critical Anthology*, ed. R. T. Davies (Evanston: Northwestern University Press, 1964), 67.

35. See Gray's treatment of this poem in his extended discussion of Snyder's reconsideration of Asian women and his behavior toward them, pp. 248-62.

36. Almon, *Gary Snyder*, 29. Also see Almon for a discussion of Snyder's interest in Tantrism, to which he was introduced during his trip to India, pp. 28-30.

37. Molesworth, 52.

38. See Castro, "Gary Snyder," 142.

39. Gray, 264-68.

40. Charles Altieri, *Enlarging the Temple: New Directions in American Poetry during the 1960s* (Lewisburg, Pa.: Bucknell University Press, 1979), 143.

41. Kanaseki, 73-74.

42. While Snyder had expressed interest in continuing to work on Miyazawa's poetry, he may have ceased his efforts when a Japanese translator that he knew took over that task.

43. Alan Williamson, "Language Against Itself: The Middle Generation of Contemporary Poets," in *American Poetry Since 1960—Some Critical Perspectives*, ed. Robert B. Shaw (Cheshire, U.K.: Carcanet Press, 1973), 62.

Chapter Five: The Waves of Household and Marriage

1. See Gray on Snyder's revisions of this essay, pp. 289-93.

2. McNeil, 43-45.

3. Snyder, *Earth House Hold*, 80. Further page references to this volume are given in the text.

4. Hertz, 52.

5. Paul, "From Lookout to Ashram," 64.

6. Snyder, *The Real Work*, 137.

7. Gary Snyder, *Regarding Wave* (Iowa City: Windhover Press, 1969).

8. Gary Snyder, *Regarding Wave* (New York: New Directions, 1970). Further page references are to this edition and are given in the text. Throughout this volume a glyph appears that looks like two three-pronged forks attached back-to-back. It is the three-pointed Thunderbolt of Vajrayana Buddhism. Its prongs stand for a series of tripartite relationships: unity of body, speech, and mind; male, female, and androgyne; husband, wife, and child; and, moon, sun, and fire; with the last three also tied to the three seed syllables of Om, Ah, and Hum.

9. Steuding, 135.

10. Bert Almon, "Buddhism and Energy in the Recent Poetry of Gary Snyder," *Mosaic* 11.1 (1970); rpt. in Murphy, *Critical Essays*, 82.

11. Steuding, 149. Gray does not see Masa as an equal participant in this poem, but more the body upon which Snyder's mythic figuration of human and planetary geography is worked out, pp. 318-20.

12. Snyder, *The Real Work*, 89.

13. Katsunori Yamazato, "A Note on Japanese Allusions in Gary Snyder's Poetry," *Western American Literature* 18 (1983), 146-48.

14. David Robbins, "Gary Snyder's 'Burning Island,' " in *A Book of Rereads in Recent American Poetry*, ed. Greg Chiasma (Lincoln, Neb.: Best Cellar Press, 1979); rpt. in Murphy, *Critical Essays*, 89-105. Further references to this work are given in the text.

15. Tom Lavazzi, "Pattern of Flux: The 'Torsion Form' in Gary Snyder's Poetry," *American Poetry Review* 18.4 (July-August 1989), 43.

16. Yamazato, "Seeking a Fulcrum," 103.

17. Steuding, 140.

18. Gray, 319.

19. Julia Martin, "True Communionism: Gary Snyder's Transvaluation of Some Christian Terminology," *Journal for the Study of Religion* (South Africa) 1.1 (1988), 69.

20. Molesworth, 87.

21. Molesworth, 84-85.

Chapter Six: Reinhabiting the Land

1. McNeil, 68-69.

2. Katsunori Yamazato, "How to Be in This Crisis: Gary Snyder's Cross-Cultural Vision in *Turtle Island*," in Murphy, *Critical Essays*, 230.

3. Paul, *In Search of the Primitive*, 274.

4. Gary Snyder, *Turtle Island* (New York: New Directions, 1974). All further references are given in the text.

5. Yamazato, "Seeking a Fulcrum," 118-19. See Snyder's essay, "The Rediscovery of Turtle Island," in *A Place in Space*, 236-51.

6. Molesworth, 8.

7. Martin, "True Communionism," 66. See Greta Gaard, "Hiking without a Map: Reflections on Teaching Ecofeminist Literary Criticism," in *Ecofeminist Literary Criticism*, ed. Greta Gaard and Patrick D. Murphy (Urbana: University of Illinois Press, 1998), 235-36, for a critical reading of this poem that argues that "the unique identities of the son and the mother were subsumed in the identity of the father."

8. Yamazato, "How to Be," 236.

9. Gary Snyder, *The Fudo Trilogy* (Berkeley: Shaman Drum, 1973) n.p. Fudōmyo-o appears in all three of the poems printed here; hence the

title of the chapbook. McNeil notes of "Smokey the Bear Sutra": "According to Snyder, he had 'Smokey' printed on the occasion of the Sierra Club's Biennial Wilderness Conference in San Francisco" and distributed 1,000 copies of it as a free broadside. As such, it can be read as an activist manifesto used politically to influence Sierra Club members.

10. Faas, 109-10.
11. Snyder comments on the kind of people depicted here in Faas, 113.
12. L. Edwin Folsom, "Gary Snyder's Descent to Turtle Island: Searching for Fossil Love," *Western American Literature* 15 (1980), 109.
13. Molesworth, 101. While I agree with his general point, I disagree with Molesworth's appreciation of "Charms." While the effort to extend a recognition of subjectivity and sensuality across species is laudable, the poem itself fails because it is marred by a sexist attitude toward women. See also Gaard's comments on this poem on p. 235 of "Hiking Without a Map." It is worth noting that Snyder has chosen not to include it in either *No Nature* or the *Gary Snyder Reader*.
14. Gray, 350.
15. Yamazato, "How to Be," 239.
16. Hwa Yol Jung and Petee Jung, "Gary Snyder's Ecopiety," *Environmental History Review* 14.3 (1990), 76.
17. The Jungs note that Snyder considered the Hopi delegation the only exception to this behavior.
18. Paul, *In Search of the Primitive*, 276.
19. Snyder, *The Real Work*, 89.
20. Sharon Ann Jaeger, "Toward a Poetics of Embodiment: The Cognitive Rhetoric of Gary Snyder's *The Practice of the Wild*" (Diss. University of Pennsylvania, 1995), 138. Necessity, in addition to compassion and pleasure, is one of the issues that complicates treatment of Snyder's hunting poems. For example, in commenting on "The Hudsonian Curlew," Gaard notes in "Hiking Without a Map" that Snyder fails to demonstrate any necessity for the killing of the curlew (p. 234).
21. Gary Snyder, *Six Sections from Mountains and Rivers Without End Plus One* (San Francisco: Four Seasons Foundation, 1970).
22. Castro, "Gary Snyder," 139.
23. Castro, "Gary Snyder," 134-35.
24. This publication history is documented in McNeil, 47-50.
25. Charles Altieri, "Gary Snyder's Turtle Island: The Problem of Reconciling the Roles of Seer and Prophet," *boundary 2* 4 (1976), 761-77.
26. Molesworth, 104.
27. Paul, *In Search of the Primitive*, 282.
28. Jung and Jung, 84.
29. Eliot Weinberger, "Gary Snyder: The Art of Poetry LXXIV," *The Paris Review* 141 (1996); rptd. in Gary Snyder, *The Gary Snyder Reader: Prose, Poetry, and Translations, 1952-1998* (Washington, D.C.: Counterpoint, 1999), 336. As Weinberger's introduction indicates, this interview was originally conducted on October 26, 1992, and then was updated in connection with the publication of *Mountains and Rivers Without End*. The remarks quoted here would have been made during the original interview.

Chapter Seven: Handing Down the Practice

1. Charles Molesworth, "Getting a Handle on It," *American Book Review* 6.5-6 (1984), 15.
2. James W. Krauss, "Appendix A, Interview 1: June 15, 1983," in "Gary Snyder's Biopoetics: A Study of the Poet as Ecologist," Diss. University of Hawaii, 1986, 173; and O'Grady, 288.
3. Gary Snyder, Letter to Dave Foreman published in *Earth First!* 1 August 1982, 2-3. In this letter Snyder criticizes the Earth First! organization for its promotion of "monkey-wrenching"—sabotage of machinery—as part of an endorsement of violent action. He emphasizes that movements in the 1960s and 1970s were heavily infiltrated by government provocateurs espousing violence and that acts of violence or of groups arming themselves, such as the Black Panther Party, played into the hands of government suppression.
4. See for instance, "Changes," *San Francisco Oracle* #7 (February 1967), 8, and "The Return of Gary Snyder" (Interview by Keith Lampe), *Berkeley Barb* 3-9 January 1969, 12-14—an edited down version of this interview appears in Snyder, *The Real Work*, 7-14. Gray discusses these texts and the social events surrounding them in some detail; see pp. 293-309.
5. Gary Snyder, *Axe Handles* (San Francisco: North Point Press, 1983), 7. Further quotations from this volume are cited in the text.
6. Julia Martin, "The Pattern which Connects: Metaphor in Gary Snyder's Later Poetry," *Western American Literature* 22 (1987); rpt. in Murphy, *Critical Essays on Gary Snyder*, 199.
7. Krauss, 173.
8. Robert Schultz and David Wyatt, "Gary Snyder and the Curve of Return," *Virginia Quarterly Review* 62 (1986); rpt. in Murphy, *Critical Essays*, 161.
9. Snyder has frequently paid tribute to Pound's influence on his work. For example, on January 19, 1973, the Academy of American Poets presented "A Quiet Requiem for E. P." [Ezra Pound] at the New York Public Library. The program of the event reprinted excerpts from publications and letters by various poets, including Snyder. In a 1 December 1972 letter to the Academy, Snyder eulogized Pound as a teacher whose vision encouraged other poets to develop their craft and their own intellectual quests (a copy of the program is in the Gary Snyder Archives).
10. Yamazato, "Seeking a Fulcrum," 168. See Tim Dean, 145-52, for a different, Lacanian reading of this poem.
11. Portions of this interpretation are based on my note "Gary Snyder's Endless River," *NMAL* 9.1 (1985), Item 4.
12. Yamazato, "Seeking a Fulcrum," 169.
13. Woody Rehanek, "The Shaman Songs of Gary Snyder," *Okanogan Natural News* No.19 (Summer 1984), 9.
14. Yamazato, "Seeking a Fulcrum, 177.
15. Schultz and Wyatt, 157; Yamazato, "Seeking a Fulcrum," 173; Eric Todd Smith in "Place and Impermanence in Gary Snyder's *Mountains and Rivers Without End*" in the "Gary Snyder: An International Perspective" special issue, guest ed. Patrick D. Murphy, *Studies in the Humanities* 26.1-2 (1999), disagrees with Schultz and Wyatt, commenting that "the Buddhist principle of emptiness, however, works in *Mountains and*

Rivers to undermine the apparent conflict between a life of transience and a life rooted in place and community" (113-14).

16. Yamazato, "Seeking a Fulcrum," 166; he cites Snyder's defining Gaia in this way in the essay "Good, Wild, Sacred," which appeared in *CoEvoluton Quarterly* about the time *Axe Handles* was published and was reprinted in *The Practice of the Wild*.

17. Schultz and Wyatt, 164.

18. Martin, "The Pattern," 203.

19. See my essay, "Sex-Typing the Planet: Gaia Imagery and the Problem of Subverting Patriarchy," *Environmental Ethics* 10 (1988), 155-68.

20. Martin, "The Pattern," 206.

21. Snyder's response to Paul's remarks is included in Sherman Paul, *In Search of the Primitive*, 299. Also, as noted earlier, Snyder has deleted a previously published passage on the Gaia hypothesis when he reprinted the essays from *The Old Ways* in *A Place in Space*. Also, he has included none of these poems in *The Gary Snyder Reader*, although he did choose two-thirds of them for *No Nature*.

22. Rehanek, 11-12.

23. Snyder, Letter to Dave Foreman, 2-3.

24. Schultz and Wyatt, 162.

25. Leonard M. Scigaj, "Dōgen's Boat, Fan and Rice Cake: Realization and Artifice in Snyder's *Mountains and Rivers Without End*," "Gary Snyder: An International Perspective" special issue, guest ed. Patrick D. Murphy, *Studies in the Humanities* 26.1-2 (1999), 133.

26. Andrew Schelling, "How the Grinch Imitated Gary Snyder," *Sulfur* No.13 (1985), 160.

27. Jack Hicks, "Poetic Composting in Gary Snyder's *Left Out in the Rain*," in Murphy, *Critical Essays*, 250.

28. Gary Snyder, *Left Out in the Rain: New Poems 1947-1985* (San Francisco: North Point Press, 1986), 5-8. Further references to this edition are given in the text.

29. Yamazato, "Seeking a Fulcrum," 189. Such skepticism goes far deeper than even this poem suggests, as indicated by the letters Snyder wrote to Philip Whalen at the time, which are available in the Philip Whalen Collection at Reed College and discussed in some detail by Gray.

30. Rossiter and Evans, 10.

31. See Scott McLean, " 'Thirty Miles of Dust: There Is No Other Life,' " in Halper, 138.

32. Krauss, "Appendix B, Interview 2: October 17, 1985," in "Gary Snyder's Biopoetics," 205.

33. Scigaj, "Dōgen's Boat," 133.

34. Krauss, 184.

35. Yamazato, "Seeking a Fulcrum," 200.

Chapter Eight: Of Wildness and Wilderness in Plain Language

1. Jaeger, 2.

2. Ray Olson, Review of *The Practice of the Wild*, *Booklist* (15 September 1990), 134.

3. Anonymous, "A Conversation with Gary Snyder," *Sallyport* 30.1 (Jan. 1971), 7.

4. Four essays from *The Great Clod* project on China, which had been previously published, are collected in *The Gary Snyder Reader*, while some work from the Ainu project has appeared but not been collected.

5. Rossiter and Evans, 13.

6. David Robertson, "Practicing the Wild—Present and Future Plans: An Interview with Gary Snyder," in Murphy, *Critical Essays*, 262.

7. For a discussion of the distinction between "nature writing" and "environmental writing," see Patrick D. Murphy, *Farther Afield in the Study of Nature-Oriented Literature* (Charlottesville: University Press of Virginia, 2000).

8. Jaeger, 1.

9. Robertson, "Practicing the Wild," 258.

10. Robertson, "Practicing the Wild," 261.

11. Gary Snyder, *The Practice of the Wild* (San Francisco: North Point Press, 1990), 4. Subsequent page references to this edition are given in the text.

12. Gary Snyder, "Editors' Statements," *CoEvolution Quarterly* no. 19 (21 Sept, 1978), np. The other editor is David Meltzer, who issued his own statement on the same page.

13. Jaeger, 2.

14. Kanetsuki Gutetsu and Gary Snyder, eds. *The Wooden Fish* (Kyoto: The First Zen Institute of American in Japan, 1961), 15.

15. Jaeger, 124.

16. Tom Clark, "Essays that echo Thoreau," "Book Review" section, *San Francisco Chronicle* 16 September 1990, 3.

17. Gary Snyder, *A Place in Space: Ethics, Aesthetics, and Watersheds* (Washington, D.C.: Counterpoint, 1995), 189.

18. Clark, 3.

19. Gary Snyder, "Letter from Gary Snyder," *Omu* 10 (1974), 26. *Omu* was published by a group called Jimusho, led by Nanao Sakaki. This issue, with the header "Nature Not For Sale," was devoted to a campaign to protect Suwanose Island from a Yamaha Corporation development scheme. This and other copies of the journal can be found in the Gary Snyder Archives.

20. In Kanetsuki and Snyder, *The Wooden Fish*, in a "Note on mealtime chanting," they write that "eating is a sacrament in Zen training. No other aspect of ordinary human daily life is treated with quite such formality or reverence in the sōdō" (p.25).

Chapter Nine: Sifting and Selecting

1. Gary Snyder, *No Nature: New and Selected Poems* (New York: Pantheon, 1992), v. Further page references are cited in the text. For years, New Directions had been Snyder's primary publisher for books. Then when Jack Shoemaker established North Point Press in the Bay Area, Snyder began publishing with him, but then Shoemaker sold North Point Press to Farrar, Straus & Giroux. Later, he established a new press, Counterpoint, with which Snyder has been publishing since 1995. In between the demise of Shoemaker's earlier press and the new one, Snyder brought out *No Nature* and, hence, its anomalous publication with Pantheon. Portions of this discussion of *No Nature* are based on my remarks about a few of the new poems originally written for *Farther Afield in the Study of Nature-Oriented Literature* (Charlottesville: University Press of Virginia, 2000).

2. Jaeger, 125-26.

3. Jaeger, 110, 112.

4. Jaeger, 23.

5. *The Diamond Sutra*, 60.

6. In an email to the author on 10 December 1995, Snyder stated that "the first lines in 'Ripples on the Surface' were said to me by the Tlingit elder Nora Marks Dauenhauer (also a published poet) who was quoting her mother, on the matter of how to read nature."

7. Yong-ki Kang, "The Politics of Deconstruction in Snyder's 'Ripples on the Surface,' " "Gary Snyder: An International Perspective," special issue, guest ed. Patrick D. Murphy, *Studies in the Humanities* 26.1-2 (1999), 100.

8. Kang, 100.

9. Kang, 109.

10. Gary Snyder, *A Place in Space*, vii. Further references to this work are cited in the text.

11. Kenneth A. Olliff, review, *Environment* 38.10 (Dec. 1996), 25; Stuart Cowan, review, *Whole Earth Review* n. 89 (Spring 1996), 74; Donna Seaman, *Booklist* 92.1 (1 Sept. 1995), 32; J. Baird Callicott, review, *Environmental Ethics* 18.3 (Fall 1996), 322, 326.

12. In addition to being published as a broadside and reproduced by a variety of people and presses, "Smokey the Bear Sutra" was published by Snyder in *The Fudo Trilogy*, which included "Spel Against Demons"— like "Smokey" originally published as a broadside, then in the *Manzanita* chapbook (Bolinas, Calif.: Four Seasons Foundation, 1972) and later in *Turtle Island* and *No Nature*—and "The California Water Plan—originally published as a broadside and not reprinted in any full-length collection.

13. Jaeger, 45; on Fudōmyō-ō, see the discussion of "Spel Against Demons" in Chapter 6 and accompanying endnotes. Jaeger provides an extended discussion of this poem, 44-52.

14. Jaeger, 47-48.

15. See Chapter 6 for an overview of its initial publication history.

16. David Robertson, "Bioregionalism in Nature Writing," *American Nature Writers*, 2 vols., ed. John Elder (New York: Charles Scribner's Sons, 1996), II: 1020. Robertson goes on to say that "as seen by a Westerner looking in from the outside, mandala has multiple meanings. It seems, for example, to designate at least three different spaces. It is, at first, a visual representation of the spatial order of the physical universe. . . . it is, at this level of meaning, a paradigm. . . . Next, mandala creates a space for dharma practice, the purpose of which is attainment of enlightenment within the spatial order of the universe. The second space of mandala allows human beings to position themselves in the first space in a way that allows them to know the truth about themselves and the world. Finally, mandala is the sacred space that comes into being at the moment of enlightenment. It is true space, the ultimately real universe" (1020). An ecosystem, then, understood as a mandala identifies a human being's environment as both the *real* place where he or she must work out her own proper understanding of the world and as a sacred place where his or her practice is fully realized, which could only occur if the integrity of the ecosystem is upheld in both its phenomenal and metaphysical manifestations.

17. Robertson, "Bioregionalism," 1020. For more on mandalas related to ecology, see *Buddhism and Ecology: The Interconnection of Dharma and Deeds*, edited by Mary Evelyn Tucker and Duncan Ryūken Williams (Cambridge: Harvard University Press, 1997), especially Paul O. Ingram, "The Jeweled Net of Nature," 71-88.

18. Joanna Macy and John Seed are deep ecology, bioregional activists who co-authored with Pat Fleming and Arne Naess a book titled *Thinking Like a Mountain: Towards a Council of All Beings* (Philadelphia: New Society Publishers, 1988).

19. Jaeger, 124-25.

20. Gary Snyder, "Regenerate Culture!" Interview with *The New Catalyst* in *Turtle Talk: Voices for a Sustainable Future*, ed. Christopher Plant and Judith Plant (Philadelphia: New Society Publishers, 1990), 16-17.

21. Robertson, "Bioregionalism," 1022.

Chapter Ten: The Calligraphy of Water on Rock

1. "Noh, a medieval play with dancing and recitation much influenced by Buddhism, is one of the most important Japanese literary elements of influence on Snyder's poetry," according to Yamazato, "Seeking a Fulcrum," 61. "Noh" and "Nō" are two different ways of transliterating the same word in Japanese.

2. Robertson, "Practicing the Wild," 259.

3. Snyder remarks in the Weinberger interview that was originally conducted in 1992 and then updated for publication in 1996 that "between 1992 and 1996, seeing the shape of the whole forming up, I put *Mountains and Rivers* ahead of everything else . . . til it was done" (p.112).

4. Eric Todd Smith, *Reading Gary Snyder's* Mountains and Rivers Without End (Boise: Western Writers Series, 1999), 30.

5. Miner, 169; see also 54-55. Miner also makes a significant point regarding Nō pertinent to *Mountains and Rivers*, when he remarks about the play *Matsukaze* that "because so much of the play—and this is typical of *nō*—is spent on recollection, there is a great deal of Brecht's 'narration on the stage.' What we hear is nonetheless also highly lyric" (p.68). *Mountains and Rivers Without End*, then, like Nō, contains dramatic, narrative, and lyric elements throughout.

6. Steuding, 95-96.

7. Yamazato, "A Note," 144.

8. Gary Snyder, *Mountains and Rivers Without End* (Washington, D.C.: Counterpoint 1996), 8. All further page references will be given in the text.

9. Anthony Hunt, "Singing the Dyads: The Chinese Landscape Scroll and Gary Snyder's *Mountains and Rivers Without End*," *Journal of Modern Literature*, in press; Smith, *Reading*.

10. Mikhail Bakhtin, "The Epic and the Novel," in *The Dialogic Imagination: Four Essays by M.M. Bakhtin*, trans. Michael Holquist and Caryl Emerson, ed. Holquist (Austin: University of Texas Press, 1981), 3-40.

11. Quoted in Steuding, 102. Steuding takes this quote from a TV interview, "Philip Whalen and Gary Snyder," Poetry U.S.A. (Bloomington, Indiana, National Educational Television interview, 1965).

12. Hunt, "Singing the Dyads," in press.

13. Weinberger, 111.
14. Smith, *Reading*, 6.
15. Scigaj, "Dōgen's Boat," 127. Scigaj provides an excellent extended discussion of Dōgen's relevance to the sequence as a whole as well as to individual parts.
16. In Smith, *Reading*, see Smith's quotation from his interview with Snyder, 14-15.
17. Yamazato, "Seeking a Fulcrum," 63; see pp. 61-63 for more on the formative influence of Nō on the development of *Mountains and Rivers*.
18. Yamazato, "Seeking a Fulcrum," 54. Yamazato quotes from the foreword to *Zen Dust* by Isshū Miura and Ruth Fuller Sasaki (New York: Harcourt, Brace & World, 1966), xiii. Mrs. Sasaki was Sōkei-an's widow, having married him, as I understand, to keep him from being interned during World War II.
19. Yamazato, "Seeking a Fulcrum," 55; Gray, 220-23. Both Yamazato and Gray rely on letters by Snyder to Philip Whalen available in the Whalen Archives at Reed College.
20. McNeil, 38.
21. The head-shaving is explained by Anthony Hunt in " 'Bubbs Creek Haircut': Gary Snyder's 'Great Departure' in *Mountains and Rivers without End*," *Western American Literature* 15 (1980)167-69. My interpretation of this poem is heavily indebted to Hunt's essay.
22. Hunt, "'Bubbs Creek,'" 169-71.
23. Tantra is "a pan-Indian religious form involving magical ritual, depending on a guru, and sometimes sexual practices," according to Robert Aitken, *The Mind of Clover: Essays in Zen Buddhist Ethics* (San Francisco: North Point Press, 1984), 199.
24. Faas, 135. Snyder refers to this as Avatamsaka, or "Flower Wreath" Buddhism, which in China is known as Hua-Yen and in Japan as Kegon.
25. See Peter Georgelos, "Post-Structural 'Traces' in the Work of Gary Snyder" (M.A. thesis, University of Western Ontario, 1987), 41-42, for this story and its relevance to Snyder's thought.
26. Yamazato, "Seeking a Fulcrum," 89. In the letter Yamazato quotes, Snyder indicates that his teacher organized a ceremony for him "to acknowledge that the student has had *kensho*, 'seeing into true nature' " (Yamazato, "Seeking a Fulcrum," 90).
27. Cf. Smith, *Reading*, for a very different interpretation of the conclusion of this poem.
28. McNeil, 52.
29. Beongchen Yu, *The Great Circle: American Writers and the Orient* (Detroit: Wayne State University Press, 1983), 223.
30. Steuding, for instance, addresses it, 105-109.
31. Julia Martin, "Practising Emptiness: Gary Snyder's Playful Ecological Work," *Western American Literature* 27.1 (1992), 9.
32. Martin, "Practising Emptiness," 9.
33. Faas, 137.
34. Julia Martin, "The Snake Person Takes on the Cock-Sure Boys: Buddhism / Postmodernism / South African Eco-politics," in *Liminal Postmodernism: The Postmodern, the (Post-)Colonial, and the (Post-)Feminist*, ed. Theo D'haen and Hans Bertens (Amsterdam, Rodopi, 1994), 347.
    For an English translation of the sutra, see Robert Aitken, *Taking the Path*, 110-11.

35. Aitken, *Taking the Path*, 108.
36. Martin, "The Snake Person," 339; see also 340-41.
37. Anthony Hunt, " 'The Hump-backed Flute Player': The Structure of Emptiness in Gary Snyder's *Mountains and Rivers Without End*," *ISLE: Interdisciplinary Studies in Literature and Environment* 1.2 (Fall 1993), 4 and 5.
38. Hunt, " 'The Hump-backed Flute Player,' " 6-8.
39. David Robertson in *Real Matter* (Salt Lake City: University of Utah Press, 1997), 100-115, provides detailed background on Snyder's acquaintance with Mount Tamalpais.
40. Robertson, *Real Matter*, 125.
41. Robertson, *Real Matter*, 133.
42. Robertson, *Real Matter*, 138.
43. The reading and interview with Lewis MacAdams took place in December of 1988 and are recorded in *Gary Snyder*, 2 vols., dir. Lewis MacAdams and John Dorr (Los Angeles: Lannan Literary Videos, 1989).
44. John Whalen-Bridge, "Spirit of Place and Wild Politics in Two Recent Snyder Poems," *Northwest Review* 29.3 (1991), 130-31.
45. On the idea of "enduring time," see Ariel Salleh, *Ecofeminism as Politics* (London: Zed, 1998), 137. Salleh takes the term from the work of Georges Gurvitch.
46. Smith, *Reading*, 39.
47. Gary Snyder, Foreword, Aitken, *Taking the Path*, xiii-xiv.

Conclusion: As Mountains and Waters Remain

1. Gary Snyder, "Acceptance Speech for the Bukkyo Dendo Kyokai Award Ceremonies, 13 March 1998. Unpublished.
2. See Gary Snyder, "Migration/Immigration: Wandering South and North Erasing Borders Coming To Live on Turtle Island," *Wild Duck Review* 4.1 (Winter 1998), 15.
3. Weinberger, 335-36.

Selected Bibliography

I. Books and Essays by Gary Snyder

Poetry

Riprap. Ashland, Mass.: Origin Press, 1959.

Myths & Texts. New York: Totem Press/Corinth Books, 1960; New York: New Directions, 1978.

Riprap and Cold Mountain Poems. San Francisco: Four Seasons Foundation, 1965; San Francisco: North Point Press, 1990.

A Range of Poems. London: Fulcrum Press, 1966.

The Back Country. London: Fulcrum Press, 1967; revised and enlarged edition, New York: New Directions, 1968.

Regarding Wave. Iowa City: Windhover Press, 1969 [limited edition]; revised and enlarged edition, New York: New Directions, 1970. London: Fulcrum Press, 1970.

The Fudo Trilogy. Berkeley: Shaman Drum, 1973.

Turtle Island. New York: New Directions, 1974.

Axe Handles. San Francisco: North Point Press, 1983.

Left Out in the Rain: New Poems 1947-1985. San Francisco: North Point Press, 1986.

No Nature: New and Selected Poems. New York: Pantheon, 1992.

Mountains and Rivers Without End. Washington, D.C.: Counterpoint, 1996.

Prose

Earth House Hold: Technical Notes & Queries to Fellow Dharma Revolutionaries. New York: New Directions, 1969, London: Jonathan Cape, 1970.

The Old Ways: Six Essays. San Francisco: City Lights Books, 1977.

He Who Hunted Birds in His Father's Village: The Dimensions of a Haida Myth. Bolinas, Calif.: Grey Fox Press, 1979.

Passage Through India. San Francisco: Grey Fox Press, 1983.

The Practice of the Wild: Essays by Gary Snyder. San Francisco: North Point Press, 1990.

A Place in Space: Ethics, Aesthetics, and Watersheds. Washington, D.C.: Counterpoint, 1995.

Compilation

The Gary Snyder Reader: Prose, Poetry, and Translation, 1952-1998. Washington, D.C.: Counterpoint, 1999.

Uncollected Essays

"On Rinzai Masters and Western Students in Japan," *Wind Bell* 8.1-2 (Fall 1969): 23-25.

"Journey to Mountains and Rivers Without End." In *Tōkaidō, On the Road: Pilgrimage, Travel and Culture*, ed. Stephen Addiss. Lawrence: The University of Kansas Spencer Museum of Art, 1982. 38-40.

"Poet." *Naropa Magazine* 1.1 (1984): 33-34.
"Beyond Cathay: The Hill Tribes of China." In *Mountain People*, ed. Michael Tobias. Norman: University of Oklahoma Press, 1986. 150-52.
"On the Road with D. T. Suzukiu." In *A Zen Life: D. T. Suzuki Remembered*, ed. Masao Abe. New York: Weatherhill, 1986. 207-209.
"Migration/Immigration: Wandering South and North Erasing Borders Coming To Live on Turtle Island," *Wild Duck Review* 4.1 (Winter 1998): 15.

II. Video and Audiocassette

Gary Snyder, 2 vols., dir. Lewis MacAdams and John Dorr. Los Angeles: Lannan Literary Videos, 1989.
This Is Our Body, audiocassette. Washington, D.C.: Watershed tapes, 1989.

III. Archives

Gary Snyder Archives: Unpublished papers and letters. Department of Special Collections, University of California Library, Davis, California.
Philip Whalen Archives. Department of Special Collections, Reed College, Portland, Oregon.

IV. Interviews and Talks

Allen, Donald, ed. *On Bread & Poetry: A Panel Discussion with Gary Snyder, Lew Welch & Philip Whalen*. Bolinas, Calif.: Grey Fox Press, 1977.
Dardick, Geeta. "An Interview with Gary Snyder." *Sierra* Sept./Oct. 1985, 68-73.
Egan, Charles. "Poetic Insights: An Interview with Gary Snyder," *Poets & Writers Magazine* (May/June 1995), 68-75.
Faas, Ekbert. *Towards A New American Poetics: Essays & Interviews*. Santa Barbara: Black Sparrow Press, 1979.
Helm, Michael. "A Conversation with Gary Snyder," *California Living Magazine, Sunday San Francisco Examiner & Chronicle* 20 November 1983, 13-17, 19.
———. "Gary Snyder Interview." *City Miner Magazine* 4.1 (1979): 9-13, 37-44.
Hertz, Un. "An Interview with Gary Snyder." *Third Rail* 7 (1985-86): 51-53, 96.
Martin, Julia. "Coyote-Mind: An Interview with Gary Snyder," *Triquarterly* 79 (Autumn 1990): 148-72.
McKenzie, James. "Moving the World a Millionth of an Inch: Gary Snyder." In *The Beat Vision: A Primary Sourcebook*, ed. Arthur and Kit Knight. New York: Paragon, 1987. 1-27.
Moyers, Bill. *The Language of Life: A Festival of Poets*, ed. James Haba. New York: Doubleday. 1995.
O'Connell, Nicholas. *At The Field's End*. Seattle: Madrona Publishers, 1987.
O'Grady, John P. "Living Landscape: An Interview with Gary Snyder," *Western American Literature* 33.3 (Fall 1998): 275-91.
"Regenerate Culture!" Interview with *The New Catalyst. Turtle Talk: Voices for a Sustainable Future*, ed. Christopher Plant and Judith Plant. Philadelphia: New Society Publishers, 1990. 12-19.
Snyder, Gary. *The Real Work: Interviews & Talks, 1964-1979*. Ed. Wm. Scott McLean. New York: New Directions, 1980.

Weinberger, Eliot. "Gary Snyder: The Art of Poetry LXXIV," *The Paris Review* 141 (1996), rptd. In Gary Snyder,*The Gary Snyder Reader*, 319-338.

V. Bibliography

McNeil, Katherine. *Gary Snyder: A Bibliography*. New York: Phoenix Bookshop, 1983. An essential reference work; also contains valuable remarks by Snyder about various volumes.

VI. Books and Journal Issues on Gary Snyder

Almon, Bert. *Gary Snyder*. Western Writers Series 37. Boise, Idaho: Boise State University, 1979. A brief overview of Snyder's work up through *Turtle Island*.

Dean, Tim. *Gary Snyder and the American Unconscious: Inhabiting the Ground*. New York: St. Martin's, 1991. A Lacanian psychoanalytic reading of Snyder in relation to the American frontier and the cultural unconscious of the mainstream population. Focuses on *Riprap*, *Myths & Texts*, and *Axe Handles*; downplays Buddhism and ecology.

"Gary Snyder: An International Perspective," guest ed. Patrick D. Murphy, special issue, *Studies in the Humanities* 26.1-2 (1999). Contains original essays by critics and translators from Croatia, Japan, Korea, Mexico, Spain, and the United States, including treatment of *Mountains and Rivers*, as well as an interview from Japan.

Halper, Jon, ed. *Gary Snyder: Dimensions of a Life*. San Francisco: Sierra Club Books, 1991. Collects over seventy essays and reminiscences commenting on the life and times of Snyder.

McCord, Howard. *Some Notes on Gary Snyder's* Myths & Texts. Berkeley: Sand Dollar, 1971. A valuable aid in reading *Myths & Texts*, with explanations and comments by Snyder.

Molesworth, Charles. *Gary Snyder's Vision: Poetry and the Real Work*. Columbia: University of Missouri Press, 1983. Analyzes Snyder's major volumes emphasizing political concerns. It contains valuable insights but is hampered by an unfamiliarity with Buddhism.

Murphy, Patrick D., ed. *Critical Essays on Gary Snyder*. Boston: G. K. Hall, 1990. Contains a bibliographical introduction, thirteen reprinted essays, four original essays, and an original interview.

Schuler, Robert. *Journeys Toward the Original Mind: The Long Poems of Gary Snyder*. New York: Peter Lang, 1994. A study that fails to realize its claim of a "comprehensive" explication of Snyder's sequences; nor does it acknowledge previously published criticism on them.

Smith, Eric Todd. *Reading Gary Snyder's* Mountains and Rivers Without End. Western Writers Series. Boise: Boise State University, 1999. A pamphlet-length study that focuses on background information and key Buddhist concepts and treats only a few poems in detail.

Steuding, Bob. *Gary Snyder*. Boston: Twayne, 1976. The first full-length overview of Snyder's life and work.

VII. Books with Chapters on Gary Snyder

Altieri, Charles. *Enlarging the Temple: New Directions in American Poetry during the 1960s*. Lewisburg, Pa.: Bucknell University Press, 1979. Compares Snyder with other American poets and argues that he writes in an "immanentist mode."

Beach, Christopher Beach. *ABC of Influence: Ezra Pound and the Remaking of the American Poetic Tradition*. Berkeley: University of California Press, 1992. Discusses the influence of Pound on Snyder.

Castro, Michael. *Interpreting the Indian: Twentieth-Century Poets and the American Indian*. Albuquerque: University of New Mexico Press, 1984. Two chapters on Snyder defend his use of Native American materials and provide readings of individual poems.

Davidson, Michael. *The San Francisco Renaissance: Poetics and Community at Mid-Century*. 1989. New York: Cambridge University Press, 1991. Includes attention to Snyder within the context of providing a cultural history of the movement.

Foster, Edward Halsey. *Understanding The Beats*. Columbia: University of South Carolina Press, 1992. Includes passing discussions of Snyder while focusing on Ginsberg, Kerouac, and others.

Kodama, Sanehide. *American Poetry and Japanese Culture*. Hamden, Conn.: Archon Books, 1984. Treats the influence of Japanese culture and experiences in Japan on Snyder.

Kyger, Joanne. *The Japan and India Journals, 1960-1964*. Bolinas, Calif.: Tombouctou, 1981. Treats Kyger's marriage to Snyder and their experiences.

McLeod, Dan. "Gary Snyder." *The Beats: Literary Bohemians in Postwar America, Part 2. Dictionary of Literary Biography*, vol.16, ed. Ann Charters. Detroit: Gale, 1983. 486-500. Particularly useful in terms of Snyder's relationship to the Beats and the San Francisco Renaissance.

Murphy, Patrick D. *Literature, Nature, and Other: Ecofeminist Critiques*. Albany: SUNY Press, 1995. Contains a chapter discussing Snyder in relation to the idea of transcendence, one comparing him with Ursula K. Le Guin, and a reprinting of "Sex-typing the Planet."

Paul, Sherman. *In Search of the Primitive: Rereading David Antin, Jerome Rothenberg, and Gary Snyder*. Baton Rouge: Louisiana State University Press, 1986. Reflects on Snyder's major works and includes Snyder's responses to the interpretations.

Robertson, David. *Real Matter*. Salt Lake City: University of Utah Press, 1997. Provides detailed background on Snyder's acquaintance with Mount Tamalpais.

Tucker, Mary Evelyn, and Duncan Ryūken Williams, ed. *Buddhism and Ecology: The Interconnection of Dharma and Deeds*. Cambridge: Harvard University Press, 1997. Several chapters provide passing or extended discussions of Snyder's Buddhist ecology. See especially the chapter by David Landis Barnhill.

Wyatt, David. *The Fall into Eden: Landscape and Imagination in California*. New York: Cambridge University Press, 1986. Devotes a chapter to a comparative discussion of Snyder and Robinson Jeffers, emphasizing a sense of return in Snyder's poems.

VIII. Critical Articles on Gary Snyder

Altieri, Charles. "Gary Snyder's Turtle Island: The Problem of Reconciling the Roles of Seer and Prophet." *boundary 2* 4 (1976): 761-77. Criticizes Snyder for shifting from the earlier role of seer to that of prophet based on an aestheticist argument.

Bartlett, Lee. "Gary Snyder's Han-Shan," *Sagetrieb* 2 (1983), 105-10.

Addresses Snyder's rendering of the persona of the Cold Mountain poet.

―――. "Gary Snyder's *Myths & Texts* and the Monomyth." *Western American Literature* 17 (1982): 137-48. Interprets this sequence using Joseph Campbell's Jungian monomyth.

Carpenter, David A. "Gary Snyder's Inhumanism, From *Riprap* to *Axe Handles.*" *South Dakota Review* 26 (1988): 110-38. Criticizes Snyder for being misanthropic.

Crunk (James Wright). "The Work of Gary Snyder." *The Sixties* 6 (Spring 1962): 25-42. Rpt. in James Wright, *Collected Prose*. Ed. Anne Wright. Ann Arbor: University of Michigan Press, 1983. 105-19. First serious critical treatment of Snyder's poetry.

Folsom, L. Edwin. "Gary Snyder's Descent to Turtle Island: Searching for Fossil Love." *Western American Literature* 15 (1980): 103-21 Explores Snyder's recycling of American culture to its origins.

Hamalian, Leo. "Beyond the Paleface: D. H. Lawrence and Gary Snyder," *Talisman* #7 (Fall 1991), 50-55. Comparative discussion of the two poets, identifying Lawrence's influence on Snyder as well as their differences.

Holaday, Woon-Ping Chin. "Formlessness and Form in Gary Snyder's *Mountains and Rivers Without End.*" *Sagetrieb* 5 (1986): 41-51. Analyzes Snyder's sequence in terms of the degree to which it is anti-teleological based on Buddhist notions of form and void.

Hunt, Anthony. " 'Bubbs Creek Haircut': Gary Snyder's 'Great Departure' in *Mountains and Rivers without End.*" *Western American Literature* 15 (1980): 167-69. An excellent reading of one poem of this sequence, which is helpful for reading other sections as well.

―――. "'The Hump-backed Flute Player': The Structure of Emptiness in Gary Snyder's *Mountains and Rivers Without End,*" *ISLE: Interdisciplinary Studies in Literature and Environment* 1.2 (Fall 1993): 1-23. A richly detailed study of this poem, as well as its implications for the sequence as a whole.

―――. "Singing the Dyads: The Chinese Landscape Scroll and Gary Snyder's *Mountains and Rivers Without End,*" *Journal of Modern Literature,* in press. Provides a thorough analysis of the history of the landscape scroll upon which Snyder bases the sequence, as well as how knowledge of the scroll aids interpretation.

Jung, Hwa Yol, and Petee Jung. "Gary Snyder's Ecopiety." *Environmental History Review* 14.3 (1990): 75-87. Focuses on the interrelationship of Snyder's ecological and spiritual beliefs.

Kahn, Paul. *Han Shan in English.* Buffalo: White Pine Press, 1989. Treats the various translations of this poet, including those by Snyder.

Kalter, Susan. "The Path to *Endless*: Gary Snyder in the mid-1990s." *Texas Studies in Literature and Language* 41.1 (1999): 16-46. A challenging postmodern dialogical feminist critique of Snyder that unfortunately ignores previous critical work already addressing the issues that Kalter raises.

Kern, Robert. "Clearing the Ground: Gary Snyder and the Modernist Imperative." *Criticism* 19 (Spring 1977): 158-77. Reads the early poetry as a reaction to modernism and a need for Snyder to shake off previous models to find his own poetic voice.

Lavazzi, Tom. "Pattern of Flux: The 'Torsion Form' in Gary Snyder's Poetry." *The American Poetry Review* 18.4 (July-August 1989): 41-47. Defines a poetics of internal tensions, particularly in relation to sexuality, and applies it to Snyder's poetry and consciousness.

Leed, Jacob. "Gary Snyder, Han Shan, and Jack Kerouac," *Journal of Modern Literature* 11 (1984): 185-93. Historical discussion of the making of the translations.

Lewitt, Philip Jay. "Gary Snyder & The Vow." *Kyoto Review* 23 (Spring 1990): 1-17. Argues that Snyder's commitment to Buddhism results in his aesthetics flowing from his ethics.

Lin, Yao-fu. " 'The Mountains Are Your Mind': Orientalism in the Poetry of Gary Snyder." *Tamkang Review* 6-7 (1975-1976): 357-91. Treats Chinese allusions and influences in Snyder's work.

Ling Chung, "Whose Mountain Is This?—Gary Snyder's Translation of Han Shan," *Renditions* 7 (Spring 1977): 93-102. Discusses Snyder's Cold Mountain translations.

Mao, Nathan. "The Influence of Zen Buddhism on Gary Snyder." *Tamkang Review* 5.2 (1974): 125-33. Points out manifestations of Zen in Snyder's poetry.

Martin, Julia. "Practising Emptiness: Gary Snyder's Playful Ecological Work," *Western American Literature* 27.1 (1992): 3-19. Provides a richly nuanced discussion of the interrelationship of Buddhism and ecology in Snyder's poetry.

———. "The Snake Person Takes on the Cock-Sure Boys: Buddhism / Postmodernism / South African Eco-politics," in *Liminal Postmodernism: The Postmodern, the (Post-)Colonial, and the (Post-)Feminist*, ed. Theo D'haen and Hans Bertens (Amsterdam, Rodopi, 1994), 331-57. Places a discussion of Snyder's work in the context of environmental justice and the relationship of Buddhist philosophy to postmodernism.

———. "True Communionism: Gary Snyder's Transvaluation of Some Christian Terminology." *Journal for the Study of Religion* (South Africa) 1.1 (1988): 63-75. Details Snyder's rethinking of Christian terminology through Buddhist and ecological beliefs.

Murphy, Patrick D. "Gary Snyder." In *American Nature Writers*, 2 vols., ed. John Elder. New York: Charles Scribner's Sons, 1996. 829-46. Overview essay of Snyder's life and writing up through *No Nature*.

———. "Mythic and Fantastic: Gary Snyder's 'Mountains and Rivers without End.' " *Extrapolation* 26 (1985): 290-99. Discusses "Bubbs Creek Haircut" and "Journeys" using Tzvetan Todorov's definition of the fantastic.

———. "Penance or Perception: Spirituality and Land in the Poetry of Gary Snyder and Wendell Berry," *Sagetrieb* 5.2 (1986): 61-72. Rptd. in *Earthly Words: Essays on Contemporary American Nature and Environmental Writers*, ed. John Cooley, University of Michigan Press, 1994. 237-49. A comparative study of these two authors in terms of Berry's Christian-based beliefs and Snyder's Zen-based beliefs.

———. "Sex-Typing the Planet: Gaia Imagery and the Problem of Subverting Patriarchy," *Environmental Ethics* 10 (1988), 155-68, rptd. in Murphy, *Literature, Nature, and Other*, 59-69. Analyzes Snyder, Jeffers, and Berry in terms of the problems of gender-typing the planet as part of transforming culture.

———. "Two Different Paths in the Quest for Place: Gary Snyder and Wendell Berry." *American Poetry* 2 (1984) 60-68. A companion to "Penance or Perception" focusing on their differing perceptions of place as wild and as cultivated.

O'Grady, John P. "Gary Snyder." In *Updating the Literary West*, ed. Thomas J. Lyon, et al. Fort Worth: Texas Christian University Press, 313-20. Reads Snyder's work through a paradigm of spiritual autobiography and Robertson's concept of "mattering."

Paul, Sherman. "From Lookout to Ashram: The Way of Gary Snyder," *Iowa Review* 1.3 and 1.4 (1970): 76-91 and 70-85. First major literary analysis of *Earth House Hold*, comparing Snyder to Thoreau. An extensive excerpt of this article is reprinted in Murphy, *Critical Essays*.

Rehanek, Woody. "The Shaman Songs of Gary Snyder." *Okanogan Natural News* No.19 (Summer 1984): 2-13. Treats *Axe Handles* in terms of the cultural function of poet-as-shaman.

Robertson, David. "Gary Snyder Riprapping in Yosemite, 1955." *American Poetry* 2.1 (1984): 52-59. Treats Snyder's development of his own poetic voice in 1955.

Scigaj, Leonard M. "Contemporary Ecological and Environmental Poetry," *ISLE: Interdisciplinary Studies in Literature and Environment* 3.2 (Fall 1996), 1-25. Sophisticated post-structuralist development of the concept of *référance* in opposition to *différance*, which includes discussion of Snyder's poetry.

Shaffer, Eric Paul. "Inhabitation in the Poetry of Robinson Jeffers, Gary Snyder, and Lew Welch." *Robinson Jeffers Newsletter* 78 (October 1990): 28-40. Comparatively treats the concept of inhabitation as realized in the poetry of these three authors.

Shu, Yunzhong. "Gary Snyder and Taoism." *Tamkang Review* 17 (1987): 245-61. Explores similarities between Snyder's views and Taoism.

Snider, Burr. "The Sage of the Sierra." *Image: San Francisco Examiner* 17 Sept. 1989, 9-12, 14, 16-17, 35. Situates Snyder within his community and the relation of art to activism.

Whalen-Bridge, John. "Gary Snyder's Poetics of Right Speech." *Sagetrieb* 9.1-2 (1990): 201-14. Interprets Snyder from a Buddhist definition of "right speech."

———. "Spirit of Place and Wild Politics in Two Recent Snyder Poems," *Northwest Review* 29.3 (1991): 123-31. Focuses on "Walking the New York Bedrock," one of the poems in *Mountains and Rivers*.

Williamson, Alan. "Language Against Itself: The Middle Generation of Contemporary Poets." In *American Poetry Since 1960: Some Critical Perspectives*. Ed. Rohert B. Shaw. Cheshire, U.K.: Carcanet Press, 1973.55-67. Discusses Snyder and several of his contemporaries, and finds Snyder the most remarkable.

Yamazato, Katsunori. "A Note on Japanese Allusions in Gary Snyder's Poetry." *Western American Literature* 18 (1983): 146-48. Includes material gleaned from Yamazato's dissertation, emphasizing Japanese folklore sources.

———. "Kitkitdizze, Zendo, and Place: Gary Snyder as a Reinhabitory Poet." *ISLE: Interdisciplinary Studies in Literature and Environment* 1.1 (Spring 1993): 51-63. Discusses Snyder's home and his reinhabitory practice there in relation to his poetry and prose.

Yip, Wal-Lim. "Classical Chinese and Modern Anglo-American Poetry: Convergence of Language and Poetry." *Comparative Literature Studies* 11(1974): 21-47. A study of the influence of Classical Chinese poetics on Snyder and other American poets.

IX. Dissertations on Gary Snyder

Gage, Maura Ruth. "Identity, Masculinity, and Femininity in the Poetry of Gary Snyder." Diss. University of South Florida, 1997. Treats Snyder's personae in his poetry by means of Eric Erikson's psychological stages of adult maturation.

Gray, Timothy. "New Lyric Worlds: Gary Snyder's Pacific Rim Communitas, 1930-1970." Diss. University of California at Santa Barbara, 1998. A sophisticated cultural studies analysis of Snyder in relation to the concept of the Pacific Rim.

Jaeger, Sharon Ann. "Toward a Poetics of Embodiment: The Cognitive Rhetoric of Gary Snyder's *The Practice of the Wild*." Diss. University of Pennsylvania, 1995. A valuable discussion primarily of Snyder's prose but also of a significant amount of his poetry using rhetorical and sociolinguistic theories.

Jungels, William J. "The Use of Native-American Mythologies in the Poetry of Gary Snyder." SUNY at Buffalo, 1973. A detailed study of the Native American sources for *Myths & Texts*.

Krauss, James W. "Gary Snyder's Biopoetics: A Study of the Poet as Ecologist." University of Hawaii, 1986. Treats the ecological dimensions of Snyder's poetry, with appendices of interviews with Snyder.

Leach, Thomas J., Jr., "Gary Snyder: Poet as Mythographer." Diss. University of North Carolina at Chapel Hill, 1974. Reads Snyder's poetry in terms of his mythmaking as a bridge between East and West.

Yamazato, Katsunori. "Seeking A Fulcrum: Gary Snyder and Japan (1956-1975)." University of California, Davis, 1987. Emphasizes the Japan and early Kitkitdizze years making extensive use of unpublished materials.

Index

Aborigines, Australian, 15, 134, 149
"Above Pate Valley," 52-53
"Across Lamarck Col," 86, 87
Acts, 22, 24
"Afloat," 205
"[After Ramprasad Sen]," 85
"After Work," 74
Ainu, 15, 149, 169
Aitken, Robert, 195, 208
"Alaska," 133
"All Through the Rains," 55
Allen, Donald, 44
Almon, Bert, 85, 95
Altieri, Charles, 69-70, 71, 121
"Alysoun," 81-82
"Amazing Grace," 168-69
"Ami 24.XII.62," 77-78
Anasazi. See Native Americans
"Anasazi," 105, 106
"Ancient Forests of the Far West," 151
"Another for the Same," 82-83
"Archaic Round and Keyhole Tombs," 97
"Arctic Midnight Twilight Cool North Breeze With Low Clouds Green Mountain Slopes, White Mountain Sheep," 200-1, 202, 203
"Artemis," 84
"As for Poets," 119-20
"Asleep on the Train," 78
"At Five a.m. Off the North Coast of Sumatra," 60
"At Tower Peak," 160
"At White River Roadhouse in the Yukon," 141
"Atthis," 137
"August on Sourdough, A Visit from Dick Brewer," 73
Avatamsaka. See Buddhism
Avatamsaka Sutra, 112, 149
Axe Handles, 11, 17, 74, 123-36, 140, 143, 156, 166, 200
"Axe Handles," 124-25

"Back," 85-87
Back Country, The, 9, 11, 13, 15, 61, 63, 65-88, 89-90, 155, 156;
Bakhtin, Mikhail, 181
Bashō, 99
"Bath, The," 107
"Bear Mother, The," 204
Beats, 7, 10, 37, 43, 67, 75
"Bed in the Sky, The," 99
"Bedrock," 116

"Before the Stuff Comes Down," 102
"Berry Feast, A," 7, 66, 67-69, 153
"Berry Territory," 126
Berry, Wendell, 126, 147, 172-73
bioregionalism 148, 167, 174-75, 176, 177, 181, 214-15
Black Elk Speaks (Niehardt), 27
"Black-tailed Hare, The," 72, 197-98
Blake, William, 101, 120, 166
"Blue Mountains Constantly Walking," 150-51, 187
"Blue Sky, The," 116, 182, 193, 197, 198, 203, 205
"Boat of a Million Years," 192
"Bomb Test," 138
Book of Odes, 124
"Breasts," 134
"Brush, The," 210
"Bubbs Creek Haircut," 184, 188, 190-92, 194, 195
Buddha, Guatama, 29, 30, 34, 37, 190, 196
Buddhism, 3, 5, 7, 8, 9, 13, 14, 15, 16, 17, 20, 23, 28, 29, 34, 36, 38, 41, 44, 56, 57, 60, 63, 66, 71, 77, 80, 81, 83, 84, 86, 90, 91, 92, 94, 95, 100, 104, 106, 107-108, 112, 115, 117, 128, 129, 135, 137, 138, 139, 141, 146, 149, 150, 152, 160, 162, 163, 164, 166, 168, 172, 176, 177, 179, 180, 181, 184, 185, 188, 190, 192, 193, 198, 201, 206, 209, 210, 215; American, 10, 83, 132, 156, 199; Avatamsaka, 91, 131; Ch'an, 16, 62, 90, 169; Hua-Yen, 192; Jodo, 16; Kegon, 16; Mahayana, 6, 65, 95, 183; mythology, 80, 183, 199; Rinzai Zen, 8, 16, 90, 154; Shingon, 108; Soto, 16, 90; Vajrayana, 65, 198, 201, 226n8; Yamabushi, 16, 150, 199; 211 Zen, 8, 9, 16, 37-38, 39, 46, 56-57, 58, 62, 80, 85, 90, 96, 120, 121, 138, 152, 162, 166, 169, 206, 214
"Buddhism and the Coming Revolution," 89, 92
Buddhist Peace Fellowship, 14
"Building," 158, 159

Bunnell, Sterling, 133
"Burning," 35-41
"Burning 1," 35; "Burning 2," 35-37; "Burning 3," 37; "Burning 4," 37; "Burning 7," 37; "Burning 8," 37-38; "Burning 9," 38; "Burning 10," 38; "Burning 11," 38-39; "Burning 12," 38-39; "Burning 13," 39; "Burning 14," 40; "Burning 15," 40, 41; "Burning 17," 40-41
"Burning Island," 97-98
"Burning the Small Dead," 71-72
Burroughs, William S., 7
By Frazier Creek Falls," 112
"By the Tama River at the North End of the Plain in April," 94
"Calcium," 140-41
California Arts Council, 11
"California Water Plan, The," 196
"Call of the Wild, The," 109, 117
Callicott, J. Baird, 164
Cantos (Pound), 41
"Canyon Wren, The," 135, 200-1, 206
"Cartagena," 60, 61
Castro, Michael, 70-71, 117, 118
"Charms," 110, 228n13
Chaucer, Geoffrey, 18
Ch'an. See Buddhism
Chardin, Teilhard de, 192
Chen, Shih-hsiang, 125
Chinese scroll painting, 179
Christianity, 28, 71, 74, 84; mythology, 52
Chuang-tzu, 142
"Circumambulating Arunchala," 84
"Circumambulation of Mt. Tamalpais, The," 199-200
"Civilization," 103
Clark, Tom, 149
Classic of Songs, 210
"Cold Mountain Poems," 18, 61-62, 155, 209
"Coming into the Watershed," 174-75, 176
communism, 6
Communist Party, 6
Collins, Robin, 4, 76, 79, 80-81
Confucius, 38

"Control Burn," 108-9
Corman, Cid, 8
Corso, Gregory, 7,
"Could She See the Whole Real World with Her Ghost Breast Eyes Shut Under a Blouse Lid?" 82-83
Cowan, Stuart, 163
"Coyote Man, Mr. President, & the Gunfighters," 142
Crandall, Jerry, 2
"Crash," 139
Creeley, Robert, 7
"Cross-Legg'd," 205

"Dance, The," 205-6
Dante, 180
Dao De Jing, 140, 159, 160, 185
Davidson, Michael, 7; *The San Francisco Renaissance*, 7
"Dazzle, The," 116
"Dead by the Side of the Road, The," 105, 106
Dean, Tim, 20, 33
"Delicate Criss-crossing Beetle Trails Left in the Sand," 128
Dharma Bums, The (Kerouac), 7
Diamond Sutra, The, 56, 72, 162
"Dillingham, Alaska, the Willow Tree Bar," 133-34
Dōgen, 150, 178, 183, 187, 200
Double Axe, The (Jeffers), 50, 60
Drinkswater, 27
"Dry Day Just Before the Rainy Season, A," 83
"Dullness in February: Japan," 138

"Earrings Dangling and Miles of Desert," 205
"Earth Day and the War Against the Imagination," 166-67
Earth House Hold, 9, 10, 11, 15, 66, 68, 89-93, 94, 96, 100, 102, 103, 143, 144, 163, 213
ecology, 16, 24, 96, 100, 112, 123, 148, 166, 167, 168, 177; ecological activism, 92 ; ecological practice, 90, 128, 133
"Earth Verse," 207
Egan, Charles, 13
"Egg, The," 111-12
Eliot, T. S., 20, 36
"Elk Trails," 137
"Elwha River, The," 189-90, 194
"Endless Streams and Mountains," 180, 184-87, 189, 198

"Energy Is Eternal Delight," 120, 166
"English Lessons at the Boiler Company," 139
"Entering the Fiftieth Millennium," 211
environmental writing, 145
epic, 180-81
Epton, Sidney, 170
Eskimos, Alaskan, 15
"Ethnobotany," 117
"Etiquette of Freedom, The," 145-47
Evans, Paul, 139
"Everybody Lying on Their Stomachs, Head Toward the Candle, Reading, Sleeping, Drawing," 98
"Exhortations for Baby Tigers," 173, 174
Exodus, 24

Fa-Tsang, 192
Faas, Ekbert, 145, 191, 194
"Facts," 110, 112
"Far East," 76-81
"Far West," 67-76
"Farewell to Burning Island," 140, 187
"Feathered Robes," 138
field composition. *See* poetics
"Finding the Space in the Heart," 178, 207-8
"Fire in the Hole," 71
"Firing, The," 79
"First Landfall on Turtle Island," 140
First Zen Institute of America, 7, 57, 139, 188
"Fishing Catching Nothing off the Breakwater near the Airport, Naha Harbor, Okinawa," 129
Flathead. *See* Native Americans
"Flowing, The," 196-97, 200, 205
Folsom, L. Edwin, 109-10
"For a Far-out Friend," 48, 49-50
"For a Stone Girl at Sanchi," 82
"For All," 136
"For Berkeley," 141
"For Example," 138
"For/From Lew," 125, 127, 131
"For Lew Welch in a Snowfall," 161
"For Nothing," 111
"For the Boy Who Was Dodger Point Lookout Fifteen Years Ago," 75-76

"For the Children" (section), 117-20; (poem), 119
"For the West," 86
"Fording the Flooded Golden River," 138
Foreman, David, 133
"Forest in the Library, The," 173, 174
Foster, Edward Halsey, 7; *Understanding the Beats*, 7
"Four Changes," 120-21, 143, 174
"Four Changes, with a Postscript," 165, 167
"Four Poems for Robin," 79
"Foxtail Pine," 72-73
free verse. *See* poetics
French, David H., 3, 4
"Front Lines," 108
Fudo Trilogy, The, 11, 107, 196

Gaard, Greta, 227n7
Gage, Maura, 222n21
Gaia hypothesis, 17, 131, 170, 220n58
Gary Snyder Reader, The, 12, 93, 136, 140, 173, 209-14
Gary Snyder's Vision (Molesworth), 73
Gass, Allison (ex-wife), 4, 75, 79, 81
"Geese Gone Beyond," 132
Géfin, Laszlo, 18
Genesis, 52
"Geological Meditation," 138
"Getting in the Wood," 129-30
Ghost Dance Religion, 183
Ginsberg, Allen, 7, 9, 54, 63, 67, 191, 199; *Howl*, 7, 67
"Go Round," 85
"Good, Wild, Sacred," 149-50
"Grand Entry, The," 132-33
Grappard, Allan, 206
Gray, Timothy, 17, 20, 24, 25, 26, 27, 29-30, 34, 36, 38, 44, 46, 51, 54, 61-62, 63, 73, 74, 76, 87, 99-100, 111, 188
Graves, Morris, 5
Great Clod, The (unfinished), 210, 211
Griffin, Susan, 19, 47

Hadley, Drummond, 75
Hagoromo, 138
Haida. *See* Native Americans
"Haida Gwai North Coast, Naikoon Beach, Hiellen River Raven Croaks," 201
haiku, 18, 99, 141
Haines, John, 19
Han-shan, 18, 27, 28, 43, 44, 61-62, 67, 191, 211

Harjo, Joy, 19
Hasegawa, Saburo, 185
Hawai'ians, 15
"Hay for Horses," 54, 55
He Who Hunted Birds in His Father's Village, 4, 20, 21
Heaney, Seamus, 213
"Heart of the Wood, The," 139
Heart Sutra, 195, 198, 207
"Heiffer Clambers Up, A," 73
Herbert, Jean, 206
Hicks, Jack, 137
"Higashi Hongwanji," 57-58
"High Quality Information," 141
Hinduism, 20, 28, 29, 33, 34, 63, 91; mythology, 14, 49, 137, 183, 191, 222n20
Hogan, Linda, 19
Hohokam. *See* Native Americans
Homer, 180
"Hop, Skip, and Jump," 86
Hopi. *See* Native Americans
"Housecleaning in Kyoto," 138-39
"How Poetry Comes To Me," 156-57
"How to Make Stew in the Pinacate Desert Recipe for Locke & Drum," 75
"How Zen Masters Are Like Mature Herring," 142
Howl (Ginsberg), 7, 67
Hsieh, Ling-yün, 210
Hsü, Fang, 25
Hua-Yen. *See* Buddhism
"Hudsonian Curlew, The," 115
Hui, Neng, 90, 107
"Hump-backed Flute Player, The," 182, 198-99, 206
Hunt, Anthony, 180, 183, 186, 191, 198, 206
"Hunting," 30-34; "Hunting 1," 31; "Hunting 2," 31; "Hunting 3," 31; "Hunting 4," 32; "Hunting 5," 32; "Hunting 6," 32, 36; "Hunting 8," 32-33; "Hunting 9," 33-34; "Hunting 10," 33-34; "Hunting 11," 33-34; "Hunting 12," 34; "Hunting 16," 34
Hymes, Dell, 5

"I Went into the Maverick Bar," 105-6
"Icy Mountains Constantly Walking," 213

"In the House of the Rising Sun," 94
"It," 101
"Incredible Survival of Coyote, The," 170-71
Indian. *See* Native Americans
Industrial Workers of the World (IWW) *aka* Wobblies, 26, 38, 126
Inupiaq. *See* Native Americans
"Is Nature Real?" 212
"It Pleases," 113

"Jackrabbit," 189, 197
Jaeger, Sharon Ann, 115, 145, 147, 159, 161, 163, 172
"Japan First Time Around," 91
Jeffers, Robinson, 4, 15, 50, 60, 91, 160, 174; *The Double Axe,* 50, 60, 137, 138
"Joanne My Wife," 139
Jodo. *See* Buddhism
"Joe Hill" (song), 125
"Journeys," 182, 194-95
Judeo-Christian, 28
Jung, Hwa Yol, 113, 121
Jung, Petee, 113, 121
Jungels, William J., 22, 23, 30, 32

Kabuki, 134-35
"Kai, Today," 99
"Kālī," 65-66, 81-85, 156
Kanaseki, Hisao, 87
Kang, Yong-ki, 162
Kegon. *See* Buddhism
Kern, Robert, 75
Kerouac, Jack, 7, 56; *Dharma Bums, The,* 7
"Kisiabaton," 161
"Kitkitdizze: A Node in the Net," 176-77
Koda, Carole (wife), 12, 159-60, 205, 214
Kodama, Sanehide, 57-58
"Kuöiwoqqóbi," 157, 158, 161
Kwakiutl. *See* Native Americans
Kyger, Joanne (ex-wife), 8, 9, 63, 64, 67, 79, 80, 84, 86, 92, 139
"Kyoto Born in Spring Song," 97
"Kyoto Footnote," 83-84
"Kyoto: March," 58, 59, 64
"Language Goes Two Ways," 171
"Late Snow & Lumber Strike of the Summer of Fifty-four, The," 46-47, 151
Lawrence, D. H., 4

Lavazzi, Tom, 98
Le Guin, Ursula K., 19
Leach, Thomas, 52, 60
Leaves of Grass (Whitman), 20
Left Out in the Rain, 11, 14, 43, 56, 88, 136-42, 156
Lenin, V. I., 38, 106
Leopold, Aldo, 163
"Little Songs for Gaia," 17, 130-32;
"Logging," 22-30; "Logging 1," 22-24; "Logging 2," 24-25; "Logging 3," 25-26; "Logging 6," 26; "Logging 7," 26; "Logging 8," 26; "Logging 9," 36; "Logging 11," 26-27; "Logging 12," 27-28; "Logging 13," 28; "Logging 14," 28; "Logging 15," 28-29, 99
Long Bitter Song, 209
"Long Hair" (section), 100-3; (poem), 102-3
"Longitude 170° West, Latitude 35° North," 138
"Lookout's Journal," 90-91
"Loops," 124-30
"Love," 102
Lopez, Barry, 19
"Love Song of J. Alfred Prufrock, The" (Eliot), 36
Lovelock, James, 170
"Loving Words," 139
Lu, Ji, 125
"Lying in Bed on a Late Morning," 85
Lynch, Tom, 23

"Macaques in the Sky," 204
Macy, Joanna, 168
"Madly Whirling Downhill," 84
"Magpie's Song" (section), 110-17; (poem), 116-17
Mahayana. *See* Buddhism
Mahā Prajñā Pāramitā Hrdaya Sūtra. *See* Heart Sutra
"Making of Mountains and Rivers Without End, The," 12, 65, 178, 184
"Makings," 138
mandala, 167-68, 177, 233n16
"Manichaeans, The," 84
"Manzanita" (section), 105-10; (poem), 110
Mao, Zedong, 129
Margulis, Lyn, 170
"Marin-an," 69, 70
"Market, The," 194
Martin, Julia, 100, 107, 124, 131-32, 193, 198

Marxism, 6, 100, 106
Masumoto, David Mas, 19
"Maul for Bill and Cindy's
    Wedding, A," 133
Mazama Mountaineering
    Club, 2
McCord, Howard, 26
McCorkle, Locke, 75, 191
McLean, W. Scott. 141
McLeod, Dan, 10
McNeil, Katherine, 66, 189, 193
"Meeting the Mountains," 102
"Mid-August at Sourdough
    Mountain Lookout," 45-46,
    51, 53, 73
Migration of Birds, The
    (Lincoln), 56
"Migration of Birds," 13, 56
Milarepa, 183, 201, 203, 207
"Milton by Firelight," 48, 51-52
Milton, John, 52, 171, 180
Miner, Earl, 179
Miyazawa, Kenji, 61, 66, 67,
    87-88, 155, 209
"Miyazawa Kenji," 87-88
modernism, 14, 20, 136; Anglo-
    American, 17
Molesworth, Charles, 73, 74,
    85, 100, 103, 105, 110, 121,
    123, 136; *Gary Snyder's
    Vision,* 73
"Money Goes Upstream," 134
"Mother Earth: Her Whales,"
    113-14
"Mother of the Buddhas,
    Queen of Heaven, Mother of
    the Sun; Marici, Goddess of
    the Dawn," 84-85
"Mt. Hiei," 77
"Mountain Spirit, The," 182,
    187, 206-207, 208
*Mountains and Rivers Without
    End,* 9, 12,14, 65, 72, 135, 178-
    208, 209, 212, 213, 214
"Mountains and Waters Sutra"
    (Dōgen), 135, 150, 178, 187
Muir, John, 37-38, 39, 138, 197
mythopoesis, 20, 26, 179
*Myths and Symbols in Indian
    Art and Civilization*
    (Zimmer), 222n20
Myths & Texts, 7, 9, 14, 20-42,
    43, 45, 46, 48, 49, 66, 69, 91,
    99, 101, 103, 137, 140, 143,
    151, 155, 178, 179, 180

"Nanao Knows," 85.
Native Americans, 15, 23, 27,
    28, 38, 53, 90, 105, 106, 109,
    122, 137, 147, 170, 174, 218-
    19n43; beliefs, 33, 37, 114,

120, 149, 193; cultures, 5-6,
    15, 67, 104, 142, 168; myths
    and songs, 14, 17, 20-21, 31,
    32, 34, 121, 131; struggles, 9,
    120; specific tribes: Anasazi,
    86, 105, 106; Flathead, 32;
    Haida, 27, 34; Hohokam; 86;
    Hopi, 86, 105, 228n17;
    Inupiaq, 148; Kwakiutl, 32;
    Piute, 157, 198; Salish, 33;
    Sioux, 27, 120
natural history writing, 171
"Nature   Green Shit," 85, 86
nature writing, 144, 145, 148,
    171
"Nets," 132-36
"Nets of Beads, Webs of
    Cells," 167
New American Poetry, The
    (Allen, ed.), 44
"New Moon Tongue," 202-3
"Night," 83
"Night Herons," 111
"Night Highway Ninety-Nine,"
    187-88, 189, 192, 194, 198
"Night Song of the Los
    Angeles Basin," 184, 195-96,
    197
Nō drama, Japanese, 14, 138,
    178, 179, 180, 186, 188, 189,
    190, 199, 206, 211, 233n1,
    234n5
"No Matter, Never Mind," 107
No Nature, 12, 14, 47, 49, 50, 56,
    58, 61, 72, 82, 88, 134, 140,
    155-63, 188
"No Shoes, No Shirt, No
    Service," 140
"Nooksack Valley," 54-55
"North Beach," 73
"North Beach Alba," 82
Norton, Jody, 71, 72
"Not Leaving the House," 99

"O Waters," 117
O'Connell, Nicholas, 1
Oda, Sesso, Roshi, 9
"Ode on a Grecian Urn"
    (Keats), 29
Odum, H. T., 142
"Off the Trail," 140, 159-60,
    188, 192
"Offering for Tārā, An" 201,
    203-4
O'Grady, John P., 12
"Oil," 73-74
"Old Bones," 187
Old Ways, The, 11, 120, 144,
    155, 172
"Old Woman Nature," 134-35
"Old Woodrat's Stinky
    House," 204-5

Olliff, Kenneth, 163
Olson, Ray, 143
"On 'As for Poets,' " 120
"On Climbing the Sierra
    Matterhorn Again After
    Thirty-One Years," 157
"On the Path, Off the Trail," 4,
    152
"One Should Not Talk to a
    Skilled Hunter about What
    Is Forbidden by the
    Buddha," 116
"One Year," 138
Oppenheimer, J. Robert, 78-79
Orlovsky, Peter, 63
"'Out of the Soil and Rock,'"
    137
"Out West," 77
"Oysters," 67, 87

"Painting the North San Juan
    School," 127-28
Paradise Lost (Milton), 51
Passage Through India, 9, 11, 63-
    65;
pastoral, 161
Paul, Sherman, 35, 36, 40, 43,
    46, 57, 59, 74, 75, 90, 91, 104,
    114, 132
Persian Gulf War, 158
"Persimmons, The," 141
Peterson, Will, 7-8, 209
"Pine River," 77
"Pine Tree Tops," 111
Piute. *See* Native Americans
"Piute Creek," 50-51, 53
Place in Space, A, 11, 12, 19, 120,
    155, 163-77
"Place, the Region, and the
    Commons, The," 147-48
"Plum Blossom Poem, The,"
    87
"Poem Left in Sourdough
    Mountain Lookout," 137-38,
    150
poetics: classical Chinese, 18,
    44; counter-modernist, 10;
    field composition, 17, 45;
    free verse, 14, 17; Japanese,
    18; "New Nature Poetics,"
    171; objectivist, 121
"Poetry and the Primitive," 94
"Poetry, Community &
    Climax," 132
"Poetry Is the Eagle of
    Experience," 140-41
poetry, modernist, 10, 41
"Politics of Ethnopoetics,
    The," 169-70
"Porous World, The," 19, 173
postmodernist literature, 41

Pound, Ezra, 4, 14, 15, 20, 125, 137
Practice of the Wild, The, 1, 11, 12, 24, 143-54, 155, 159, 163, 171, 187
"Praise for Sick Women," 47-49, 50
"Prayer for the Great Family," 107, 110
"Public Bath, The," 77, 78

"Rabbit, The," 198
"Rainbow Body," 98
Range of Poems, A, 87
Rapges, Tashi, 168
"Raven Beak's River at the End," 205
Reading Gary Snyder's Mountains and Rivers Without End (Smith), 198, 207
Real Matter (Robertson), 199
Real Work, The, 132
"Real Work, The," 110-11
"Record of the Life of the Ch'an Master Po-chang Huai Hai," 90
"Rediscovery of Turtle Island, The," 176
Regarding Wave, 9, 10, 11, 17, 66, 93-103, 140, 150, 156
"Regarding Wave," 99, 100
Rehanek, Woody, 17, 128, 132
"Reinhabitation," 151, 172-73
"Removing the Plate of the Pump on the Hydraulic System of the Backhoe," 133
renga poetry, 179
"Revolution in the Revolution in the Revolution," 100
Rexroth, Kenneth, 15, 217n21
Reynolds, Lloyd, 3
"Right in the Trail," 160-61
Rinzai Zen. *See* Buddhism
"Ripples on the Surface," 159, 160, 162-62
Riprap, 7, 8, 9, 13, 18, 20, 43-61, 65, 72, 90, 91, 137, 138, 151, 155, 160
"Riprap," 59, 61
Riprap and Cold Mountain Poems, 43-62
"River in the Valley," 125-27
Robertson, David, 145, 168, 177, 199, 200, 211, 233n16; *Real Matter*, 199
"Robin," 82
"Roots, 98
Robbins, David, 97
Rossiter, John, 139
"Running Water Music," 101

Sakaki, Nanao, 9, 231n19
Salish. *See* Native Americans
San Francisco Renaissance, 7, 15
San Francisco Renaissance, The (Davidson), 7
Sasaki, Sokei-an, 188
Sasaki, Ruth Fuller, 7, 138
"Sather," 75
Schelling, Andrew, 136
Schultz, Robert, 124, 129, 134
Scigaj, Leonard, 135, 142, 183-84, 206
Seaman, Donna, 163
Seed, John, 168
"Seed Pods," 94
"Seeing the Ox," 138-39
"Sestina at the End of the Kalpa," 142
Shamanism, 17, 27, 91, 106, 117, 131, 137, 166, 193, 198
Shapiro, Robert, 120
"Shark Meat," 98-99
Shingon. *See* Buddhism
Shoemaker, Jack, 232n1
Shugendo, 108
Shinto, 71, 149, 206
Silko, Leslie Marmon, 19, 219n43
"Single Breath, A," 169
Sioux. *See* Native Americans
Six Sections from Mountains and Rivers Without End, 63, 116-17, 178
Six Sections from Mountains and Rivers Without End Plus One, 178, 187, 192
"Six-Month Song in the Foothills," 13, 69-70
"Six Years," 80-81
Sixteen T'ang Poems, 209
Smith, Eric Todd, 179, 180, 183, 195, 198, 206-207
"Smokey the Bear Sutra," 108, 164
Snyder, Anthea, 1, 64
Snyder, Gen (son), 9, 126, 174
Snyder, Harold (father), 1
Snyder, Kai (son), 9, 99, 102, 112, 124-25, 126, 138, 157
Snyder, Lois (mother), 1, 2, 112
"Song of the Cloud," 96
"Song of the Slip," 96
"Song of the Tangle," 96
"Song of the Taste," 96
"Song of the View," 96
Soto. *See* Buddhism
"Source," 110
"Sours of the Hills," 101
"Soy Sauce," 128

"Spell Against Demons," 107-8
Spretnak, Charlene, 50
"Spring, The," 70, 73
"Spring and the Ashura," 88
"Spring Sesshin at Shokoku-Ji," 92
"Steak," 105, 106-107
Stein, Gertrude, 4
Steuding, Bob, 48, 57, 58, 66, 94, 96, 99, 179, 180
"Stone Garden, A," 58-60, 64
"Straight-Creek-Great-Burn," 114-15
"Strategic Air Command," 129
"Summer of Ninety-seven," 213-14
"Surrounded By Wild Turkeys," 158-59
"Survival and Sacrament," 153-54
"Suwa-no-se Island and the Banyan Ashram," 92
"Sweat, The," 158

"T-2 Tanker Blues," 60-61
Takasago, 180
Taking the Path of Zen (Aitken), 208
Tales of Ise, The, 60
Tanahashi, Kazuaki, 183-84
"Tanker Notes," 92
Tantra, 85, 91, 96, 191, 235n23
T'ao Yuan-ming, 210
"Target Practice," 103
Tarn, Nathaniel, 20
"Tawny Grammar," 148-49
"There are those who love to get dirty," 141-42
"Thief," 88
"Thin Ice," 54
"This present moment," 214
"This Tokyo," 83
Thoreau, Henry David, 22, 60, 144, 165; *Walden*, 22, 41, 60, 144
"Three Poems for Joanne," 139
"Three Worlds, Three Realms, Six Roads," 188-89
"Thoughts on Looking at a Samuel Palmer Etching at the Tate," 161
"Through the Smoke Hole," 86-87
"To Fire," 101-2
"To Hell With Your Fertility Cult," 76, 81-82
"Tōji," 57
"Tomorrow's Song," 117
"Toward Climax," 118-19
"Trail Crew Camp at Bear Valley, 9000 feet. Northern

Sierra—White Bone and Threads of Snowmelt Water," 72
"Trail Is Not a Trail, The," 140
"Travelling to the Capital," 161
"True Night," 129
Tsang, Hsuang, 193, 198
Turtle Island, 11, 15, 104-22, 123, 125, 129, 132, 136, 140, 143, 155, 156, 161, 165, 166
"Twelve Hours out of New York After Twenty-Five Days at Sea," 86
"24:IV:40075, 3:30 PM, n. of Coaldale, Nevada, A Glimpse through a Break in the Storm of the Summit of the White Mountains," 132
"Two Fawns That Didn't See the Light This Spring," 115

Uehara, Masa (ex-wife), 9, 12, 66, 90, 92, 94-95, 96, 97, 98, 99, 100, 116, 138
"Uluru Wild Fig Song," 134
Understanding the Beats (Foster), 7
"Unnatural Writing," 171
"Uses of Light, The," 112

Vajrayana. *See* Buddhism
"Vapor Trails," 77
"Village Council of All Beings, A," 167-68
"Voice as a Girl, The," 94-95
"Volcano in Kyushu, A," 78-79

Walden (Thoreau), 22, 41, 60, 144
"Walk, A," 70-71
"Walked Two Days in Snow, Then It Cleared for Five," 132

Walker, Alice, 19
"Walking Downtown Naha," 211-12
"Walking the Great Ridge Omine, on the Womb-Diamond Trail," 211
"Walking the New York Bedrock Alive in the Sea of Information," 201-202, 212
"Walking Through Myoshin-ji," 128-29
"Walls Within Walls," 210
"Walt Whitman's Old 'New World,'" 173, 174
Watts, Alan, 120
Waste Land, The (Eliot), 36
"Water," 52-53
"Wave," 94-95, 96, 97
"Way West Underground, The," 105, 106, 110
"We Wash Our Bowls in This Water," 206, 208;
Weinberger, Eliot, 215
Welch, Lew, 4, 125, 188
Whalen, Philip, 4, 64, 187, 199, 209
Whalen-Bridge, John, 202
"What Happened Here Before," 118, 120
"What Have I Learned," 133
"What's Mean By 'Here,' " 120
"White Devils," 94
White Goddess, The (Graves), 5, 135
Whitman, Walt, 137, 173, 174
"Why Log Truck Drivers Rise Earlier Than Students of Zen," 116
" 'Wild' in China," 210
"Wild Thing" (Lawrence), 36
Wilderness Society, 2

"Wilderness, The," 120
Williams, William Carlos, 4, 15
Williamson, Alan, 88
"Wiper's Secret, The," 73
"Without," 105, 106
Wobbly. *See* Industrial Workers of the World
Woman and Nature (Griffin), 47-48
"Woman Who Married a Bear, The," 19, 153, 160
Wood, Charles Erskine Scott, 4
Wooden Fish, The, 146, 206
"Word Basket Woman," 160
"Work To Do Toward Town," 79-80
"Working on the '58 Willys Pickup," 129-30
Wovoka, 183, 198
Wright, James, 43
Wu, Tse-Tien, Empress, 192
Wyatt, David, 124, 129, 134

"Xrist," 84

Yakamochi, 60
Yamabushi. *See* Buddhism
Yamamba (Seami), 179
Yamazato, Katsunori, 46, 76, 79, 81, 97, 99, 104, 107-108, 112, 125, 126, 128, 129, 138, 142, 180, 188, 192
"Yogin and the Philosopher, The," 165-66, 172.
Yu, Beongchen, 193

Zen. *See* Buddhism
Zen Center of San Francisco, 8
Zendo, Ring of Bone, 16
Zimmer, Heinrich, 222n20;
Myths and Symbols in Indian Art and Civilization, 222n20